To the members o
Our Redee

MW00917232

Enjoy my story!

Harry G Kapeikis

May 4, 2013

Exile from Latvia

My WWII Childhood
from Survival to Opportunity

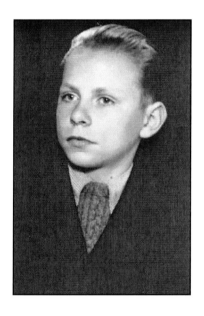

by
Harry G. Kapeikis

Trafford Publishing
Victoria, BC, Canada
www.trafford.com

ELCIC's Global Hunger and Development Appeal
www.elcic.ca/ghda

Partial proceeds from the sale of this book benefit the Evangelical Lutheran Church in Canada's Global Hunger and Development Appeal.

Photos: Hermine Krauja Photography; Rudis Smits
Title page photo: Harijs, Christmas 1948, Hermine Krauja Photography
Editing, layout & cover design: Gillian (Jill) Veitch. Kelowna, BC
Cover Image: PJ Perdue
This book is typset in Book Antiqua & PrestonScript.

Order this book online at www.trafford.com/07-1299
or email orders@trafford.com

Most Trafford titles are also available at major online book retailers.

Note for Librarians: A cataloguing record for this book is available from Library and Archives Canada at www.collectionscanada.ca/amicus/index-e.html

Printed in Victoria, BC, Canada.

ISBN: 978-1-4251-3400-6

We at Trafford believe that it is the responsibility of us all, as both individuals and corporations, to make choices that are environmentally and socially sound. You, in turn, are supporting this responsible conduct each time you purchase a Trafford book, or make use of our publishing services. To find out how you are helping, please visit www.trafford.com/responsiblepublishing.html

Our mission is to efficiently provide the world's finest, most comprehensive book publishing service, enabling every author to experience success. To find out how to publish your book, your way, and have it available worldwide, visit us online at www.trafford.com/10510

Trafford
PUBLISHING™

www.trafford.com

North America & international
toll-free: 1 888 232 4444 (USA & Canada)
phone: 250 383 6864 ♦ fax: 250 383 6804
email: info@trafford.com

The United Kingdom & Europe
phone: +44 (0)1865 722 113 ♦ local rate: 0845 230 9601
facsimile: +44 (0)1865 722 868 ♦ email: info.uk@trafford.com

10 9 8 7 6 5 4 3 2

Dedicated to:

Mr. and Mrs. Gunars Salins (Jautrite). Teachers who, under difficult circumstances, worked beyond their call of duty and gave much of themselves, taking special interest in all my elementary school classmates in Haunstetten, near Augsburg, Germany from 1945 to 1950. Their influence gave us a positive direction early in our lives. We thank them a million times.

Also to JoAnn, my wonderful "help meet" in life, for the countless hours spent helping me write this book and searching for my classmates.

Foreword

WE ARE BORN with little or no cognitive memory. The dim, warm comfort of the womb vanishes to a harsh blaze of light and the dry coolness we know as air. We gasp and, with our birthing cry, unconsciously ignite the process of breathing. We do not remember how or when we become aware of our self. We do not remember the taste of mother's milk, nor the need that prompted us to nurse. This we learn when we observe our own first child, or a sibling born much later. We observe the baby's eyes gaining focus, and then witness the wonder in those eyes as she starts to observe and react to her surroundings, beginning to remember and recognize things, sounds, words, mother.

This process develops into a complexity of interdependent phenomena we call growth and development. We observe, perceive, and remember which, in turn, modifies what we observe, how we perceive - what and how we remember, eventually leading to whom we are now.

We are our memories. If we have no memories, we are nothing. If we have fond memories, we are rich. How we perceive influences what we remember. What we remember influences how we perceive our present. How we perceive our present affects what we expect of our future.

Welcome to my memories of a boyhood before, during and after World War II. Someone else with the same experiences may have perceived and remembered differently. We all are unique individuals.

Children in war zones tend to mature quickly and become little adults sharing adult thoughts and concerns. In Latvia I had very few toys. When we fled, I had none. My mom had no need to tell me to pick up and put away my toys. Instead of living in Toyland, I listened to adults talking about atrocities committed by dictators, as well as casualties, military maneuvers, air raids and daily survival. I was as much concerned about having something to eat and staying alive as my mom and dad, and so were my friends; friends I lost because we had to move on. A child in a war zone grows up a breadwinner at an early age, not by choice, but necessity.

In writing this memoir, I had six documents stimulating my memory, in addition to photographs, letters, event programs and personal notes. Of terrific value was my mother's diary where she recorded, to the precise hour, departure and arrival dates. Also, my uncle's monthly magazine, published in Germany from January, 1946 through December, 1948; the pages of twenty-four of these publications reminded me of issues, concerns and events that took place in Displaced Person's (D.P.) camps. As I was rummaging through photographs and precious artifacts, preparing to write, I discovered two logs or notebooks, records to the day and hour, of two years' activities of the Boy Scout Patrols of which I was a member, recorded by several "patrol scribes" or "chroniclers." How did I manage to keep them? One explanation; I was the last chronicler writing detailed accounts of events, games played, and the when, where and who of my patrol.

Also among my artifacts I rediscovered a copy of the farewell journal, *Kamolins*, which roughly translates as, "a little clew of precious yarn". It was a collection of short stories and poems written by my Haunstetten Elementary School classmates and myself about our experiences, hopes and dreams. Finally, I kept a diary from the day I left the

D.P. camp to the day I arrived in New York harbor.

Pure memory can easily misplace exactly where or when an event happened; the recorded events in these logs and diaries were invaluable.

This book is not intended to be a chronological record of history but a collection of memories about people, events, issues, concerns as I remember them and the lessons in life that I have learned.

While writing the manuscript, I enjoyed reliving my boyhood experiences in Latvia and Germany; I was there in spirit. I would like readers not to observe my experiences from the distance of a half century and more, but to experience with me what I was reliving. I have taken the liberty of employing narrative-style creative non-fiction, recreating dialogue in an attempt to bring to life not only events but also the emotions, feelings, hopes and dreams I associate with them. There were no tape recorders in the 1930's or 40's, therefore my memories may portray people I remember well as composite persons, speaking about issues of someone else's concern. For that, I ask forgiveness. Read on and enjoy!

Harry (Harijs) G. Kapeikis.

Riga

Latvia

Germany

Bremen

Haunstetten · Binabiburg
Munich

one

Riga to Binabiburg

BINABIBURG, GERMANY, MAY 1945

I WOKE EARLY IN THE MORNING on a day I would long remember. I felt cozy and warm wrapped in my old blanket, lying on a canvas cot instead of the usual hard floor in some auditorium of a school or abandoned barn, or worse, shivering on the grass under open skies.

Mom and Dad, covered with a blanket, were sound asleep and snuggled close in a single bed. Bed, yes a real bed, in the privacy of our cubicle in the corner of a large room above a barn of farm animals; some cows and a pig. There was a roof above us and four walls, two sporting rough grey boards and two formed by sheets of grey canvas. The vertical sheet at the foot of my cot could be slid open to serve as a door.

We were in a little Bavarian village named Binabiburg. The war was not over but rumors that it soon would be were heard everywhere. Aware of the other families in the large room, thanks to their distinctively dreamy snores, I began to daydream, reminisce and remember.

I was good at this mental time travel. I did it often. Sometimes I would imagine an invisible friend day-dreaming with me, that way it was even more fun. The two of us seeing, feeling and experiencing my memories all over again; flashbacks of unforgettable, memorable, remarkable events. We'd zoom through space back to my beloved Latvia…

RIGA, LATVIA: JUNE, 1941

"DAD, HOW MUCH LONGER must we stay in the shelter? We've been in here for two dreadful days."

"I don't know, Harij*. The German Army is already in Latvia and heading our way, and according to last night's news, they're closing in on Riga."

"They're going to shoot it out in Riga, aren't they Dad - that's why you built this shelter," I surmised.

Dad looked at me with tired, anxious eyes and said, "The onslaught has begun."

"The onslaught?" I asked.

"Yes, Harij, the invasion of Russia through Latvia that we have talked much about. We can only hope the Germans will liberate us from the Communists, from Stalin."

"The Russians are going to get it, aren't they Dad?" The Panzers can drive through a building and level it," I exaggerated.

"The Panzer divisions are unstoppable," said Dad, "First the Luftwaffe and long range artillery pound the Russian positions, then come the tanks and infantry to pulverize Russian defenses, one after another."

"They're going to attack Riga through our yard, Dad?"

"That's why we must stay in this shelter." Mom added.

(Years later we learned that the invasion of Russia was code named "Operation Barbarossa" and that the German forces near us were the 16th and 18th Armies, spearheaded by the 4th Panzer group, in what came to be known as

---

* pronounced *Harry*.

blitzkrieg, the lightning war.)

Just then I heard planes.

"Messerschmitt fighters!" exclaimed Dad, "Flying low and fast toward Russian positions outside Riga." Earth shaking explosions started at once; more explosions, more planes and more explosions, so close, so close.

The Russians are getting it, I thought. German pilots are accurate. The Stuka dive bombers, deadly.

Soon after the intense but brief air strike on Russian positions, we heard a distant rumble. That's the Panzers, I thought.

We lay on the musty dirt floor of the shelter. Dad had laid thick wooden planks over it and covered the planks with a mound of soil a meter thick. Good protection from shrapnel and small arms fire but no protection at all from a direct hit by a bomb or the metal treads of a Panzer. Dad had placed a white flag above our shelter to plead to the German tank commanders not to drive over and crush us.

The Panzer divisions bypassed Riga; the Soviets were routed. Riga was liberated from an occupation that had begun on June 17, 1940, when the Red Army marched into an undefended Riga and ushered in a year of terror; a year of arbitrary mass arrests, physical torture, confiscation of properties and the sexual exploitation of young women and girls. Deportations and executions became daily events. Farms were collectivized and factories nationalized, dismantled and shipped to Russia. The great nations of the world did not know, did not care or were helpless to stem the horror in Latvia. We welcomed the Germans as liberators.

The 4th Panzer Group, including the 16th and 18th Armies, was on its way to Novgorod and Leningrad. Indeed they were unstoppable.

Assured and certain of German victory, my dad dismantled the shelter, filled it with soil, replaced the topsoil and gave me the area as my first and very own vegetable garden.

A gardener I became though only six years old. I did not have many toys, just a few wooden blocks that Dad had cut for me, a rubber sailor doll that bathed with me, a tricycle, a wooden rocking horse and a metal wheel barrow which came in handy for gardening. Gardening was important to my family more out of necessity; we weren't poor, neither were we rich, but growing our own vegetables, garden greens, chickens and rabbits meant more abundant meals. I felt grown up pretending I was "Dad" in my garden. Being able to contribute my share of produce to the family root cellar, from potatoes to sunflower seeds, made me feel good. When asked what I wanted for my birthday or Christmas, I asked for a new spade, or a smaller rake or some other gardening tool.

I began my schooling in 1942 at the age of 7 in "The 35th Elementary School of Riga" and completed 1st and 2nd grades before the war closed all schools in Latvia in the fall of 1944.

From 1941 through to the fall of 1944, the three and a half years of German occupation, it was my garden and school that kept me busy and the pleasure was enhanced with parties and visits with uncles, aunts, cousins and the older girl across the street – she was nice.

Late in fall of 1942, Father splurged and brought home a radio – a powerful eight tube radio that could tune in to distant stations. A new habit developed in my family. In the evenings, an uncle or aunt would come over and my dad would turn on the radio. All of us would sit around it and listen; first to music from a German station, then news about victories and conquests by the S.S. These broadcasts always ended with names of soldiers wounded, killed or missing in action.

At first there were just a few names, but as time went on, the number of names increased to what seemed an endless list. We listened carefully for Latvian names. We could tell which they were, as Latvian names mean something – for example, Janis Eglite (John Fir Tree) Juris Mucins (George Barrel) etc. Yes, there were Latvian names among the German, but none that we knew.

Then one evening we heard the Red Army had gone on the offensive and encircled the German 6th Army; enforcements were on the way, we were told, to stop the Red Army. The German S.S. was on a temporary tactical retreat. Suddenly the broadcasting station went off the air.

The news became local – Russian planes were making nightly air raids on Riga. Late in the summer of 1944, for our safety, we contemplated leaving the city until the German counterattack.

GOODBYE HOME, RIGA AND LATVIA

MY FAMILY, including my mother and father, Erna and Arvids, along with my mother's sister, Marta, whom I call by the endearing term Tinte, and her husband, Rudolfs, who prefers the nickname Rudis, ended up traveling for a long time, mostly by train, since we left Riga in the fall of 1944.

Because my dad worked in a foundry supplying products needed by the German army, he had to stay in Riga when Uncle Rudis, Tinte, Mom and I first left. We departed our beloved home in Riga thinking that it was just temporary, that the well-disciplined and heavily armed German army would prevail over the Communists, as they did at the beginning of the war.

We had lived under Stalin's oppressive rule until June 22, 1941, when the German *blitzkrieg* liberated Latvia from Russian tyranny. "The Communists will not win. Stalin must not win the war!"

Thinking the Germans would prevail, we took with us

only the clothes and provisions for our immediate needs: soon we shall return to our home in Riga. But our temporary flight was extended again and again as Russian forces kept advancing, as if they were following us, bound and determined to catch and terrorize us again.

We fled from Riga by truck to a water-driven flour mill in the country, and from there to Liepaja (Liebow). We crossed the Baltic Sea on October 14, 1944, on a German battle ship, arriving in Germany the following day. The crossing was an adventure for me and a scare for my mom. Our ship, one of five destroyers, was attacked by British Spitfires and a Lancaster dropped bombs that fell close to the ship on both sides. My mom screamed, and frankly, I, too, was scared. It was good to be on a solid shore, again. If I was to die, I preferred the land over the sea.

Traveling, traveling, always on the move – new places, new people. What a way to live. Many a night we just spent outdoors since we could not find shelter. Often we stayed on a train, crowded with many refugees trying to escape to the west, toward the advancing American and British forces. We hoped that one lucky day we would be captured by them, and not by the Russians. Then World War II would be over for us.

SOMEWHERE IN BAVARIA: APRIL, 1945

THANK GOD THE SNOW HAD MELTED. The dirt road was muddy with the kind of puddles I would splash through lightheartedly in summertime if I were at home. But here, I wanted to stay dry and as clean as I could.

I hadn't bathed for weeks and hadn't eaten for several days - literally. I was very hungry and feeling tired and weak. In the German city we had left, there was nothing to eat. Nothing. The city with a name unimportant to us was in smoldering ruins. Even the train tracks were destroyed.

The train could go no further west, so when we realized we had to leave the city, we left on foot.

Dad found a damaged wheelbarrow in a bombed out warehouse. He pushed it, loaded with all our earthly belongings: four suitcases and three backpacks. We walked in silence. What was there to talk about? The unthinkable had happened. The once unstoppable German armies, spearheaded by Panzer and Tiger tanks and the swift Luftwaffe, were losing the war and we were about to starve to death.

No place in particular to go since the Red Army's advance into Latvia, just *'west'* and away from cities. We would advance toward the setting sun, hoping and praying our helpless and hopeless predicament would set with the sun below the horizon of human hostility and, with the sunrise, a bright new day of freedom and peace arrive.

The silence on that muddy dirt road in April, 1945, was broken by the roar of four British Spitfires in a dive toward us. Their machine guns opened fire as they banked to the left. I wondered what they were shooting at. In spite of our misery I was glad it wasn't us. I heard an explosion, and a column of black smoke rose into the sky behind the bend in the road, about a kilometer back, from where we had just come. The fighter planes didn't return. They had made their kill, and we continued our pitiful trek.

Soon a German army truck was overtaking us. It had a shattered windshield from a bullet hole on the passenger side. The truck stopped and the driver, a young German soldier, asked us where we were going. Dad answered that we really didn't know. "West," Dad said. The soldier offered us a ride. He was going to Binabiburg, to a guest house there. His face was bloodied from a cut on the forehead. There were shards of glass on the bench seat in the cab, also some blood. We climbed into the back of the truck. It was empty but there were two gaping bullet holes in the floor.

Mom and Dad stirred. "Harij, it's time to get up," Mom said.

"I've been awake for some time, thinking," I replied.

"About what Harij?" inquired Dad.

"About many things, like Riga, the air raid shelter, our travels, the days we had nothing to eat, stuff like that," I replied.

"Let's finish the loaf of black bread this morning, we are out of bacon grease, so water will have to do," said Mom.

"That's okay Mom, at least we have some bread," I replied. "Are we going to get some more from the guest house owners?"

"I don't know Harij," answered my dad with sadness in his voice, "I don't know."

Little did any of us in the upper room know that the day had come when our lives would change forever.

The weather was sunny and warm, a perfect day for me and my two new friends to go fishing. About two weeks ago we were brought to this tiny Bavarian village by the wounded German soldier.

War for a nine year old boy means daily excitement, but for grown-ups, I'm told, it is tragedy. Much destruction, much heartache, death and grief, added to changing governments, social status and culture. All this, I must try to remember and learn from, if we survive.

But after my breakfast of bread and water, that morning was perfect for going fishing with my new friends, Juris (George), ten years old and Janis. (Not a girl - I wouldn't be seen with a girl. Janis translates to John.) Janis was a sprouting bully at fourteen years old. There we were, Harijs, Juris and Janis with freshly cut willow sticks for fishing rods on our shoulders, marching single file to the little river a mile or so from our guest house in Binabiburg – guest house, if one can call a large room over a cattle barn a guest house. It was normal for people in Bavaria to live above their farm animals, saving on heating bills in winter, and plugging their noses in summer.

The three of us counted ourselves very privileged to be able to go fishing that sunny May morning. We needed fish. There wasn't much to eat, and the Germans allowed kids to fish for food, but not adults.

My catching fish was survival. We cut willow tree branches for fishing rods and for hooks, used bent straight pins we begged from the lady who allowed us to stay in the large room over her barn; one learns to improvise in times of war. But the worms we dug up last night were real and fat. The fish will like our worms, and our families will like the fish. Fresh fish for supper tonight. What a treat when one hasn't had a good meal for days.

"Janis," I said, "did you see those two American fighter planes fly over the village yesterday? Man, they flew low. For a moment I thought they might strafe us."

"Yeah," Janis replied, "I was outside and thought they were coming for me, it scared me half to death. I could see the pilot looking at me."

"Seeing and hearing the planes roar overhead reminded me of the time my folks and I were on a train which stopped in the woods to avoid detection by fighter planes protecting a flight of bombers," I said, "but the American fighter pilots spotted the train anyway and came at us, guns ablaze. We jumped out of the train and ran for our lives."

To get further away from the train, we ran across an opening in the woods. The pilots saw us. They mistook us for German soldiers. Two planes turned around and came after us, but we made it across the opening and into the trees, so they just flew over us without firing. We sure were lucky to get away."

"I think they knew exactly who you were – refugees," inserted Juris. "The Americans want to kill us to please the Russians. My mom and dad were talking about what happened in Dresden. Dad said the British and the

Americans knew Dresden was full of refugees from Latvia and other countries, and they leveled it. Destroyed it completely. Mom said thousands of people died in the resulting fire storm."

"I hate to think the Americans want to kill us but I do remember that air raid well," I said. "We had just left Dresden in a train. We wanted to stay there but there was no room. Every place was full of people. Wasn't there a festival of some sort that also brought in many German people as well?"

"Yeah, there was," affirmed Janis, "but I don't remember what it was. Something to do with the arts, I think. Perhaps it was a music festival."

Then I shared what I recalled of the night of February 13-14, 1945. We left Dresden February 12th on a crowded train but that night we had the fortune of finding a place to stay in a little village quite similar to Binabiburg, about a hundred kilometers from Dresden. The night of February 13th we heard the planes, hundreds of them. They sounded like British Lancasters. Wave after wave flew over us. There wasn't a single German fighter to harass and attack them. My dad said Dresden wasn't defended because it wasn't a military city. Soon we heard what sounded like a rumble, like an earthquake, a distant thunder. Then more Lancasters above us. The horizon in the direction of Dresden began to glow; red then yellow. Soon the smell of smoke, the odor of burning trees and explosives reached our nostrils. Still more Lancasters. No one slept that night.

In the morning we saw hundreds of American Flying Fortresses heading in the direction of Dresden. We also saw the escorting fighters, and we took cover in a nearby air raid shelter. Not a good idea to be outside and be spotted by the fighter pilots as they returned with lots of machine gun ammunition left in store. For days after that vicious attack we found pieces of burnt clothing and documents in trees – even pieces of burnt money, all blown in by the wind. After sharing this with my friends, I said, "How are we to trust the British, or the Americans when they take over from the Germans?" In unison they answered, "I don't know."

"It's going to happen soon," I said, "everyone knows the Germans are retreating. You saw the German trucks pulling big guns heading away from the American front, probably heading toward Berlin to shoot at the Russians. Sure hope the Russians don't catch us."

"They won't," said Janis.

Juris added, "Hope you're right, Janis, but if you're wrong we'll find some guns and shoot them ourselves if they come. Right?"

"Should we go and look for some guns in the woods?" I added smartly, "The Germans sometimes leave a few behind when they retreat in a hurry. People have found rifles and ammunition."

"No, silly Harijs, let's do our fishing and bring home some fish and have something to eat tonight," advised older Janis.

"Janis! Juris! Look! Up the road by the bend, there's a bunch of German kids coming this way. That's too many for us to mess with. We got to scram. Hide."

"No way!" Janis growled at me, "I'm not afraid of them. They'll know who we are. They'll know I can fight like a boxing champ. They'll leave us alone."

"Come on, Janis. Don't be a fool, let's run," added Juris, "Harijs is right. They outnumber us, and that'll make them brave. Let's run."

Just then we spotted a culvert that went under the road ahead of us. Lucky for us.

"Come on, into that tube, fast," I whispered.

And in single file, we crawled into the tube. It was just big enough for us to crawl to the middle. We laid still and quiet until the group of boys passed over. Luckily for us, they hadn't spotted us. Ha! They ware singing a patriotic song and marching. Hitler Jungen playing soldiers. We did that, too, at times. Marching like soldiers made us feel big, strong, important and tough. We even pretended to carry guns. They were just wooden sticks, but from a distance they looked like real rifles. Some of the older guys said they had found real guns in the woods and knew how to use them. We believed it. Of course, they didn't carry real guns when they marched. They knew better. The Gestapo would confiscate them.

The rhythmic strut of the Hitler Jungen above us knocked the dirt off the metal tube and unto our backs. After the marching and singing squad passed over us, we crawled out of the culvert and laughed; but we should have cried. Our clothes! We looked at our poor clothes. From head to foot we were covered with dirt. Now what? What else but head for the river and take a swim, clothes and all. It was a warm and sunny day. Without saying a word, that's exactly what we did. The water was ice cold.

"Look at us," said Janis as we crawled out of the water. "We're wet and cold, but the dirt is gone."

Right he was; not a big accomplishment when one is wearing little old patched shorts and a plain cotton shirt with not much, if anything, under them. We were smart enough not to get our wooden soled sandals wet. We wore no socks.

At about eleven in the morning we started to fish in the bend of the river about a stone's throw from a wooden bridge. A little late for serious fishermen, but we didn't know that. A big part of fishing was having fun and we had already had some.

There we were, three new friends standing riverside under a huge oak tree, willow sticks in hand, fat, juicy worms on hooks in the water, waiting for the big one to strike. We were having a good time laughing, joking and sharing stories of past experiences.

Suddenly tears were forming in my eyes. The scene

reminded me of a fishing trip in my beloved Latvia. I can't remember the name of the river, but it was by the flour mill where we found refuge after leaving Riga. Latvia is not a mountainous country. Compared to the majestic slopes and cliffs of the Bavarian Alps, Latvia is flat. I could see quite far down the road; anything approaching was visible from a distance. Birch and maple patches were about all that could block my view. Why did memory of that scene draw tears to my eyes? Joyful tears.

When we left Riga, my dad had to stay behind. He was not allowed to come with us because he was employed in the Terauds foundry which, in place of farm machinery, was producing critical iron products for the German war machine. Producing what the army needed put my dad under the same discipline as any soldier. You did not abandon your post. We left and he stayed behind. That was sad enough, but thinking we would soon return to our home made it bearable. I loved my dad, and I remembered how much I missed him the first night we parted. We had been at the flour mill for about three weeks when it became obvious it would be a long time before we could go home. The Red Army had intensified attacks, and we heard Riga was under constant air and artillery bombardment. Riga would soon fall into Russian hands. Would we ever get to go home? Where was my daddy? Was he alive? So many people were being killed daily. Would I ever see my daddy again or were we parted forever? I didn't want to live without my daddy. I loved him so much and he loved me.

Then it happened. I saw a tall, slender figure coming down the road towards the mill. Who could it be? It was a man! He was carrying something on his back. He was wearing a grey coat like my daddy's coat. He was my daddy! Did I ever run. Head over heels and so did he. We literally collided. Had he not picked me up in his arms he would have knocked me over.

"Daddy! Daddy!" I cried, "I love you, I missed you!"

"I love you too, Harij!" He said, "I missed you, too!"

"You got out of Riga," I said. "How did you find us? Did you know we came to this mill out in the country?"

As the days grew more chaotic in Riga and the Russians were almost at the city limits, my dad escaped. Yes, he deserted his post at his work-bench. I never found out how he found us.

Suddenly my memories were interrupted.

"Hey Harijs! What's with you?" That was big Janis' voice calling me back to reality. "Are you gonna wet your pants? Are you?" He giggled at me. The strong emotions must have been showing on my face.

"They are wet. And so are yours, unless they are silk, like some dumb girl's!"

"You want to rumble with…"

I was saved by the sight and sound of two cars on the dirt road, immediately catching our attention and ending Janis' irking. How insensitive can he be? Just because he's fourteen and I'm only nine he acts so big and almighty. No, I don't want to rumble with him, nor anyone, really. I don't like to argue, much less fight.

"Look, there are two cars on the road!" Juris called out.

Cars were a novelty. Only army officers and rich people had cars. There were no rich people in and around Binabiburg who could buy cars, much less gasoline. Gasoline was for the military. Even military vehicles were found abandoned by the roadside, out of gasoline. We did see the occasional truck or a bus with a wood burning gas generator strapped on its rear, but not cars. Certainly not two cars at the same time. Ordinary people traveled on bicycles, farmers on wagons pulled by two oxen. What was going on? Two cars on the road! Our eyes were bulging. How exciting!

"They're going fast." I noted. "Look at the dust!"

"Who do you think is riding in them?" Juris asked.

"What a strange color they are? What would you call

it?"

"Olive drab," was my comment.

"See the white star on the door," Janis noted.

Without slowing down, the cars drove across the wooden bridge and were gone, leaving us in utter amazement. What important event could cause two cars to drive so fast on the road out of Binabiburg?.

"My uncle had a car," I said.

"What, your fat uncle Rudis had a car. Rudolfs Smits, the German."

"No Janis, not my uncle Rudis and don't call him fat, and he's not German."

"So, how come he speaks German so good if he's not a German, Harijs?"

"Because he's smart. Yes, Janis, he's smart. He was even appointed a Lager Fuhrer (Camp Director) and he did a good job. Got extra food for all in the camp."

"Now I know he's German for sure. No Latvian, Estonian or Lithuanian would be appointed a Lager Fuhrer. Sure he's not a Nazi as well, Harijs!"

"Janis, leave my uncle alone, he's neither…"

"Stop it you two!" shouted Juris. "Tell us about your uncle who had a car, Harijs."

"You really want to know?" I was getting irritated and ready to go home.

"Yes, I want to know. Any Uncle who has a car is my kind of a man. Did you ever get to ride in it? Is that uncle rich?" Juris went on but Janis turned his back to us and jiggled his fishing line.

"I don't think my uncle was rich. His name is Edwards. We call him Edis. He's my mother's brother and we don't know where he and my aunt are. Her name is Anna. I don't know why he didn't want to travel with us. It may have something to do with one bomb killing all of us."

"That's dumb, Harijs. You can travel together; just don't bunch up during an air raid. Anyway, if your uncle wasn't rich, why did he have a car?"

"He had a bakery in Riga...."

"Then he was rich," Juris cut me off. "Anyone who owns a bakery is rich."

"I don't think he owned the bakery. He leased the building. I know he worked long hours. He also had a motorcycle."

"A motorcycle and a car and a bakery! Harij, he was rich!"

Uncle Edis' bakery. Riga, 1944.

"Yes, he had more than my dad and mom. We lived in a duplex on the outskirts of Riga with my so-called 'German' Uncle Rudis and Tinte." I sneered at Janis, "Uncle Edis and Aunt Anna lived in a brick apartment building near the center of the city. Yes, he was richer than my mom and dad, Juris."

"Why did he have a car and a motorcycle?"

"I really don't know why. He didn't have them at the same time. I never saw his motorcycle. My mother said he took her for a ride once."

"Really? Was she scared?"

"Oh, yeah, she didn't ride with him again." Both Juris and Janis laughed.

"Uncle Edis did take Mom and me for rides in the car. He even let me steer it once."

"Really!" responded both of my friends.

"When was that?" asked Juris.

"Oh, yeah, I remember. Aunt Anna ran away from him, to her relatives who lived on a farm. Uncle Edis asked my mom and me to go with him to get her back. When we were on a country road he let me steer for a whole kilometer."

"Wow Harijs! You drove the car?"

"No, Juris. I sat close to my uncle, reached over, and held the steering wheel."

"You are lucky Harijs: rich uncle, motorcycle, car, bakery. Did your aunt come back?"

"Oh, yeah, she did. Come to think of it, he didn't have the car all the time. Can one own a car some of the time, and not all of the time?"

"Hey guys," shouted Janis, "I think I have a bite! Yes, I do! It's a big one! Come on Betsy, Janis' got ya! Out you come!" And with that, my friend Janis landed a large trout on the grass right at my feet.

Inspired by Janis' success, we re-baited our improvised hooks with fat, fresh worms, reset our bobbers (a cork from a bottle) and sinker (a rusty nut from a machine bolt) to the depth that Janis was fishing, and threw them into the stream, anxious to outdo Janis. I remembered my mom saying "there's more than one fish in the sea." She sure wasn't talking about our little river. We waited and waited. After a couple of hours our eager anxiety turned to boredom and disappointment.

"Let's head for home," I said. My companions agreed. "Let's head for home."

We pulled our lines out of the water, tied them to the willow poles and secured the ends by sticking the sharp end of the hook into the wood. Janis tied his big, wonderful, beautiful, magnificent fish to the top end of his pole, and threw the pole over his shoulder, the fish dangling as proof of his success. He started for home. Juris and I followed a couple of meters back with jealous respect.

Well, well, well! Wouldn't you know; there were three German boys near the bridge. We could tell they were German by their fine clothes "Lederhosen" (leather shorts) with ornamental suspenders, nice shirts with collars, knee high stockings and brown leather shoes. With clothes like that one wouldn't want to dive in the river to wash off some dirt.

Compared to us in our worn duds, these boys looked like kings. We didn't know how long they had watched us from the bridge. We had their full attention as we approached them. One was sitting on the bridge railing, while the other two were standing below him on grass that sloped steeply towards the river. They were about our age and size, though Janis was the biggest.

"Was hast du?" asked the guy who was sitting on the railing, looking at Janis' big fish.

"Hast Du keine Augen? (Don't you have eyes)" replied Janis.

"Du hast unser Fisch! (You have our fish!)" stated the bridge guy.

"Nein! Nein!" (No! No!) Janis shouted back. I began to feel uncomfortable.

"That's our river," said one of the guys on the steep slope.

"But we're allowed to fish here, the fish is mine! Mine!"

"You'd better give it to us or else!" The exchange was getting hotter.

"Or else – what!" shouted Janis, as he took a step forward. "What's your name up there, you puny Kraut?"

"Deb," said the guy on the bridge railing.

"What kind of a name is that? Deb yourself. When the Americans come this will neither be your river nor your country. The Americans will cut your throats!"

Janis made a cutting motion across his throat. I froze. I saw the guy on the bridge leap off the railing towards Janis. Janis let go of his fishing rod. The fishing rod, fish and the German hit the grass at the same time. The German slipped on the grass, fell backwards and somersaulted into the river. What followed was most unexpected. The five of us remaining on the shore burst out in hilarious laughter. We three helped the two Germans pull the wet one out of the water. We shook hands as the wet one asked us, "Didn't you see the two cars?"

We answered "Yes, we saw the two cars."

We went our way towards Binabiburg and the Germans the other way across the bridge. I wondered, as we walked and talked about many events, why the wet German asked us about the two cars.

"Guys," I said, "strange how us kids can't get along, while their parents treat us with kindness, while their country is being destroyed and their army is losing the war and all."

"I think the German kids envy us," said Juris. "They know we get to travel a lot, see many places, big cities, destroyed city centers. They must stay home and help their mothers with chores, their dads being in the war and all."

"Right. Especially farm kids," I said. "When they're not in school they're out in the fields helping their moms. We don't even have school. I was in a German school in Hamburg. That was scary. I wasn't there long because we had to move on. I learned some German words there."

"You got it made, Harijs," said the big fish. "Your uncle can pass for a German, that's why they're nice to you. They're not nice to my family. My folks don't like Germans. They want to go home to Latvia. I do, too. We had things there, a farm, animals, lots of milk and meat. We have nothing here."

"Okay Janis," Juris came on, changing the subject, "Tell us the truth. We promise to tell no one. Are you the one who broke the glass on the memorial in the village square, the one with photos of local German soldiers killed in the war? Are you the one who broke the glass? Tell us the truth, Harijs and I won't tell anyone. Right Harijs?"

"Absolutely. Nobody."

"Hey, guys, I said I don't like Germans. I didn't say I hate them. Nor do my parents hate them. No, I did not break the glass. I had nothing to do with it, believe me."

"Okay, we believe you. You didn't break it. People that do things like that make it difficult for us. Germans suspect us. Remember how nice German people were to us when we were starving on the trains. How long will they have people with pots of hot soup in train stations when our trains come in. I'm thinking about my stomach. I know what it's like to be hungry."

"Yes, Harijs, we all do, that's why we fish," Janis said looking down at me.

"All right," I said, "just let's remember to be nicer when we meet Germans. They're the ones who saved us from the Russians. The communists. Stalin. They allowed us to come to Germany. We must thank them."

We came out of the whispering maple tree grove, and around a bend in the road, giving us a clear sight of pretty little Binabiburg resting in warm sunlight, and the guest house with its big, very big yard. The yard was full of strange trucks and vehicles I had never seen before. All in olive drab, the same color I had seen on the two cars on the road. All of the fifty or more vehicles had a white star painted on the doors. Americans! Americans!!! We were finally captured! That's why the Germans asked if we had seen the two cars. They knew but didn't tell us. The war is over! Now, can we trust the Americans? I had never seen an American.

Slowly, but steadily we walked towards our guest house. Janis, with his big fish, fell back so that all three of us walked side by side, giving us a sense of security. My heart beat faster, palms sweated, chest tightened, giving me a choking feeling in my throat. No one spoke. Janis was biting his lower lip. Juris' fists were clenched. As we got closer to the strange vehicles, a small group of soldiers emerged from behind them with rifles on their shoulders, their uniforms olive drab. They surrounded us. One of them, pointing at Janis' fish started to say something–

"Nuw loooks th leete boob haazs bega fschh….etc. etc"

I didn't understand a word he said. Two more soldiers came. One of them had a sack of chocolate bars in his hand. I couldn't remember when I had eaten some chocolate, but I was so surprised I could have wet my pants! The hands giving me the chocolate were totally black on top. Only the palms were white. The smiling face revealed the whitest teeth I had ever seen, but the face was completely black with big white eyes. Had he been burnt in the war? What had happened to the man? He had a helmet on, cocked to one side. I saw tight black curls where his hair should have been. Then I saw my mother running flat out, skirts a-flying. She grabbed me, pulled me away from the black man, picked me up and ran with me in her arms. Before I knew I was in the large upper room we shared with ten other families. I was in front of a trembling Mother, tears flowing down her blushed cheeks. Tinte Marta was by her side.

"Harij, do you know that man could have eaten you! They are cannibals!" My mom was shouting at the top of her voice. I could hear her above the noise of many other excited voices in the big upper room!

So ended one war, but for me another had just begun.

two

Binabiburg

EVERYONE WAS TALKING in various degrees of excitement and nobody was listening. There was Tinte Marta, Mom, Dad, Uncle Rudis and adult representatives from all the families who shared the large upper room of the guest house. Janis was there in the company of his parents, likewise Juris with his. The spontaneous combustion of voices was trying to tell Janis, Juris and me frightening news, but to which voice should we listen? And what were the voices talking about? I heard a jumble mumble of words like,

"Save Black Cannibal"
"Savage Army Harijs Janis Cannibal"
"Truck Juris Children Eat"
"Cannibal Our Rita With Americans Long ago Africa"

Finally, as the commotion settled I could hear my mother's lecture as she repeated over and over again, "Harij, I was scared. You weren't coming home. I was afraid the Americans, the American army, the Americans had taken you away. No one can understand what they're saying. None of us can speak American, and then you were with the Americans and the two black cannibals were coming to get you. I was so scared. You weren't coming home....I was scared... etc. etc..."

"Mother, I'm okay. They didn't hurt me nor did they try to. I think they're nice soldiers. They were smiling, especially the two hurt, burned ones... they were black...they gave us chocolate bars. Where are mine, mom? He gave me two."

"I have them. But I don't think you should eat them."

"Why not Mom, I like chocolate."

"The chocolate may be poisoned." (By now we were dispersed in family groups.)

"Why would they poison the chocolate?"

"Let me see them." Tinte Marta took over as Mom handed her the two bars. She opened the end of one, smelled it, and pinched off a tiny piece and put it to her lips, tasted and ate it.

"The chocolate is fine. Sweet. Oh, for goodness sake, let Harijs eat them. One now, save the other for later."

"I'm afraid, Marta," pleaded Mom.

"I want to eat one, now. Please."

"I'm afraid," Mom said it again.

"I want one now, it's been so long since I..."

"Let Harijs eat one," it was Dad's turn to speak. "Americans don't poison chocolate bars to hurt children."

"American chocolate is very good. We imported boxes of it in Riga," said Uncle Rudis who had worked for a shipping and importing company in Riga as a bookkeeper. He was smart; knew his chocolates.

"Mom, I want the chocolate, Mom!"

"Here, but eat it slowly, piece by little piece," Tinte Marta handed me the bar.

"Marta! No!" cried my mom.

Too late. I grabbed the bar and ran to Dad and Uncle Rudis for protection. That stopped Mom in her tracks. Uncle Rudis was seated so I jumped in his lap.

With the greatest of anticipation I unwrapped the bar

and, following Tinte Marta's suggestion, broke off a little piece and put it into my mouth. Oh! Oh! What a taste! Heavenly! I had actually forgotten the taste of fine milk chocolate.

"Aren't you going to share it?" asked Uncle Rudis.

"Rudolph!" exclaimed Tinte, "Really!"

"Want some, Uncle?"

"No, no, I was just teasing."

Mom stood beside Dad, who had his arm around her. She was watching me as if I was about to drop dead any minute. Oh, but the taste of American chocolate!

"The black man gave the chocolate to Harijs as bait. I saved Harijs. The cannibals would've drugged him into…"

"Erna," interrupted my uncle. "Black Americans aren't cannibals."

"How do you know that? I've read Robinson Crusoe. They're cannibals, savages."

"Erna, that book is about the 17th, maybe 16th century Africa, These men aren't from 17th century Africa. They're from present day America."

I was eating my chocolate piece by little piece, slowly and listening, all ears, to this conversation about the black men. I'd never seen a black man before. Obviously neither had my mom. There were no black people in Riga, perhaps not in all of Latvia. In America are there black women? Wow, black moms? Black boys? Maybe even little black girls with big white eyes. Very interesting. Black people.

Now I got it. I'm not going to tell anybody I thought the two black soldiers were hurt, burned, injured in the war. I was dumb thinking only people of my skin color lived in the world. Latvians, Lithuanians, Estonians, Germans even Russians have the same skin color. I hadn't imagined some Americans were black.

"I am afraid of them," said my mom.

"Ah Erna you're afraid of everything," noted Tinte, shaking her head.

"Afraid or not, love," Dad came back into the conversation, "we're with the Americans now and we're going to live with them no matter what color they are. Just remember they're not Russians, and not Communists. We have to trust them. They'll protect us."

Now that was pretty wise of my dad, I thought, but what would it be like to have a black boy as a friend. If I had a black boy as a friend and the two of us would come upon a white girl who was pestering me, would she be afraid of my black friend, like my mom, and run away?" A most entertaining idea. A black friend is all I need to keep the girls away. Hmm.

"Erna, Harijs," said Uncle Rudis as I was finishing the last little piece of my first delicious American chocolate bar. I felt safe now to get out of my uncle's lap, chocolate bar in my tummy, and be on my own in the midst of my family.

"Listen to me. I haven't seen black Americans before. But someone from the shipping firm I worked for, who had traveled to America, told me about them. He said they used to be slaves and lived mostly in the southern areas of the United States."

"Slaves, were they," said Mom. "Who and why anyone would want them as slaves?"

"Farmers with big cotton and produce farms on large plantations. Cheap labor. Just like we were, and like our own ancestors were for the Russians and later the German Barons. Cheap labor. Slaves. We can relate to that."

"Slaves in the Army? American Army?" inquired Mom.

"No, no, black people aren't slaves any more, but my colleague at work did say that they live in separate sections in cities, or on farms. They keep mostly to themselves." (I could understand that. I kept mostly to myself in my big yard in Riga with the solid three meter wooden fence all around.)

"Then what are they doing in the Army?"

"What does anyone do in the Army? They were drafted

to fight the enemy, just like our boys were drafted by the Nazis to fight the Communists."

"Well, Rudi, I just don't know. I don't like them and I don't want them around my boy."

"Believe me Erna, they won't hurt him or anybody, today nor tomorrow. Erna, they're probably better people than you or me. Just think Erna if it wasn't for the Germans and now the Americans, including these black Americans, we would be slaves in the Soviet Union - Siberia, where our own people were shipped to work and die. Remember, Erna, the cattle railroad cars in the train terminal in Riga; bolted shut, Latvians in them barely alive, being shipped like pigs to Siberia. Remember why we left Riga."

This is getting interesting, I thought. Now I knew why we had to leave Riga. As I was listening to my uncle Rudis advancing the cause of black Americans, something happened that drew the attention of all of us in the large upper room.

I heard a small group of people coming up the stairwell. I heard girls' voices, giggles, laughter and men's voices, but I couldn't make out what the men were saying. The double doors opened and in came three girls who were very much a part of our extended upper room family, smiling from ear to ear, slightly blushed to match the shades of pink of their short straight cotton dresses. Each girl carried a parcel in her hands. They were followed by three American soldiers also armed with parcels. Our guest house owner, all dressed up in lederhosen, was the last to walk in. The tallest of the girls, almost as tall as Mom and actually quite pretty, said, "The Americans want to help us with dinner tonight. They want us to know they're our friends and mean no harm to us."

"In my box is bread and in Vilma's (the tall girl) is some butter and jam," said the second tallest, also quite pretty, the breeze folding her dress between her legs.

Then one of the American soldiers stepped between the

girls, placed his parcel on the floor, pointed to his chest then to the insignia on his helmet and said, "Loitnant" in German (Lieutenant). Again he pointed to his chest and said, "Jack. Lieutenant Jack." Then he pointed to the first soldier behind him, then to the stripes on the sleeve of his jacket, "Sergeant Ron." Then he pointed to the second soldier, a tall, thin man, "Private Ken."

Then he pointed to the parcels and extended both arms towards us, drawing a semi-circle in our direction, and said (translated by the Guest house owner), "These are for all of you for tonight." He took a step back from the girls and, unbelievably, saluted the girls, then motioned to his two men and the guest house owner to follow him. The four left our big upper room. Someday I'm going to like pretty girls.

Each family returned to their cubicles: the large room had been sectioned with old blankets along the four walls to give families some privacy.

That night we ate like we had never eaten before in all our travels since we left Riga. White bread with strawberry jam on top of the butter. A slice of delicious canned ham and a cup of potato soup. All from America.

After we had eaten our best supper in a long time, Janis came into our cubicle with one more surprise. "Harijs, my mom wants you and Juris to come over and help me eat my fish."

German forces in Italy surrendered on May 2, 1945.

Early in the morning of May 7, 1945, General Alfred Jodl of the German High Command entered Allied headquarters in a school building at Reims, France. On behalf of his government he signed terms of unconditional surrender. Lieutenant General Walter B. Smith, Eisenhower's Chief of Staff, signed for the Allies. On May 9th, a ceremony in Berlin ratified the terms of surrender. After five years, eight months, and seven days, the European phase of World War II was over.

The most costly and deadly war in history:

Estimated cost in 1950's dollars: over $1.15 trillion.

Loss of life: Over 55 million people, civilians and military.

No estimates of the number of wounded, maimed for life or psychologically disabled.

three

Binabiburg:
End of May, 1945

THE CHOPPING BLOCK! Look at the big chopping block a half meter in diameter, I said to myself. The owner of the guest house was using it to save his back. I wondered how tall was the fir tree from which it was cut.

The kind owner was chopping wood for the wood fire stove in the large kitchen of his guest house. He placed a log on the center of the block, picked up the big axe, lifted it high over his head and, thud! The big axe came down on the log and it fell to the ground in two pieces. The owner was a big strong man but, dressed in his woodcutting pants, he looked old. He looked shabby like the rest of us. I volunteered to help him pile the wood. In turn, he allowed me to watch him chop. Chop! And another piece split in two. He was strong.

Sitting on a log nearby, I thought about the day the war ended for us. We learned that the war had actually ended earlier, but we just didn't hear the news until the day the soldiers arrived. That explained why there was no shooting or bombing the day the Americans came to Binabiburg. The Germans had already surrendered.

We also learned that the American unit that occupied the guest house yard and the warehouse on the other side of the yard from the guest house was not infantry but a supply unit, bringing food, ammunition and medical supplies to combat troops. Since the war was over, the lieutenant could be generous and benevolent toward us.

The American unit stayed four days and gave us more food upon leaving, which we divided according to the size of each family. We made the rations last until order was restored and food became available.

I will never forget the days before we came to Binabiburg when we had nothing to eat. There was no food in bombed-out city grocery stores, and the soup pot that always seemed available at the train stations was gone. There was only destruction and chaos. No one had food. There was no reason to expect there would ever be anything at all to eat. There were no crumbs under the table and, if there had been, I would have gladly dropped down on my knees like a dog, and licked them up. We prepared ourselves to die of starvation. That experience taught me the meaning of hunger. I'll never forget it. Food is precious. Food is sacred. Food is life.

When we arrived at the guest house, the strong old man who was splitting wood gave each of us a slice of black bread with bacon grease on it. He saved us. My uncle had a gold pocket watch from Latvia. He gave it to the man.

Knowing the war was soon to end, the guest house owner allowed us to stay and promised to help us with food as best as he could. This amounted to a bowl of soup a day for each of us, a loaf of black bread for the five of us and some lard and bacon grease. We supplemented our simple diet with an occasional egg we begged from nearby farmers, also potatoes, rutabagas and cabbage we gleaned from the fields.

He was a good man, I was happy to help him with the wood. Later in the day I had planned to hunt mushrooms in the nearby woods. It had been raining and I overheard Rita's dad saying mushrooms were starting to sprout. A bit early in the spring, I thought, but it wouldn't hurt to try.

Maybe Janis and Juris will come with me? I wasn't sure I wanted Janis to come, but Juris, yes.

During the four days the Americans were in the guest house yard, I learned a few things about them. Americans did Church. I wondered if they were Lutherans like us, but I knew they did Church. One morning they were sitting on the grass in a semicircle, with a soldier wearing a cross on his uniform standing in front, first reading then speaking. They sang. The soldier with the cross made the sign of the cross and they all stood. I knew it was church. I hadn't been to church since we left Riga. On one occasion a Latvian pastor did come aboard the train we were on and served the Lord's Supper to the adults, including some Estonians who didn't understand a word he said. We prayed every night before we went to bed. We prayed the Lord's Prayer. We prayed for peace, for something to eat, a safe night and to be alive and well in the morning.

I also learned soldiers cleaned their rifles. At first I didn't know what they were doing. They assembled two metal rods to look like a big needle, inserted a piece of cloth in the eye, dripped something like melted butter on the cloth, and then pushed it into the business end of the rifle. I asked Dad. He knew right away, "Cleaning and oiling their rifles," he said.

Dad was in the Latvian Army after the First World War. He was a messenger (later signal corps) whose duty was to deliver orders and instructions from the commanders to the troops; a most dangerous assignment in the front lines during war. At discharge he was awarded a citation for his outstanding performance of duty.

I had learned a lot by observing the soldiers. Americans didn't march like Germans. In fact they didn't march at all in the courtyard. Only once did they stand in formation when a high ranking officer came in a jeep to visit them. In the courtyard they walked like normal people. German soldiers marched wherever they went. I thought the

Germans looked more like soldiers. Americans were relaxed. They even put their feet up on desks when they sat. I saw Lieutenant Jack in the warehouse sit with his feet on his desk. The door was open.

When an American soldier had a chocolate bar or some other treat in his hand and said something I couldn't understand, I'd nod and say "Ya" or better yet, "Yes" and he'd give me the chocolate or the cookie. I had eaten more than ten chocolate bars and many tasty cookies since they had arrived. (I didn't tell Mom.)

The most amusing and puzzling thing I learned was that Americans didn't speak American. They spoke English. I wondered how did that come about? Latvians spoke Latvian, Estonians spoke Estonian, Lithuanians spoke Lithuanian, Germans spoke German and Russians spoke Russian but Americans spoke English. If we Latvians spoke Russian among ourselves, it would mean we had lost our historic language, culture, traditions, folk songs and stories – in other words, everything, to Russia. Victorious Americans spoke English. Amusing! Had they lost their culture? In some way did the English rule America? What will I learn next? That I, too, must speak English?

The good, kind and strong guest house owner stopped working and was waving to me. I was glad to help him stack the wood he had chopped with the big, big axe on the big, big chopping block. Maybe he'll give me something for helping. He didn't. Oh well, it's not wrong to hope.

"So I see you're collaborating with the Germans," Janis' voice startled me from behind, just as I was finishing stacking the wood. The owner had left the job all to me.

"What do you mean collaborating?" I spat back in disgust.

"Nice boy, aren't you, piling wood for them and all."

"So what's wrong with that? This wood is for the big oven in the kitchen to bake bread for us; for you. You've eaten bread baked in the big oven."

"Yes, I have. But it's not very good, not near as good as my mother used to bake on our farm in Latvia."

"Would you rather have nothing at all to eat?"

"No, but must they mix sawdust with the flour. I'm sure they do. The black bread tastes so woody."

"They do not. Maybe they don't have the good flour mills like we had." I thought of the flour mill we had stayed at where my dad caught up with us.

"Yeah, Harijs, Yeah. You make a good advocate for Germans. Go ahead, plead for them, be their defense attorney, they'll like that. Anyway, I hear you're going mushroom picking later on today. Is that right, Harijs?"

"Where did you hear that? By the way, the war *is* over, or haven't you heard?"

"What does it matter, I mean what does it matter where I heard about you going after mushrooms. Well, if you are, I want to go with you for your protection. You know it's not safe to go alone."

"You got me there, but let's ask Juris to come along, okay Janis?"

"Suit yourself."

After this delightful conversation, I found Juris and asked him to come along. He said he was happy to, but had to ask his dad. I was surprised that my mom and dad had allowed me to go mushroom hunting by myself, or possibly they had overheard Rita's dad talk about mushrooms and thought I was going with her family to pick them? Rita's family! Yeah sure. Parents just don't understand anything. Rita's family, yeah right. Go mushroom hunting with a girl. Girls can't even run across a road or jump a ditch or a mud puddle without tripping, falling or asking for help. Rita's family. Right.

Later in the afternoon the three of us were on our way, not toward the river but the other way, over a little hill to the woods, with home woven wicker baskets under our arms. My dad had woven them. He was good at making things. Many people said he was a good handyman.

"Harijs?" asked Janis. "Who told you mushrooms are growing already? Usually they grow late in June. It's only the end of May."

"Who told me? No one. I overheard Rita's dad speak to Rita's mom. They may be going too. We may meet them in the woods. We better keep a watch out. Don't want to run into them."

"Rita!" Janis exclaimed, "Rita is going mushroom picking with her folks?"

"I didn't say that, Janis. I just overheard her folks talking about mushrooms, that's all."

"Harijs!" exclaimed Janis, "That's why you were planning to go alone. You were scheming to join up with her folks. With Rita. You like Rita!"

Rita was the youngest of the three girls that were with the American soldiers on the famous "end of the war" feast day.

"I do not! You like her, Janis!"

"If I liked her would that stop you from… from….from liking her? Would it?"

"How come you're stuttering? Even if I did like her what good would that be? I don't play with girls, but I think you'd like to play with girls, especially Rita! Wouldn't you, Jani?"

"She is kind of pretty," injected Juris.

If the truth were told, I did think Rita was pretty. But I wasn't going to admit it. She was only a girl. I wondered where she got her pretty dresses. Clothes were hard to come by and were very expensive, but not in terms of money. No one sold anything for money, but if you had something to trade, food for example, or jewelry, American chewing gum or even cigarettes, then you could get things. I wondered how many loaves of bread does a pretty dress cost?

"Okay I like her a lot," admitted Janis.

"What about the other two? Vilma, Zenta. You like them too, Janis?" I asked.

"They're too old for me," answered Janis. "They could be my mothers."

"You want two mothers?" joked Juris. "Eighteen and nineteen year old mothers?"

"I'm not interested in any of them," I lied, thinking that Rita really was pretty, "but what I am interested in is, how did they manage to get the Americans to give us the food we're living on?"

"I wondered about that too," said Juris. "You don't suppose Vilma (the oldest) knows a little American?"

"Juris," I said, "Americans don't speak American. Americans speak English."

"Harij," said Juris, "that's the same language. American and English are the same language."

"You sure, Juri?" I wanted confirmation on this enlightenment. "That's queer, how come?"

"Long time ago the English established colonies in America," explained Juris, "but soon the English forgot how hard it was to be a colonist. The English were mean to the colonists so the colonists got mad at the English and rebelled. Attacked them."

"Really? The colonists in America fought the English," I said, "then what?"

"The colonists won and decided to be Americans."

"But the English made the colonists speak English like the Russians wanted to force us to speak Russian?" commented Janis.

"No, no, being of English descent the colonists themselves decided to continue to speak English. They just pronounced some words differently. Shortened some, abbreviated others."

"How do you know all this?" asked Janis.

"My dad told me. He's a school teacher," answered Juris.

"Yeah, but that doesn't really explain why American is the same as English," I noted. "Don't Americans have their own literature, stories, folk songs, identity?"

"Harij, I don't know. They probably have. Every nation produces memorable literature and music during their times of struggle. I should ask my dad." Juris continued. "Yeah, Dad said Americans even fought among themselves to free people who had become slaves in America."

"Slaves, like the black people?" I asked.

"Yeah, I think that's what my dad said," answered Juris.

"Juri," I asked, "did we fight among ourselves in Latvia?"

"Not lately, Harij. Maybe a long time ago under legendary leaders. Lately our conflicts have been with the big neighboring nations who'd like to think our fertile farm lands, the Baltic seashore and the year round ice-free port of Riga is theirs. Somebody always thinks we should be their servants. Slaves."

"Juri," I said, "you sure know a lot."

"Well, it's my dad. He says he must teach me because we have no school."

"When your dad is teaching you about these things, can I join you in listening?"

"Why not, I'm sure that'll be okay with my dad."

"What about you Janis? Are you interested to learn from Juris' dad?" I asked, but he hadn't listened to Juris and me.

"Hey, I know how Vilma, Zenta and Rita got through to the Americans!" He exclaimed jubilantly, changing our chat back to our previous subject, "they used body language."

"What do you mean by body language?" I asked.

"Well, in body language you point to things. You move, you use your body to say things, like a smile could say that you're happy or approve, or you could point to your tummy if you're hungry, things like that," answered Janis.

"To say you want to eat because you're hungry," I tried to develop the idea, "you'd point to your mouth with one hand, and with the other clutch your tummy?"

"Harijs, that would be saying, kiss me and hug me," interrupted Juris.

"Now we're talking," said Janis, with a big grin on his face. "That's how we got the food from the Americans. The girls used body language. A girl can say more with her body than with words. The girls got the Americans to like them and when a guy likes a girl he'll do anything for her. When you grow up Harijs, you'll know what I'm taking about. Body language, dummy."

I knew exactly what Janis meant. Body language! You bet! Body language!

That's when we met Rita on the trail, (the pretty dress hugging her body under an open coat was speaking loudly). She was leading her family. All three carrying two baskets each full of mushrooms. They told us they had found them in a shady marsh beyond the hill just ahead of us. Rita's dad advised us to go a little further into the marsh under the tall trees, where we'd find lots of big light brown mushrooms. With that information under hat we were on our way to success. Too bad Rita had to go the other way with her parents.

"Harijs, why are you gawking after Rita?" Janis was glaring at me.

"I'm not. I was looking at her basket full of mushrooms," I lied.

"Oh sure, with your mouth open and hand in your pocket?"

"Yeah, her mushrooms, I tasted them on my tongue, fried."

"Just keep your tongue in your mouth, eyes on the trail and your hands away from Rita. Rita is mine and don't you ever forget that. Got it, little Harijs."

"Yes, Janis I got it. But you get it, too, I've no interest in girls."

"Keep it that way for your own good, you runt."

"Okay, okay," I said to end the conversation, "no interest in girls."

As we walked along the first marsh, I saw where Rita's family had cut their mushrooms. I also saw Rita's footprints in places where the forest floor was covered with damp green moss. (Even her footprints were speaking.) Better not look at her footprints too obviously; I didn't want Janis to rib me again about pretty fifteen year old Rita. (Body language!) Janis had just turned fourteen. I should tell him Rita was too old for him.

As we walked through the ground zero of Rita's mushroom success and out into the clearing beyond, I saw the grove of tall trees we were told about. I made a proposal. "Let's spread out. Janis, you take the center. I'll go about a hundred meters to the right. Juris, why don't you go about a hundred meters to the left. We'll have a better chance of finding the mushrooms."

"Good idea," they agreed and we spread out.

As we went I imagined we were soldiers and the mushrooms, prisoners of war who had escaped. We're going to find, capture and bring them in. Hey, pretending and imagining was fun!

I pretended my dad's pocket knife for cutting the mushrooms, was a bayonet. The wicker basket that soon would be full of mushrooms was an ammunition magazine containing hand grenades and rifle shells.

"Harijs! Juris!" I heard Janis calling, "come here, look at this, quick!" We came running to our center Scout.

"Look!" and Janis pointed to what looked like tank track imprints in the ground just on the edge of the grove of the tall trees.

"It went that way," Janis said, "around the grove, and it looks like it drove into the thicket of shrubs just beyond the rise."

"Let's go see what it is," I suggested.

"Okay," they both agreed and we ran fast. We followed

the tracks in the ground over the rise, and yes, whatever it was had gone into the thicket. Out of breath, we arrived at the thicket of brush. What was this battered, abandoned vehicle? My imagination went into action. I shouted, "It's a tank! A real tank. A Panzer, a German Panzer, abandoned in the brush."

"Come on, men!" I heard Janis take command, "We'll make them surrender. We'll capture the tank."

"Forward!" he commanded. And we charged the thing, branches scratching our arms and legs. Our baskets fell to the ground. "Over the treads and into the turret!" shouted Janis.

No sir, no way, enough pretending and imagination for me. This object is real, but what is it? I'm not climbing on it nor in it. Feeling like a deserter, I watched Janis climb up, open a big hatch, and disappear into it.

"Hey guys! This is great! Come see!" Janis shouted from inside.

"No Janis!" shouted Juris, "we shouldn't. Better not mess with the thing." And I agreed but said nothing.

"Why not? I'll look around inside here." Janis' voice, dampened inside the walls.

"No, Janis, get out of there," shouted Juris again.

"How in the world do you start this thing?"

"Start? I don't know," Juris replied, "I don't even know how to start a car. Janis, get out of there. Don't start anything."

"I'm going to press this red button. Here it goes." But nothing happened. The big thing just laid there. I saw rust on the chains.

"Hey, there are two levers. They look like sticks, I want to see how they move."

"Janis, get out of there," Juris was pleading now.

"Those sticks don't move, but the pedal on the floor goes up and down."

"Janis, get out of there. Please listen to Juris," I was

pleading too.

"You two little chickens. Hey, what's this? I think I've found something. Look at this." Janis poked his head out of the hole and in his uplifted arms were two real hand grenades. One in each hand.

"Put those things back. You fool. Don't you dare throw them!" screamed Juris as Janis was waving the grenades above his head. I said nothing but felt hollowness in my stomach.

"Don't worry. I won't throw them. Besides, they don't explode until you pull this pin. See the pin is there," he pointed to it.

The grenades were centimeters apart now. What if he dropped them by accident? Right at our feet. Kaboom! There'd be but pieces left of three dumb boys.

Janis disappeared again into the thing. Second thoughts flashed in my mind. I had heard of soldiers using hand grenades to stun fish in lakes and rivers. Might be a good idea to keep some grenades. I could stun and collect lots of fish with them. But, no. I didn't have a boat. I wouldn't be able to retrieve the stunned fish.

Janis popped up out of the tank-like thing and I saw boxes of ammunition in his hands. Real ammunition in Janis' hands. "Look guys! Bullets! There are lots of bullets here. Small caliber. I think they're for hand guns. Let's take these. Maybe we can trade them for something. There are people who hunt. They could use them. What do you think?"

"No, Janis," Juris replied firmly.

"Juris," I said, "I think Janis has a good point."

"That a boy, Harijs!" and with that Janis dismounted the thing on tank treads, holding a box of one hundred small, shiny copper shells in his hand.

"If you don't want any Juris, Harijs and I'll split this. You'll be sorry."

"I don't want any," Juris said. "I don't want anything to

do with the bullets. You keep them all. We better leave the thing alone and get back to our mushrooms before someone else picks them."

We agreed. We walked away from the big thing, looking back more than forward, until the mighty tank was hidden from our view by the thick brush. Fearing our parents' wrath for playing with dangerous things we told no one about this. It was much later that I learned from photographs of army vehicles that it was a wrecked German all terrain armored truck.

Soon we were back to the marshy grove of tall trees where Rita's dad had said we would find mushrooms. I felt the fresh coolness of the shade, created by the tall trees, on my neck and bare arms. I stared not because it was darker in the trees but because I saw mushrooms. Hundreds of them. Beautiful mushrooms. Brown, yellow and red.

"Wow!" I heard my companions.

"Have you ever seen so many mushrooms?" I exclaimed as I dashed to the nearest cluster, reaching for Dad's knife to cut them.

"Never," said Juris, "but do we know which ones to pick. There are poisonous ones, you know."

"Don't worry about it. My mom and dad know all about mushrooms. They'll wash them and throw out the poisonous ones. Your folks can check with my dad. But I know the light brown ones are the best."

"Right!" Juris answered, "Let's pick the light brown ones."

Without wasting more time talking or joking we got to work. With visions of deliciously sautéed mushrooms in my mind, I could already taste them as I sliced and gathered them into my wicker basket. "No doubt about it, we'll feast tonight," I thought. Lightly fried mushrooms were simply delicious.

The war over, and with food on the table, life was improving. There was hope. Perhaps Dad will get a job.

Yes, but will we get to go home to Latvia? Not if the Communists rule. I knew my parents would not live under the rule of Communism, especially Stalin's Communism. Nor will I, I thought. Stalin's Communism is evil.

"How're you doing, Juris, Harijs?" I heard Janis' voice. "My basket is almost full. We can't pick all of them."

"I know, that bothers me. I don't want them to be wasted," I answered.

"Me neither, let's come back tomorrow and pick the rest," suggested Juris.

"Good idea," I said, then changed my mind. "But don't you think we should tell the other families about our find. Rita's dad told us."

"Lots of mushrooms, yes, but not enough for everyone," replied Janis, "let's think about it, okay."

"Janis, I doubt we have a choice. Rita's dad probably has told everyone already," observed Juris. "He's generous you know." Janis didn't answer.

During hard times, and war is the hardest of all, people became generous, unbelievably generous. People shared what they had. They shared food and they shared housing. It was nothing unusual to see families share their homes, apartments, even shacks that didn't leak, with other families. From our traveling days I remembered seeing from our train window, as it went slowly through a totally destroyed city center, two families sharing a protected hole in the rubble of a bombed out brick building. Yes, there were two families sharing the hole. I saw a blanket in the middle of the hole dividing it in two. But when times start to get better, greed begins to rear its ugly head. "Okay let's think about it," Janis had said.

"Okay. Let's think about it," I repeated as we started for *home* – the cubicle in the shared big upper room above farm animals; some cows and a pig, a typical Bavarian guest house.

"Hey guys, I'm a bit tired," confessed Juris, "let's sit

under the fir tree and rest a bit."

"No way!" protested big Janis, "we have to get the mushrooms home."

"Oh come on Janis we've time," I supported Juris.

"All right babies, let's rest," consented Janis. "So you two can think about your mommies?"

"Might not be so bad if you thought about yours sometime, Janis," I joked.

"Harijs!" Janis glared at me. "Just sit down, shut your mouth and rest. Okay."

"Sure, Janis, sure. Anyway, sorry," I apologized.

We sat in the shade of the fir tree. I felt the cool spring air. The light breeze was compelling the grass and underbrush to sway like submerged seaweed. The fragrance of the lush green foliage added spice to the musty smell of freshly cut mushrooms in the basket by my side. Too bad that Janis got on my nerves, and I seemed to get on his. That could have been a memorable moment, resting under the fir tree, already tasting the dinner to come.

I began to day dream. I did that a lot. All at once we were soldiers, Janis, Juris and I. Soldiers of a crack Latvian unit sent out on a patrol to find Communists. Juris and I had repeating rifles, Janis was pulling a machine gun on a cart. We had lots of grenades. We were moving like foxes, swiftly and quietly. Then we heard them. Communists! They were coming toward us. A platoon of Communists supported by a monstrous tank. I could see them, the red star on their garrison hats. Garrison hats, not helmets. A red star on the side of a monstrous tank in the shape of Communist Russia. A big Communist manning the machine gun in the turret was sitting, unprotected. He had a thick mustache, and wore a flat topped hat with a bill and a double breasted coat. There he was, the number one Communist, dictator, monster. Juris and I took our positions. Janis deployed his machine gun. At the right time we opened fire. The number one guy at the machine gun on the tank fell immediately. We were aiming at the red stars on the garrison hats, like bull's eyes on a target. We were mowing them down like flies. The tank opened fire on us but missed. There were no more red stars to aim at, but the tank was advancing. It fired again and missed. The tank was almost upon us. Juris and I pulled the safety pins of our grenades as Janis kept firing at the tank. At the right moment Janis ceased firing, Juris jumped on the tank and pulled open the hatch and dropped his grenade into the tank. Simultaneously I jumped and slid a grenade down the tank's smoking barrel. There was a double explosion as Juris and I hit the ground. The tank was engulfed in black smoke, its mighty barrel lying helplessly in mud by the tracks of the tank, mangled in the form of a hammer and a cycle.

"Guys, we better head for home," said Janis as he stood up, taking his basket.

"We got 'em!" I shouted, and then realized I was out of context.

"Got what?" asked an annoyed Janis.

"The mushrooms," I said, coming back to reality.

We've had an exiting day, I thought. I didn't even get into a really serious argument with Janis. Well, almost, because of Rita. Am I changing my mind about girls? Anyway, Janis is abrasive at times but he's brave.

Whatever made me pretend the strange abandoned wreck was a German Panzer? My day dreams? We were now at peace, but in my mind remained flashbacks from the war. Scenes from news reels, magazines, newspapers. In my heart the war wasn't over because Latvia wasn't free.

What are Janis and I going to do with the bullets we found, I was thinking. Can we really show them to anyone? Not my parents.

As we walked it seemed we had run out of things to talk or argue about. That was fine with me. In Latvia I lived in a house with a huge yard. We had front, back and side fields where we grew vegetables and harvested hay for our chickens and rabbits. The huge yard had a high fence around it. I had no sisters or brothers. Most of the time I played alone, in silence, protected by the high fence. Walking with these two guys without talking was comfortable for me. I was a loner.

I was lost in memories of my yard in Latvia when we came to the place on the trail were we had met Rita earlier that afternoon. Rita, yes Rita. She reminded me of Irene, the girl who lived across the street from my fenced yard in Riga and came to play with me from time to time. Play? Not really. She helped me tend my garden. She helped me weed and water, and advised me on pruning. I liked to garden. My parents liked to garden. In my garden, I pretended I was my dad. Irene also came when Mom and Dad couldn't take me with them when they went to required political meetings. That was nice of Irene. She read stories and we talked about dumb things like dolls and shoes and hair styles for girls. But I liked her anyway.

One day I got in trouble with my mom because of her. In our yard was a high pile of lumber; the heavy timbers and boards my dad had used for the ceiling of the air raid shelter. From the top of the pile I could see Irene's yard and the porch of her house. One summer I noticed from the top of the lumber pile, that on sunny afternoons, Irene came out of her house and laid down in a recliner on her porch or on the green grass. As she lay down, the hem of her dress or skirt floated up to her slender waist. That happened often. I regretted I didn't have money to buy one of those thick glasses sailors use to look for land and other ships. When Irene lay on the grass, or on the porch I couldn't see what I wanted to see. I got in trouble, a spanking no less, when my mom caught me watching her. Mom told me, "Don't you ever do that again!" I had no idea why my mom was angry with me. And then there was Rita! Rita's body language explained why. Appreciate me, it said, but treat me like a gentleman would treat a lady, with kindness, consideration and respect.

In remembrance. From Irene.
Riga, December 5, 1942.

"Janis," I asked, "Do you know, I mean, have you ever seen what's inside a rifle cartridge?"

"No, why do you ask?"

"What is it that makes the noise and smoke and shoots the bullet out of a gun?"

"Inside the cartridge is gun powder. It burns fast, like in a split second, like an explosion."

"You think we can open one of the cartridges and see what gunpowder looks like?"

"Pretty hard to pry out the bullet without tools."

We stopped and Janis took out one of the shiny little

cartridges from the box and gave it to me as Juris looked on. I tried to wiggle the bullet but it was solid. It didn't move. I put the cartridge to my ear and shook it. I heard nothing.

"The gunpowder must be solid. It doesn't slush about. I wonder what color it is? Janis, have you ever fired a rifle?"

"Yes, in Latvia."

"You have!" I exclaimed, "You fired a rifle!"

Juris expressed his surprise, "You fired a gun!"

"Yes. My old man, all of the men in my family, were hunters. We had lots of rifles and pistols in the house. All kinds of ammunition too. My dad liked to hunt wild boars."

"You shot a wild boar?" asked Juris.

"No, no. To tell you the truth they didn't want me to go hunting with them, but my old man let me shoot at targets. Pieces of wood. You should have seen the wood fly apart when I hit it."

"You're a good shot, Janis?" I inquired.

"Not bad, not bad."

"But you have never seen gunpowder?"

"No, Harijs, the cartridges are always empty when they come out of the rifle."

We were getting close to the guest house; I could smell the pig on the first floor. I wanted to prepare myself for praise and adoration over my impressive harvest of golden-brown mushrooms, and my friends did too. I changed the subject but not without making one last suggestion.

"Janis, let's hide the cartridges in the wood pile as we go by it, find some pliers, and come out after we've delivered the mushrooms. I want to see what gun powder looks like. Juri, don't you dare tell on us."

"You want me to lie, Harij?"

"No Juri, just don't bring up the subject. Okay."

My dad must've spotted us. He was standing in the door of the guest house smiling from ear to ear. Confident of a banquet of mushrooms tonight provided by his son, he was wearing what he called his Sunday outfit, grey pants and a white linen shirt. I was smiling too as I held in front of me my basket full of beautiful fresh golden brown mushrooms.

"Good boy!" Dad said as he took the basket from me. "I knew you'd be successful, especially after Rita's dad told us he met you on the path. He was sure you'd find a lot of mushrooms too."

"We did and there are lots more there. Can we go tomorrow again and get some more?"

"Yes, a good idea, but let's talk to Mom first. But now let's get these mushrooms washed so Mom can start cooking. Seems everybody is using the wood stove in the kitchen tonight and cooking something."

"Want me to help with the washing?"

"No, you have done plenty today. Run along, get cleaned up for supper, rest a bit."

"Not tired, Dad. Think I'll go see if the guest house owner wants me to pile more wood. Oh Dad, do we have a pair of pliers?"

"No, we don't, you know that I had to leave all my tools in Riga. Why do you ask?"

"Ah... I... I need to pull a nail."

"Where?"

"In... from... I mean the box where I keep my things."

"If the box is coming apart you don't want to pull out the nail, you want to hammer it back in. You need a hammer, and we don't have a hammer either. Find a rock, or maybe the guest house owner can lend you a hammer for helping him with the wood."

"Okay Dad, I'll do that ... or find a rock." My dad left. I got out of there quickly. How stupid of me. I told Juris not to bring up the subject and I myself just about blew it. I'm a dummy, a real dummy. But how was I to get the bullet out of the cartridge? I wanted to see what gun powder looked like.

I walked away from the door, and back to the wood pile. Thank goodness no one was there, not even Janis. I located the ammunition box, took out three cartridges and admired them. They were shiny, made of brass, felt cold. There was a red dot on the blunt end. A rounded bullet in the other. I couldn't budge the bullet. It was in there tight, very, very tight. What was I to do? I wanted to see some gun powder - stuff so powerful that it not only dislodges the bullet from the cartridge, but also throws it a long long way. Powerful stuff. I want to see what it looks like.

Aha! Aha! I saw the guest house owner's big axe. Could I lift it? I lifted it. Yes I could. Could I lift it over my head? Yes I could. I knew what I must do to see gun powder. I must smash the cartridge with the blunt end of the axe. I carefully placed one of the shiny brass cartridges on the big chopping block. I lifted the axe over my head and let it come down upon the cartridge. Kabooom! There was a flash of fire, smoke and I heard something hit the woodpile. I moved the axe, and under it was a cracked and flattened cartridge but no sign of gun powder, just a blackened area, that's all.

Well, if at first you don't succeed, try again. I placed another shiny cartridge on the big chopping block. This time I was going to use the sharp end and cut the cartridge in half. I hoped I could hit the little target. I picked up the axe again and, just as I was about to lift it over my head, pandemonium broke lose. I almost dropped the axe on myself. The kind guest house owner, and behind him a group of people, were running towards me shouting, "Halt! Halt! Ah Do Dumkopf! Knabe! Halt! Halt!" ("Stop! Stop! O you dumb-head! Boy! Stop! Stop!") The big axe fell to the ground with a thud. On the chopping block was the brass cartridge, and another one between my teeth, protruding through my lips like a little brass tongue, and by the woodpile, a whole box full of little brass cartridges, and on my shoulder was my father's heavy hand. "He is my boy and I will deal with this," my dad spoke to the owner of the guest house. "I am very sorry about this. I don't know where my boy got the twenty-two caliber cartridges. I hope he didn't steal them from you."

"No, they don't belong to me."

"Then do accept my apologies for my boy's stupidity, and do take the cartridges. I assure you, Sir, this will not happen again."

With his heavy hand on my shoulder, my father led me through the crowd of people, aghast; my mom, Tinte, Uncle Rudis and Rita among them. He led me through the back door of the guest house to our cubicle in the upper room. That evening, mushrooms I did not get. What I did get, I wanted to forget.

four

Binabiburg:
End of June & July

WEEKS PASSED. It might as well have been a million years since the rifle cartridge event, but the silence directed at me from my one-time friends was intolerable.

In our big yard in Latvia, which I missed terribly, I could play by myself all day long and enjoy the silence, hear the wind, listen to the sound of rustling leaves, smell the fragrance of Mother's flowers, watch our vegetables mature for the harvest. Silence was welcome there but in our cubicle in the upper room, this new silence was not comforting. I could see and hear my friends but they wouldn't speak to me. When I walked by their cubicles or approached them they turned, looked and went the other way. They avoided me. They gave me the silent treatment.

The only significant young people who spoke to me were the three girls. But even conversations with them ended with said or unsaid pre-drawn conclusions: "How stupid of you, Harijs." "You could have been wounded, Harijs." "You could have been killed, Harijs." What was so surprising about that? Since 1939 I could have been wounded or killed any day or night. We had grown to accept danger and death as an everyday fact of life. What's so terribly unacceptable about a little explosion of a twenty-two caliber rifle shell compared to the explosions of tons and tons of high explosive bombs? If I did a stupid thing, what should I call the actions of strong leaders like Hitler who started the awful war or Stalin and his cronies who devastated my Latvia? The Americans had leaders who decided to drop bombs on refugees in Dresden. I was in Dresden, perhaps a target missed by a few hours. Oh yeah, what I did was stupid only because I was nine years old.

I was lonely. I was disgusted and angry with the adult world. I was told I must learn from the war. Who should learn? Me? No, the grownups should. The leaders. The generals. But will they? They didn't learn a thing from the 1st World War. "I'll learn. Yes, I'll never forget. I'll be different when I grow up." I wanted to change the world. I wanted to build homes and buildings, not destroy them. I thanked God for the women who welcomed refugee trains in railroad stations, with the big pots of vegetable soup, usually without the smallest morsel of meat. We would have died of starvation without the soup. "God, bless the people who kept us alive," I prayed, "let nothing bad happen to them ever." Yes, I resolved to help people not hurt them. Yes, I did.

There was one good result to the exile. I grew closer to Mom, Dad, Uncle and Tinte. They talked a lot with me. But it didn't ease the pain of having to be around friends who didn't speak to me any more; my performance at the chopping block also reined trouble upon them that led to the disclosure of Janis boarding the armored vehicle and playing with the hand grenades. But it was good to learn, in spite of everything, that my parents, Tinte and Uncle loved me and cared for me. They said many times taking turns, "Harij, I love you." "Harij, I care for you." "You could have been wounded at the chopping block; all three of you could have been killed if one of the grenades exploded and set off all the others. You should have known better."

In self defense I reminded them how I had saved our

lives in Liepaja. They acknowledged that event and were grateful as we recalled the dreadful memory.

It was evening and the weather, threatening. Not knowing what we might find in the train station in Liepaja, Uncle Rudis took out of his brown suitcase a fat ham and loaf of black bread, making a sandwich for each of us. This was our usual simple but delicious supper. The train was slowing and came to a stop at the station. This was the end of the line for the train. We had to disembark and find a place to stay. As the train was pulling into the station I noticed a military train along with several other trains, stopped at the station. The military train caught my attention, "Uncle, look, a military train. Tanks and guns on flatcars."

"The closed freight cars may have ammunitions in them," commented Dad.

"Is this what they call an Ammunitions Train?" I asked.

"Yes," concluded Uncle Rudis.

"It's a long one, too," Dad added.

"Wow!" I rejoiced when I saw the Panzer tanks, "All that armament should be able to stop the Communists dead. Look at the big guns."

"For a little while, a little while, Harij," Uncle commented sadly. "I'm afraid that at this time the Red Army has much more, many more guns and Armor divisions."

The time came for us to leave our train. We each picked up two suitcases and a back pack; the sum total of our worldly goods from home. Mine were smaller than Mom's, Dad's, Tinte's and Uncle's. We entered the station. It was big and there were lots of refugees. Uncle Rudis spotted an empty bench and quickly we claimed it. We put our loads on the floor. My parents, Uncle and Tinte sat down. It was nice and warm in the station. With some hesitation I sat down too.

"Aren't we going to find a place to stay?" I asked.

"We have found a place to stay," declared my uncle with authority.

"This is good enough for tonight." Tinte supported Uncle Rudis.

"Yes, Marta, I think so too," my mom agreed.

"What do you think about that, Dad?" I asked.

"We couldn't ask for more. It is nice and warm in here." Dad also spoke in support of staying the night in the station.

"What? Stay here!" I objected.

"Yes. Stay here," Mom declared.

"No way," I objected again.

"We're staying here," Tinte scolded me. "We're staying here because it's cold and dark outside and we don't know of any better place."

"What's the matter with you, Harijs?" Dad asked.

"Dad, you saw that ammunition train parked alongside the train we were on," I pleaded.

"Yes we talked about it, it may pull out," said Dad.

"Dad, but what if it doesn't pull out?"

"If it doesn't pull out it doesn't pull out."

"Calm down Harij," counseled Mom, "I'm not going out in that threatening dark night to look for another place to stay. The station is good enough."

"No, Mom! I am not staying here! The ammunition train. The Russians will bomb it. I know they will. Please let's get out of here, please! Now!"

We argued back and forth. My adults didn't seem to get the point. A stationary ammunitions train is a prime target for an air raid. Russian bombing was as inaccurate as inaccurate could be. We knew that. The station was in great danger and so were we and all the people who would stay. Finally, after all the fuss I had made, Uncle Rudis agreed with me. "Maybe Harijs is right. That train is a target. Let's move on. If nothing else we'll stay in an air raid shelter."

Good news, I thought.

Even though both Mom and Tinte objected, when Dad finally agreed to go, we picked up our heavy loads and left the station. We had walked not even five minutes when the sirens commenced a warning of an imminent air raid. We increased our pace. My mother and Tinte started to fall behind. I urged them on. Dad spotted a sign giving directions to an air raid shelter. We ran. We heard the distant hum of many airplanes. The planes were getting closer. They were closing in on us. Yes, I heard it, the whistling of falling bombs. The whistling stopped. That meant the bombs would fall very close or upon us. "Was this it? My end!" We were at the entrance of the air raid shelter. Dad pulled open the door. Mom fell, Dad helped her up and pushed her into the shelter. People in the shelter shouted at us, "Close the door!" Of course we did. No sooner had we closed the door when an ear shattering blast, followed by a compression shock wave, reached the shelter, hitting my chest like an iron ball. Another. Another and yet another. I counted, yes I could still count. I counted twenty-five. The lights went out. It was quiet in the shelter, deathly quiet. No one spoke. The dead silence gave way to the crackling sounds of a nearby fire. Through a crack in the door caused by the blasts, we saw the flickering glow of fire. In a while we heard the sirens of many fire trucks. The sirens ceased nearby. The air raid sirens sounded the all clear signal. Someone opened the door and closed it at once. The glow of fire was all around us. We were in the midst of the target area.

We stayed the night in the air raid shelter. There were about fifty people in close proximity sharing the protection of the shelter. Dawn's early light penetrated the shelter through the cracks in the door. Mom noted she had lost a suitcase, the one where most of her dresses were packed. She remembered dropping it when she fell. When we came out of the shelter the suitcase was nowhere to be found. What we did find was fire and smoke billowing all around us, especially thick and black from the rubble of the nearby railroad station. The trains were still burning and smoldering. The box cars of the munitions train had exploded. In the spot we had occupied the night before was a crater excavated by a high explosive bomb.

"Harij," said my dad, "you saved our lives."

Mom agreed. Uncle Rudis agreed. Tinte Marta agreed. Harijs saved our lives. But now I wondered, "What for?"

I heard a crash. Boards breaking, falling. A woman's voice screamed. Suddenly Janis appeared in the opening to my cubicle. His brown eyes wide open, it looked like any moment his black hair would stand upright.

"Harij, Mr. Kapeikis, Mrs. Kapeikis please come help! My mom fell through the floor boards into the pig pen below! Please help!"

"What!"

"Yes she did! She fell. She sat on her bed. The bed and all broke right through the floor and she's below by the pig!"

"Your mom fell on the pig below? My folks aren't here. They went to the warehouse. Why didn't anyone tell me the Americans had returned? The Americans are handing out shoes and clothes to those who can prove they need...."

"Come! Let's go help!" Juris yelled as he ran by.

Without saying a word Janis and I followed Juris as fast as we could through the door and down the stairs out into the courtyard around the corner of the guest house to the double doors of the barn where the pig pen was. Others were following. Out of the corner of my eye I saw Mom and Dad coming out of the warehouse. I saw my dad had a pair of shoes in his hands, and my mom had a blanket. That could wait. "Was Janis' mom hurt?" I wondered. She was a big woman.

We threw open the barn doors and flew in. Janis in the lead, then Juris and his dad, then me. I was the slowest.

I saw Janis' mom lying on the straw next to the pig, bed boards and floor boards all around her. Janis cried out and raced to his mother, "Mom!" He slipped on some manure and fell next to his mother. "Mommy, are you alright? Mommy! Oh Mommy! Say something! Please!"

A number of people had gathered in the pig pen. I was gazing at the gaping hole above, through which I could see Janis' belongings. Then, with concern, I looked at Janis' mother, who lay in the straw. Was she alive?

I saw no blood. Neither her arms nor legs showed any signs of fractures. Her legs only revealed lose flab where her well padded thighs met her underwear. Yikes! Is that what happened to girls' slender legs. That hadn't happened to my mom's legs. My moms' legs were nice and firm, long and slender.

Mom and Dad had joined the crowd in the pig pen. Yes, I saw Dad had new shoes in his hands, his size, I noted. Mom had a new blue wool blanket. Janis' mom moved and a sigh of relief echoed through the little crowd. She was alive. But was she seriously hurt?

"Mommy, are you hurt?" moaned Janis with tender tones of love and concern for his mother. Well, I thought, Janis is human after all. But I was glad it wasn't my mom laying there by the pig. I began to be aware of the smell. The pig was big. Janis was getting up now. He had pig dung on his pants and shirt. Served him right. Janis' dad pushed through the crowd. "Velma, my Velma!" He started to sit her up. She uttered a quiet moan, "Ooohhh."

"Say something, Velma, say something," said Janis' dad, supporting Velma by her shoulders.

"Yeah, say something, Mommy," begged Janis.

"My back hurts." We barely could hear Velma. She moved her arm to brace her attempt to stand.

As Janis and his dad helped her stand, we breathed with relief.

"What happened?" she asked.

"Mom, you fell through the floor. You sat on your bed and the floor gave way and you and the bed fell through the floor. Lucky there was some straw where you landed. You could've been hurt."

"I am hurt. My back hurts, bad." She rubbed the small of her back with her hand, "but I don't think it's broken. Thank God nothing seems broken."

Janis, with his dad and mom, started taking slow steps towards the wide open barn doors. The little crowd parted and the big pig saw her chance. She squealed at the top of her lungs and lunged for the open door, knocking Janis into the dung and almost colliding with our kind guest house owners who managed to stay upright by grabbing each other in an awkward embrace.

"What's going on?" he asked in German, but saw for himself. No one needed to give an explanation.

"Oh my God!" exclaimed Frau (Mrs.) guest house owner. "This is terrible! Is anyone else hurt beside Frau Velma?" she asked.

Janis' dad answered, "No one else is hurt and my wife Velma is more in shock than hurt. She complains about her back, so we should get a doctor to examine her. Do you know if the Americans have a medic?"

"Yes, they do, I'm sure they have," answered Herr (Mr.) guest house owner. "Among their vehicles is a van with a red cross painted on its side. That must be an ambulance. There should be someone among them with medical knowledge."

"Arvid," said Janis' mother (Janis and I had fathers with the same name), "Arvid, take me to the Americans. I want a doctor to check my back and my side."

She pointed to her right side where a little spot of blood was showing through her grey A-line dress.

In my isolation I hadn't noticed, and no one had told me, that a detachment of Americans had returned to the warehouse. We feared a registration, or perhaps an interrogation of refugees was in the works. In the past such question and answer sessions had never gone well for us. One had to know the right answers to avoid trouble, arrest or even persecution. How should we answer the Americans who are friends with Stalin and his communist party? I felt my dad's big hand on my shoulder but not as firm as last time by the wood pile.

"Let's go upstairs Harij. See, I got a new pair of brown leather shoes from the Americans. There were no shoes your size. No children's shoes. I'll make you a new pair of wooden sandals if you want."

"This blue blanket is for you, Harij," said Mom, "It's wool and it will be warmer than the one you have now." True, I thought, but I didn't like wool. Wool is scratchy, but I only said, "Gee, thanks mom. Can I still keep the old one?"

"Sure, why not," she answered.

I wanted to say something to mom about my liking the old blanket when I became aware of Juris and Janis at my side. They just stood there looking at me. They said nothing. Then I heard Janis' dad speak to my dad, "Mr. Kapeikis, can my boy stay with you while I take Velma to see the American doctor? I sure hope they have one."

Janis looked at me and gave a pleading nod as my dad answered, "I see no reason why not."

There were three boys following my mom and dad out the barn door, back around the corner of our guest house, in through the front door and up the stairs to my cubicle. Janis stopped in the bathroom to clean himself up then joined us in my cubicle. His pants and shirt were a little wet in places and not very clean, but who cared. The moment was special and precious.

"My Uncle Rudis showed me how to make paper airplanes that really can fly. You want to learn? I'll show you."

Later the three of us had fun helping catch the runaway

pig. I liked chasing squealing pigs. "Some day I'll eat one for breakfast!" I thought of bacon and eggs. "Someday, yes someday, I'll have bacon and eggs for breakfast, like in Riga." Until then a slice of black bread with bacon grease remained a delicacy.

Janis' mom was examined by the American doctor. He treated the bad scrape on her side, gave her a red rubber hot water bottle to put on her back and some aspirin for her pain. She hadn't injured her back, only her pride. She, too, like Janis, had to clean up in the bathroom where there was a water pump, but some one had to pump it. The job fell to Janis and me in the unisex bathroom.

In time the floor was repaired, but in the mean time Janis slept with me. (They didn't want Janis sleeping near the edge of the hole in the floor. Did they think he might scare the big pig below?)

Before the day was over we got the word from the Americans via our guest house owners. "The Americans want to register all of you starting tomorrow morning at nine. They'll see one family at a time. They'll have a translator, but the translator doesn't speak Latvian, so Herr Smit (my uncle), will you go first so you can be available as translator for those who can't speak German."

"Yawol," my uncle agreed. The guest house owners left and all of the adults huddled immediately. My uncle took charge.

"All right, folks. Tomorrow morning Marta and I will go at nine. Is there anyone else who can't speak German and needs me to translate?"

I knew my parents would want Uncle Rudis to translate for them. They could speak some German, but I was sure they would like Uncle Rudis around for a sense of security. I was surprised three other families wanted Herr Smit to help. They could speak German better than I did. I thought it strange that adults needed someone for a sense of security, just like kids.

As one of the families asked my uncle to help them, Janis gave me a curious look and whispered, "Herr Lager Fuhrer again, your uncle." But this time he said it with a smile in his voice and I acknowledged with a smile on my face thinking: "Well, Janis, now you know my uncle is smart."

The order of appearance before the *American Tribunal* was quickly arranged (by my uncle). My parents and I would follow Marta and Rudis, then Janis' family, Juris' family, Rita's family etc. etc.

"What do you think they will ask us?" questioned Rita's dad. "No doubt they will want to know why we left Latvia," he added.

"No doubt about that," affirmed Rita's mom. "It's easy for us to say why we left our farm. Some crazy arsonist burnt it down right to the ground while we were shopping in Riga. Both the house and barn; we lost everything. Furniture, clothes, everything. But it's entirely another reason why all of us left Latvia, isn't it?"

"That's for sure," Rita's dad supported his wife.

"We can't say we left Latvia because we didn't want to live under the Communists," stated my uncle, and everyone nodded in agreement.

"The Americans think of the Communists as their allies, friends and comrades," he added and everyone continued to nod in agreement.

"You think we can say that we didn't want to get caught in a crossfire between the Germans and the Russians," I heard Vilma's voice, the tallest of the three girls.

"There was heavy fighting over every meter of Latvian soil," she added, "especially in Liepaja where our boys defended our land to the last man. But I know we can't say our boys fought on the German side, against the Communists," she concluded.

"Well said, Vilma." Vilma's dad praised her and was proud of Vilma. "Let's say we continued to flee the continuously approaching battle zones and eventually ended up in Germany," he added, "like Vilma said, we didn't want our families to be caught between the front lines."

"That could be a way of explaining why we left Latvia," summarized my uncle. "But they may not even ask us that. Maybe the Americans just want to know who we are. Our names, occupations, things like that. Maybe they want to help us? We can't stay in this guest house forever, you know."

The communal conference went on for a long time. We three boys listened. During war you quickly learned to listen or you may not be living very long. You also learned talking gets you into trouble. I wondered if the adults had forgotten the lessons we learned about keeping one's mouth shut. What if there was a spy here who was listening and reporting to the Americans? There may not be a need for the tribunal tomorrow, should we all be in jail. But yes, what should we say about leaving Latvia, and how do we explain why we won't go home when we really and truly want to go home with all our heart and soul?

The morning came after a night of dreams; nightmares actually. I dreamed the Americans arrested Uncle Rudis and Dad. The pair were sentenced to hard labor in a dangerous coal mine in America, and forced into old cattle cars like the ones the Russians used to deport innocent people from Riga. My Tinte cried and begged the Americans not to take Rudi and my dad away. My mom cried and tried to say my uncle and dad had done no wrong. They both were good and kind; we'll be lost without them. But the Americans didn't listen. They threatened to shoot my dad if Tinte and Mom continued to annoy them with their sobs and tears. They threatened to nail my mom's tongue to a board if she didn't shut up, just like the Russians had done in Riga to some people they had arrested.

Why did I dream such terrible dreams? It scared me. I knew Americans weren't like the Communists. Americans were good people. They gave me chocolates. They gave us good food. Was I like my mom? Did I also fear the Americans like she feared the black Americans? Will she ever get over her fears? I didn't want to be afraid. I wanted to trust the Americans. I didn't tell this dream to anyone. No one needs to know I had nightmares like those.

No one said much during breakfast. There was a strange sense of numbness, like a wet blanket cast over the upper room. Was everyone trying to forget a nightmare they didn't want to tell? Did we fear what the Americans may do to us? Was this our last meal of black bread with bacon grease and water before the world as we knew it, ended?

"Marta," Uncle Rudis spoke at last, "it's just about nine, are you ready?"

"Yes," she answered, "just have to put the bread away. Then let's go and face what comes. We've done it many times before."

"The inquisition is what comes," said Mother, "I'm afraid not much will change for us."

"What do you mean?" asked Dad.

"The Americans will question us until we say something wrong, something they can hold against us," she explained. "Don't you recall, Arvid, how these inquisitions have gone before?"

"Erna, the Americans aren't like the Gestapo and certainly not like the Communists. They'll be fair to us," answered Dad, adding, "don't be afraid of them Erna."

"Okay Marta, let's go, we're first," said Uncle Rudis.

"Oh, Rudi, please be careful. Please." Pleaded Mom, "Just agree with them, okay?"

"We'll do well, just wait and see," Uncle Rudis spoke positively and turned to Tinte, "Come Marta. The future is about to begin."

They left and headed to the warehouse where the

Americans, with the German translator, were waiting for us. My father was pacing the floor as if I was about to get a baby brother. Mother was sitting motionless, staring at the floor. And me? I was tapping the floor with a little stick I had cut from a bush.

"Cut that out!" Mom said, nervously. "Cut out that awful noise! Tap! Tap! Tap! It's driving me crazy!" she complained.

"Oh, Erna, leave Harijs alone," Dad protected me, "he's not doing anything wrong."

"I'm worried about Marta and Rudis. That noise is annoying me."

"Okay Mom, I won't tap the floor. Didn't mean to upset you. What time is it?"

"Oh my God, it's after ten and Marta and Rudis are still there. Now I am getting scared," she spoke. What else is new, I thought.

"Harij," Mom said, "you'll behave when we're before the Americans." I wondered what my behavior had to do with it?

"Yes, Mom. I won't speak unless I'm spoken to."

"Erna, leave Harij alone. Why are you picking on him?" Dad asked.

I knew why she was picking on me. She was afraid. That's why. It had happened before. That was my mom. I saw Tinte Marta and Uncle Rudis come out of the warehouse doors. They were talking and gesturing, but I couldn't hear what they were saying. They looked excited. As we had agreed, when we saw them come out, we headed for the warehouse. We did not want to annoy the Americans by having them wait for us.

"Good luck to the Kapeikis family." We heard from the other cubicles as we walked by.

"Good luck."

"God be with you."

"All will go well."

We went down stairs and out the front door, as Tinte and Uncle climbed the steps of the porch.

"How did it go?" asked Dad.

"What did they do to you? What will they do to us?" asked Mom with a voice of concern.

"Everything is fine, Erna." said Tinte, "Don't worry Erna. Rudis will go with you. They know him now. It won't be as long for you."

"Yes," said Uncle Rudis with a grin. "I had a hard time convincing the Captain that I was Latvian. In all my papers I couldn't find my birth certificate. He thought I was German. But you won't have that problem. Let's go. Let's not keep the council waiting."

We walked across the yard. Uncle Rudis came with us and Tinte went back to the upper room where she faced anxious questions from our fellow countrymen.

As we climbed the steps of the warehouse porch I noticed my mom's hands were shaking and her upper lip quivered. She was scared and so was I.

There were only three men in the room. Two soldiers in very neat light brown uniforms and the German translator, who was wearing a black tailored suit, complete with a black tie. He looked like a man who could be trusted. He was sitting near the end of a desk occupied by an officer – a captain, my uncle had said. I saw two silver bars on the shoulders of his uniform, and in front of him on the desk, a sharp looking hat with the image of an eagle as insignia. To the left of the captain sat a sergeant behind a desk piled high with papers. I recognized the chevrons on his sleeves. Same as the ones Sergeant Ron had, the sergeant with Lieutenant Jack and Private Ken, who gave us the food. The Captain looked at us and spoke. The translator motioned for us to come forward and sit down on the chairs the sergeant was bringing forward. We sat in a semicircle facing the captain. The captain spoke and the translator, in German, asked my father for his name. Uncle Rudis didn't need to interpret. My dad understood and answered, "My name is Arvids Verners Kapeikis."

The next question was about Dad's place of birth. My dad placed our birth certificates and their marriage certificate on the Captain's desk. The Captain picked them up and examined them. His observations, spoken and translated, were encouraging.

"Good. You were born in Ezere, Latvia, on June 18, 1907. This also shows that you both are citizens of Latvia, registered in the city of Riga. Your wife's name is Erna Doroteja Anna, born Riskus, in Riga on the 21st of August, 1908. These look like authentic documents. When and where were you married?"

"We were married in Martin Lutheran Church, Riga, in 1931 on the 24th of June," answered Dad.

"Good. That's what is on your marriage certificate." The translation followed a question from the Captain, "Tell me about the boy."

"He is our son, Harijs Gastons, who was born to us in Riga on July 22, 1935."

"Has he been enrolled in school?"

"He completed grades one and two in Riga. No schooling since then." (Not true, I thought. For two weeks I was in a German school.)

"And your education, Arvids?" The captain called Dad by his first name. The Germans wouldn't do that.

"I finished grade four and then had to go to work."

"Hard times for the family? What kind of work?"

"At first I learned shoe making and shoe repairing. Then I had the opportunity to learn the trade of making forms or molds in a foundry - the forms into which molten metal is poured to make parts for farm machinery."

(Hey Dad, better watch what you say, I thought. You're getting close to 'parts' for the Nazi war machine.)

"What foundry did you work for and where?"

"I worked in Riga. The foundry's name was Terauds.

(Watch it Dad, you'll spill the beans.) My tension eased when he addressed my mother.

"Erna, tell me about yourself. Your schooling and your occupation."

"I finished grade six in Riga. I'm a dressmaker. I worked at home in Riga and took care of my family."

"So you are a seamstress and a homemaker."

"Yes," she answered.

"You both seem to be in good health. Given the opportunity, are you both willing to work for the American Military Government of Germany?"

"Yes, of course," my parents answered. (He hasn't asked why we left Latvia. I prayed in my thoughts that he wouldn't. So far so good.)

"I have just one more question." (Oh, no, here it comes.)

"Arvids, Erna, tell me the absolute truth for I will have you back your statement with an oath. Have you ever served with or in Nazi armed forces?"

"No," they answered simultaneously. "We have not served in the Nazi armed forces," confirmed my dad.

Another "good" from the captain. "Sergeant, prepare the Military Government of Germany identification forms for this family. We'll skip the oath." Turning to us he said, "As of now, you are registered with the American Occupational Force as Displaced Persons. The Sergeant will take your fingerprints and you will each be issued a certificate of identification before the end of the day. Do not leave the guest house. I repeat, do not leave the guest house. Thank you. After being finger printed you may go."

The captain stood up and came around the desk to shake hands with us, as did the sergeant and the kind looking translator. We left feeling that a heavy load had been taken from our shoulders. Something good was in store for us. Uncle Rudis didn't need to come with us to interpret. I was proud of my parents.

That's how the day went for all ten families. No one was

asked why they left Latvia. The Russians were never talked about and all of us were declared Displaced Persons. The biggest and worst problem was Rudis – his last name being Smits, and his ability to speak German so well always did make people think he was German.

Late in the afternoon the sergeant came with our Displaced Person papers. He and the translator entered the upper room, but the sergeant himself read our names and handed out the papers. I held back giggles as he called our names with an American accent. Funny. Very funny! I was glad they left. I couldn't hold back laughter much longer. I laughed loud and was joined by others.

We examined our papers, but what did we read? Military Government of Germany: Temporary Registration. I was looking over my mom's shoulder. Yes, I could read. "Name: Kapeikis, Erna. Permanent Address: Riga, Lettland (Latvia). Present Address: Binabiburg – Rothenwort b. Staddler." But what was printed after that - "The holder of this card is duly registered as a resident of the town of (Binabiburg) and is prohibited from leaving the place designated. Violation of this restriction will lead to immediate arrest. Registrant will at all times have this paper on his person."

I heard moans, women's voices crying, someone was pounding a table.

"We are imprisoned."

"We can't leave Binabiburg."

"We have to stay here. We can't go fishing."

"We can't hunt mushrooms any more," Rita was crying.

"We can't leave the village to trade with farmers." The village was at an intersection of two roads.

"What in the world are the Americans doing?"

"The Americans have placed us under house arrest."

The heavy weight lifted from my shoulders was replaced by a crushing load. Tears were welling in my eyes; a lump was in my throat choking me.

If I had trouble sleeping last night, with bad dreams and nightmares I couldn't tell anyone, what would this night bring? The Americans had disappointed me. My hopes had betrayed me. Mother is right in fearing them. What will they do with us? Oh, yes, the captain asked, "Are you willing to work for the American Military Government of Germany?" Slaves, we'll be slaves like the black people were in America. Slave laborers like the people deported to Siberia. Cheap labor like we were for the Russian nobility, and the German Barons.

D.P. identification papers.

five

Binabiburg to Haunstetten

WE WERE NOT ARRESTED. Confronted with a language barrier, we misunderstood the intent of the registration and, conditioned by past experiences with the Gestapo, assumed the requirement to stay in Binabiburg was a house arrest. In the past, a breach of this order would lead to prosecution if not persecution. We did not know Displaced Persons Camps were proposed in various locations throughout the American zone of occupation in Western Germany. Therefore it was imperative that we, now Displaced Persons or D.P.'s, cease our sojourns and stay put so we would be easily found when it came time for American authorities to pick us up and take us to a camp.

Good news. Exciting news. "What will these camps be like?" became a popular question, and "Where will they be?" Another popular question.

More good news for us three boys. Our fishing spot was within the boundaries of Binabiburg. We could fish again. Since food was still a precious commodity, we resumed our fishing at our favorite spot, under the large oak tree, a little ways down river from the wooden bridge. Our lines were in water, our minds indulging in the topics of the day.

"Janis," I said, "Isn't it great that we're going to have a place to live?"

"Sure, but what kind of a place? Every place is bombed

out, burned to the ground. Anything livable is occupied by Germans. Will Germans give up their homes for us? I doubt that. What can Americans do?" questioned Janis.

"Maybe they're setting up tents for us," said Juris, "we'll live like soldiers in the field. I'd like that."

"My mom wouldn't," I said, "she wants a kitchen, inside bathroom and a bedroom like we had in Riga."

"Where would they set up the tents?" questioned Janis, sarcastically suggesting, "Under the Brandenburg Gate or on Wilhelmstrasse in Berlin."

"What're you talking about, Janis?" I asked.

"You don't know what the Brandenburg Gate is?" Janis was looking at me again as if he was my superior.

"It's a landmark in Berlin," Juris answered in my place. "Built in the 1700's I think."

"Good for you, Juris. Completed in 1791," declared Janis in a know-it-all tone. "Little Harijs has a lot to learn."

That remark made me angry enough to foolishly ask, "Gate to where?"

"Gate to nowhere, stupid. It's a landmark, didn't you hear Juris?."

"I heard, but what's so important about...what strasse?" I didn't know when to quit.

"Wilhelmstrasse! Dummy! That's where Hitler had his headquarters. Don't you know anything, Harijs?"

"How would I know that? I haven't been to Berlin, besides I don't believe you. That would be kept a secret," I defended myself.

"Everything's a secret, Harijs, until someone finds out. I overheard some Germans talking about a document that's been found. They were talking about Hitler as if he had been living on Wilhelmstrasse. Okay, I'm just guessing."

"You shouldn't guess about things like that," said Juris. "People have been arrested for saying even less."

"That's right, Janis," I said, looking for a way out. "We shouldn't talk about German secrets. We could be arrested.

Juris is right."

"Alright, but are you both forgetting the war is over?" Janis said.

"I'm not forgetting, but I don't think Americans will have us live by the -- gate nor on Hitler's street," I said.

"Brandenburg Gate, Harijs and Wilhelmstrasse. You sure don't learn very well," Janis said. "Yeah, but where will they put us? Beats me," he added.

I was about to say Americans will find some place nice for us, but was cut short by Janis' exclamation, "I've got a bite! Out you come!" and Janis landed a large trout on the grass near my feet.

"Hey, I got a bite too!" I shouted, as my cork disappeared under the water and my line went tight. As I pulled in my line Juris shouted with excitement.

"I got a bite!" Juris cried out and jumped for joy. Simultaneously Juris and I landed our fish on the grass near Janis' feet. They weren't as big as Janis' fish but just as beautiful in our eyes. We re-baited our hooks, fished some more but after an hour of no luck decided to go home. It was a good day, I thought.

When we get relocated to a D.P. camp I hoped to find a better friend than Janis. Here in Binabiburg I had no choice. There were only the three of us boys. Juris I will miss.

Supper was delicious. Mom had fried my fish perfectly. She cut it in three pieces and gave me the piece I liked best, the tail. Crunchy. I scraped the meat off the bone and put it on a slice of black bread. Sucked every trace of meat and cartilage from the bone and enjoyed my delicious fish sandwich to the fullest. I savored every little bite. We even had dessert. Chocolate chip cookies that Frau guest house owner had given us. Life is improving, I thought. It's going to be even better when we're moved to a D.P. camp.

"Harij," my mom addressed me. "We had a surprise today. A letter from Uncle Edis. He was able to locate us because of the American registration we were so upset over.

American authorities have directories now, listing all D.P.'s and where they are located. Edis and Aunt Anna are..." my mom reached under the pillow of their bed and pulled out a letter. "They are in Haunstetten, near Augsburg. Edis wrote that he has asked the American authorities to bring us to Haunstetten where he is. Uniting families is a priority with Americans. Isn't that wonderful. We'll be together again!"

"Where is Haun..." I couldn't remember the long name.

"Haunstetten is not far from here, it's towards Munchen," Dad explained. "We'll get there in a day."

"We're going to walk?" I asked.

"No, no. We'll probably get to ride in an American Army truck," said Dad.

"Wow! When? Dad."

"Don't know. We'll just have to wait. The Americans will let us know."

"Uncle Edis also wrote that he has found the Kraujas," Mom stated.

"Who are they?" I asked. "I don't remember any Kraujas."

"Oh. Richards and Hermine and they have a son, Ojars, who is a year and a half older than you. Richards is my second cousin. You'll remember them when you see them. They were at your ninth birthday party in Riga," Mom said.

"I don't remember any Ojars," I said.

"Oh, right, Ojars wasn't with them," Mom corrected herself.

"Ojars didn't come to my birthday party with his parents? Why?"

"I don't know, Harij. They just didn't bring him," Mom said.

"They came to my birthday party but didn't bring Ojars. That's weird," I said.

"Maybe he was being punished for something," Dad said.

"He was punished? Sounds more like they were

punishing me. Maybe I'm not good enough for Ojars. I just don't remember Ojars."

"You did meet him. He was with Hermine and Richards when they came to say good-by to us the night before we left Riga," Dad said.

"I don't remember him. Was I ever at one of his birthday parties?"

"Probably not," answered Mom. "We didn't see them very often."

That was weird. I wanted to change the subject back to the Americans.

"Kraujas will also come to Haunstetten," Mom said to Dad. "They are in Austria now."

"Then I'll meet Ojars in Haunstetten," I concluded. "But when will we get moved?"

"We don't know. We must wait. That's why we aren't allowed to leave Binabiburg. The Americans may come any time," answered Dad.

"That place where Uncle Edis is – that's a D.P. camp? I asked, "Are there tents for us to live in?"

"No, Edis wrote it's a nice place. Two story apartment houses; inside bathrooms with running water. Edis is working with the Americans. He is confident we'll be moved there soon."

"I want to go there tomorrow!" I exclaimed.

Rudis and Tinte came and suggested we go outside for a walk around the guest house yard. We did. It was a nice, clear evening.

I was right about going to Haunstetten tomorrow. We didn't move that day, but received the notice to be ready to relocate in a week. A truck was scheduled to take us to the D.P. camp in Haunstetten. Juris' family received notice they would be transported to Lauingen, and Janis' to Eichstadt. At least in part I got my wish. Good-bye, Janis!

Another notice came informing us of the day and hour of our departure. Three trucks were to pick up all the D.P.'s housed in the guest house and take us to our respective camps. Sad to think that I will not see Juris and Rita any more.

Parting had become a common experience for me. Hello and goodbye. The sadness at losing friends this time was moderated by knowing that in Haunstetten we would not be met by falling bombs and strafing airplanes, but by Uncle Edis and Aunt Anna. Life will be better. Yet I longed for the day when the friends I made would be friends for life. Would that day ever come? It would be a day of peace and stability; a day when we wouldn't have to worry what we shall wear or eat. Mom read words like that from the Bible yesterday.

There wasn't much to pack. I had a pair of winter boots, two pairs of wooden soled sandals Dad had made, three pairs of mended socks, one pair of long pants, three shirts, one of them with long sleeves, one sweater, three sets of underwear, one brown Russian leather hat, one winter coat, two blankets, a little pillow, a towel and a toothbrush. The rest of my clothes I would wear. My fishing rod (willow stick) and makeshift tackle I gave to the guest house owner. All my belongings were in my backpack except for one pillow and the blanket which I would roll up in the morning. I was ready for the trip. D.P. camp – here I come!

The morning the trucks arrived was exciting. Our luggage was loaded quickly. We milled around and said goodbye to everyone. Everyone was good at this. We had all done this many times before. "Goodbye Juris. Goodbye Janis."

Then a surprise; a first in my life. Rita ran up to me and said, "Goodbye Harij," hugged me and put her head on my shoulder, pressing her cheek against mine. I put my arms around her. I had never done that, except to my cousins in Riga. This felt different. Her hair felt soft against my cheek and radiated a pleasing fragrance. I liked it.

"Goodbye Rita. I hope we'll meet again."

"I hope so, Harij," she whispered in my ear. "You be good now and don't you ever smash rifle shells again."

Without looking at me she pulled away, turned and joined her parents who were standing near the Eichstadt truck. I watched her for a while, knowing it was the last time I would see her. She was wearing the pretty dress I had seen her in the day I met her on the trail, the day I picked mushrooms, the day Janis found the rifle shells. I looked up and saw Janis glaring at me.

I joined my parents as they were about to climb into the back of the truck bound for Haunstetten. Our truck was smaller then the other two. Then another surprise; the driver beckoned me to climb into the cab. My mom's eyes widened and, shaking her head in disapproval, she whispered, "No, no! I want Harijs with me."

"Let him ride in the cab," said Tinte, "It'll be warmer for him."

"Yes, Erna, let him," Dad echoed.

That's all I needed to hear. In a flash I was the assistant-driver-next-to-the-real-driver, admiring the sticks, pedals, gismos and clock-like instruments. Exciting! Exciting! Will I get to steer? I wondered as I looked out the window and saw the guest house owners watching our departure. They looked so lonely, so old. They had been good to us. Will they miss us? I wondered. I glanced through the rear window into the back of the truck. Mom, Dad, Tinte and Uncle Rudis were seated on the benches along the sides of the small truck. My mom looked nervous, that fearful look on her face. Why does she get so frightened at times like this? I thought. This is fun.

The driver walked around the truck as if he was looking for something, then climbed in behind the steering wheel. He gave me a big smile and said something I couldn't understand. He pulled a chocolate bar out of his pocket and said something again. I answered with a firm "Yes," and nodded. He gave me the chocolate. Body language, I remembered. It worked every time. I unwrapped the sweet milk chocolate and gobbled it up.

The driver took what looked like a very tiny metal saw out of the chest pocket in his uniform and inserted it into a little slot between the clock faces under the front windows. He turned it and at the same time pushed something curved into the floor with his left foot and pressed a gismo on the floor with his right foot. The truck went Brrrrrrr...I noted there were two metal sticks with knobs sticking out from the floor. His left hand was on the steering wheel and with his right hand he moved one of the knobbed sticks forward and the other backward. His left foot let the curved gismo come out of the floor. His right foot pressed down a flat piece of metal toward the floor. The truck went bRRRRR... and with a little lurch, began to move forward.

I remembered what Uncle Edis told me. The flat piece of metal was the gas pedal. It made the truck go faster or slower. One of the knobbed sticks was the gear shift, but which one? With his left foot, the driver pushed the curved gismo into the floor again and moved one of the knobbed sticks. That gave it away. I knew I could figure it out. One day I'm going to drive a truck just like the American soldier. What I couldn't figure out was why he pushed the curved gismo into the floor every time he shifted gears? And what did a gear look like? Where were they? How many? Were they all lined up like soldiers, or in a circle like dancing girls, under the truck's nose? How did they shift? Every time he shifted, the truck lurched a little, and went faster, changing the BRRRR.... I had many questions. I wished I could speak English and ask them.

The truck was fascinating; so powerful and fast. It could catch a horse in no time. It was going ten, maybe twenty times as fast as an oxen-pulled farm wagon. Wow! The countryside was sliding past like I was sitting in a fast train. I liked riding in trains. But sitting up front in a truck, watching the road slide under you was a thrill.

Go! Go man, go! I glanced at one of the clock-like faces which had one hand and a circle of numbers: 0, 10, 20, 30, 40, 50, 60. The hand was oscillating over 40. What are these gauges and dials? Soon I'll see Uncle Edis. He knows how to drive. I'll ask him. He'll tell me.

It will be good to see Uncle Edis again. I liked him but I was also a little afraid of him. He was stern, not mean, but serious and demanding as a teacher; ambitious and self educated. He was tall and strong with black hair and bushy eye brows. He wore a mustache when I last saw him in Riga.

Uncle Edis was in Moscow in 1917 and took part in the October Revolution that overthrew the Czar and brought the Communists to power. He said the Czar was very mean to workers and farmers. My uncle sided with the Communists who called upon the workers of the world to unite and do away with the Czar. Uncle Edis talked about his experiences in Russia many times when he came to visit us in Riga and also at parties. He said the teachings of Karl Marx promised a democracy, a classless society. Uncle Edis joined the revolutionaries.

But what Karl Marx promised did not happen, he told us. The Communists, after coming to power under Lenin, became worse dictators than the Czars. My Uncle Edis realized he had been deceived by Marx and the Communists. He escaped from the ranks of the Communist Red Army, came back to Latvia, joined the newly formed Latvian Army, and fought against the Red Army which he had helped to form. To make a complete break with his past he changed his surname from Riskus to Raudupe.

Uncle Edis liked to teach me. He taught me history. He'll definitely teach me about cars, trucks and gears.

Mom, Uncle Edis & Tinte.

six

Haunstetten

LARGE AREAS OF AUGSBURG, as in most large cities, were destroyed.

The main streets were cleared of rubble allowing the few cars and trucks to drive unhindered. Devastation everywhere. A wall of scorched bricks was standing amidst twisted steel beams, broken concrete and burnt timbers; on the other side of the street stood the remains of a fireplace and a chimney.

Our truck was driving slowly through this conglomeration of destruction. There were small groups of people rummaging for whatever could be of use, like we had done and would do some more. One man was holding up a metal pot. A woman had gathered an armful of wood. Two boys were throwing stones at a mangled kitchen stove. Someone had built a shelter in the corner of a roofless building by stretching canvas into roof and two walls. Across a field of crumbled walls stood Gothic arches of sacred granite, the remains of a cathedral; a silent witness to the merciless Godlessness of war. Where in this destruction was a D.P. camp?

We drove slowly through this cemetery of man-made ruins that once was a beautiful city with historic buildings. As we drove on I was relieved to see not everything had been destroyed. There were undamaged houses and two story apartment complexes that were slightly damaged, but occupied. Children were playing in the streets and yards. Three men were repairing a roof. A woman was painting the repaired stucco siding on a house. Another woman and a boy were working in a garden. That gave me hope. We might have a garden in Haunstetten. The outlying area we were driving through was not damaged. Then a complex of two story stucco apartment houses that looked like those described by Uncle Edis came into view. We had arrived! The driver pointed to a sign that read: "Displaced Persons Camp – Haunstetten." This was to be our home. The truck turned into an area surrounded by army barracks and stopped.

"I hope these barracks will not be our home," I mumbled to myself, "I want to live in a nice two story apartment building." There was a sign on one of the barracks that made no sense to me. It read "UNRRA."

The driver turned the little metal saw-like thing I figured was the key and the Brrr…stopped. He opened his door and motioned for me to open my door and climb out. I obeyed. My dad had already opened the back gate and was climbing down, followed by Mom. Uncle Rudis was ready to pass down the luggage but before he had the chance to do so, a door opened and out of the barrack came Uncle Edis and Aunt Anna. They looked great. Uncle Edis wore a brimmed hat and neck tie and Aunt Anna wore a black coat and silver earrings. I ran to them. Uncle Edis picked me up saying, "You little rascal, where have you been? What have you done?"

Aunt Anna went to greet Mom and Tinte who were running towards her.

"Uncle," I said, "I rode in the cab of the truck. What are all those gismos in front of the driver that look like faces of clocks? How do gears shift?"

"Easy, easy, little rascal, later for that. First tell me

where you've been since you left Riga. Then I'll tell you all about cars and trucks. Did Uncle Rudis take good care of you?"

"Oh, yes. Real good care. He could pass for a German so we were treated well by the Germans. He was even Lager Fuhrer once."

"Doesn't surprise me at all. Did Aunt Marta spoil you, Harij?"

"No, but she did stick up for me when my mom wouldn't let me do things because she was afraid something might happen to me."

"Those are my sisters alright. I'll put you down now. Must give them a big hug. We'll talk about cars later."

It was nice to see Uncle Edis and Aunt Anna again even though, overwhelmed by this reunion, they ignored me. The six adults had much to share – stories to tell of our travels. I listened as Uncle Edis told about his escape from Latvia. He had left Riga about the same time as my dad. The Red Army was near the city limits. My uncle, aunt and another couple left Riga in a car. The car belonged to a motor pool that had ceased to exist. No one was on duty to take it back. They took the car and drove almost to the town of Saldus where they were about to run out of gasoline. They met a farmer who took the car and gave them two large hams. The farmer drove them to a train station. The rest of Edis and Anna's travels resembled ours. Trains, trucks, farm wagons pulled by oxen and on foot.

The American Army truck left. They were still talking when a young woman came out of the door below the UNRRA sign and motioned us to come in. We had a surprise! She spoke Latvian. There were two other persons in the UNRRA office; a woman and a man, both in uniform. They spoke English. Our business was simple. Uncle Edis had done the required preliminary paper work. There were questions about our earthly possessions, willingness to work and health. We would be scheduled for a physical examination. The young Latvian lady told us our rooms (one for us and one for the Smits) were in the same apartment as the Raudupes. The three families would share a kitchen with dining space and a bath room. In the basement of the building was a storage room we were allowed to use. She welcomed us to the camp and said that Anna and Edis would take us to our new home. We picked up our belongings and eagerly walked to our new home; Finkstrasse 6, Apartment 2.

Finkstrasse 6, Apartment 2.
Third fourplex from left.

The building was a fourplex, with two apartments on the first floor and two above. The common front door led to a corridor and a staircase. Uncle Edis unlocked the door to apartment two, which was up some steps and to the left of the front door. He motioned for us to go in. I went first. Wow! It was nice! The bathroom with running water was to the left; kitchen, with eating area, straight ahead. To the right of the eating area a door led to a bedroom occupied by Aunt Anna and Uncle Edis. Across from the bathroom was a bedroom through which was access to a third bedroom. To my surprise in the first bedroom a cot and a double bed were ready for occupancy. The second bedroom contained only one made up double bed. That bedroom was for Tinte and Uncle Rudis, the bedroom with the cot was for my parents and me. All was planned and supplied by Uncle Edis. It didn't take us long to move in. We were home!

Aunt Anna had supper for us the first night. Beef stew, complete with potatoes, carrots, onions, celery and parsley. White bread with margarine and strawberry jam from a plain greenish tin can marked U.S. Army, and tea. Where had she gotten all this? Especially the beef in the stew and the kitchenware, the dishes? We had our own knives, forks and spoons but no dishes. In Binabiburg we ate American food out of the can and saved the can to be reused as a cup or a dish. The first night in Haunstetten our meal was on dishes and we sat around a table. At the end of an evening of lively and animated conversation, we thanked God for preserving us through the war, reuniting the family and for the food we had eaten. We prayed the Lord's Prayer. We hadn't done that before as a family. Aunt Anna was Catholic and I couldn't remember if Uncle Edis went to church in Riga. Usually it was Mom, Tinte and my grandmother Lavize who took me to church.

After the Lord 's Prayer there was silence and we looked at each other.

Uncle Edis broke the silence, "It's getting late. Let's go

to bed," and looking at me he added, "little rascal you'll sleep well in your army cot."

"But Uncle, you haven't taught me about cars and trucks. I want to know how gears shift."

"Tomorrow. I'll teach you tomorrow after you tell me about your trip from Riga. Good night, Harij."

"Good night, Harij," said Aunt Anna.

"Oh, Aunt Anna, where did you get all the food for tonight? The beef stew tasted great. Once we stayed in a schoolhouse where I thought they served us beef stew. The following day as I was rummaging through the garbage behind the school's kitchen, I found the skin and head of a Husky dog. Was it real beef we ate tonight, Aunt Anna?"

"Yes, Harij, yes. It was real beef. I saved it from our rations for this special night. Now go to bed."

seven

Haunstetten:
The First Day

I SLEPT WELL the first night in Haunstetten. The cot was very comfortable and I was warm with the extra blue wool blanket from Binabiburg. I was living in luxury. This couldn't be compared to the places I had slept in when we traveled. The usual sleeping place was the floor, with my back pack as a pillow.

I was fortunate to have a wool blanket. I could undress and didn't have to sleep in my clothes, like many other boys who had no blanket. Last night I went to bed in our own warm room with a tummy full of good food. Completely undressed, I crawled between fresh linen sheets under two wool blankets and slept like a king, dreaming about cars, gears and trucks. I was driving fast…

"Time for breakfast," Mom was calling me. She and Dad had gotten up earlier, allowing me to sleep longer my first night in Haunstetten. I crawled out of bed and dressed quickly, discovering as I went into the kitchen that the adults already had eaten. Did this mean all the goodies on the table were for me? There were two slices of white bread, margarine, the can of jam we had the night before, a boiled egg and, I couldn't believe my eyes, a glass of milk with a full jar of milk beside it! I couldn't remember the last time I had milk. Riga? No. Once a farmer gave me a glass of milk when I was begging to buy some eggs; I couldn't remember where. Last night beef stew, this morning milk. I felt blessed. As I sat to enjoy this bountiful breakfast, without anyone urging me, I prayed silently the prayer my grandma had taught me, "Come Lord Jesus, be our guest, and let these gifts to us be blessed. Amen."

As I was enjoying breakfast I noticed Uncle Edis wasn't home. Mom, Dad, my two aunts and Uncle Rudis were in the kitchen talking, but no Uncle Edis. "No lessons about cars this morning," I said to myself, and then asked aloud, "Where is Uncle Edis?"

"He went to work," answered Aunt Anna.

"To work!" I exclaimed, "I didn't know he had a job."

"Uncle Edis doesn't have a job, as such," said Aunt Anna. "He's talking with the people from UNRRA about publishing a magazine."

I wanted to ask about UNRRA but didn't get the chance.

"A magazine!" exclaimed Mom and Tinte almost simultaneously, and I noticed that Dad and Uncle Rudis sat up and raised their eyebrows.

"Edis says we Latvian D.P.'s need something like that to keep us informed and give us identity," said Aunt Anna. "It will keep us together." My first thought was that he would be away and busy, with no time to teach me about gears, cars and trucks.

They talked for a long time about the magazine my Uncle Edis was planning to publish. From their conversation I learned it wasn't easy to publish a magazine. I didn't understand all he must do. I did learn he had purchased a typewriter. I wasn't sure what a typewriter was; something that was used in big offices? The idea of seeing a typewriter fascinated me. More questions for Uncle Edis. More questions for everybody. What in the world is UNRRA?

I finished my delightful breakfast and listened to the adults talk about Uncle Edis' magazine for about an hour.

Then I decided to go back to our room, lay down on my cot and daydream about gears, cars and trucks. I slipped out of the eating area in the kitchen unnoticed. As I entered our room, out the window I saw a boy about my age playing an interesting game with two smaller boys.

They had two sticks, one about thirty centimeters and the other about sixty centimeters long and two red bricks on the ground about twenty centimeters apart. The my-age boy placed the shorter stick across the bricks, then used the longer stick to propel the shorter stick towards the younger boys who tried to catch it, but didn't. The catcher closest to where the shorter stick fell, picked it up and from that place threw it at the longer stick that was now placed crosswise on the bricks, trying to knock it off the bricks, but he missed.

The my-age boy then held the shorter stick in his left hand and with the longer stick in his right hand hit the shorter stick towards the younger boys who again tried to catch it, but didn't. Again the catcher closest to where the short stick fell tried to knock the longer stick from the bricks, but didn't. Then the older boy held both sticks in his right hand, released the shorter stick and hit it with the longer stick propelling it toward the younger boys, who again tried to catch it, but didn't. Then the older boy, using the longer stick as a standard, measured the number of stick lengths the shorter stick fell from the bricks and wrote down the number on a piece of paper. The game started over again. (Later I learned that the number was how many points the batter earned toward winning the game. I also learned if someone caught the shorter stick, the batter was out and whoever caught the stick was up. Also, if you knocked the stick off the bricks by throwing the shorter stick at it, the batter was out and the thrower was up. The idea was to survive one's position at the bricks for the third and scoring shot when both sticks are held in the right hand. If no one catches it, the batter measures for points.

One point for every length of the longer stick to where the shorter stick had fallen.)

Whoever had the most points at the end of the game was the winner. There was one problem. When should the game end? Usually it was played for an agreed length of time: like a long time, a short time or till a Mom called. We had no watches. The nice feature of this game was that any number of people could play it. And we played it a lot. We only needed two bricks and two sticks. This was the Bricks and Sticks Game.

Back to my bed room – and the rest of my first day.

But it wasn't long before I decided to be brave and go out and meet these boys, especially the my-age one. I went into the kitchen to ask my mom if I could go outside. They were still talking about Uncle Edis and his proposed magazine. I decided to risk a possible reprimand and interrupted.

"Mom," I said, touching her arm, "May I go outside for a while? Three boys are playing an interesting game in the yard behind our building. I want to meet them, maybe learn the game they're playing."

"No, Harij, I don't think so. I can't go with you now and I don't want you to go alone."

"Mom, I'm almost ten years old. I can take care of myself. Besides they look like good boys. One is about my age, two are younger."

"I don't want you to go by yourself," she sounded firm.

"Oh Erna, let him go," Tinte came to my defense, "we can watch Harijs from the window."

"Tinte, please no," I said in despair, "You don't need to spy on me." Then, turning to my mom, "Ten minutes, fifteen maybe. Please."

"Let him go," Dad also came to my defense, "We're among Latvians now. Go, Harij, fifteen minutes, twenty. Go."

That's all I needed to hear. Before my mom's protests

ended, I was outside. Twenty minutes. Great. What did that mean? I didn't have a watch.

But making new friends wasn't as easy as overriding my mother's fears. I had made new friends many times before. I was confident I would do it again.

Slowly I walked around our fourplex to where the three boys were still playing the stick and brick game. I stood at the corner watching them. Hit! Throw! Measure! Hit! Finally one of the smaller boys caught the stick. The older boy surrendered his place at the bricks and began to trade places with the boy who caught the stick. As he was walking away from the bricks, he noticed me and started to walk towards me.

"Hi," I said.

Coming toward me, he responded, "Hi. You new in camp?"

"Yes, I arrived yesterday afternoon. I'm Harijs."

"I'm Imants, nice to meet you, Harijs. What's your last name?"

"Kapeikis, what's yours?"

"Mackus, and these two are my kid brothers." The two younger ones came up to meet me as well.

"Hi, kid brothers," I said. "I like the game you're playing, Can you teach me? But I can stay out only twenty minutes. "

"Ahhh!" said Imants, "Strict mother?"

"Nah," I replied, "Not strict, scared. She always worries about me getting in trouble."

"Do you?" inquired Imants.

"No, not usually, but sometimes," I replied.

"Don't we all," said Imants. "Do you have brothers, sisters maybe?"

"No, I don't. Just Mom, Dad, me, and two sets of Uncles and Aunts."

"You moved in with the Raudupes?" asked Imants. "My parents met them when they moved in about a month ago."

"Yes, we did. When did you come here?" I asked.

"Just a few days before your uncle. The camp had just opened."

"This is a nice place. I like it," I said.

"I like it too, much better than the ruins we had to live in when we were running from the Russians," said Imants. "So you want to play the game?"

"Yes, I do."

The game was briefly explained to me – the terms, the rules, the goals and we started to play. Twenty five minutes went fast. I didn't even get to bat before my dad came out to call me.

"Harij, twenty minutes was five minutes ago. Come in now."

"Sorry, Dad, I don't have a watch you know."

I introduced my new friends to Dad. He said he was glad to meet them.

Not to upset Mom, I followed Dad to our room.

In spite of Mom limiting my outdoor play time, it had been a good day. I had made my first friend in Haunstetten and learned a new game. Then I waited for Uncle Edis to come home and tell me about cars, gears and trucks. He came home just before supper.

We had another great meal; wieners, sauerkraut, potatoes, carrots and a dessert of white bread with margarine and strawberry jam. The adults drank tea and I had two glasses of milk. Wonderful! Wonderful! Wonderful! I loved the white bread with jam and milk. No more hunger pains. No more anxiety and fear of starving to death.

I'll never forget the days when we had nothing to eat, and no one had any food to sell or give us. On the trains, many evenings came when we hadn't eaten anything that day. No breakfast, lunch or dinner. But usually the following day the train would stop at a station and "angels" would be there stirring a big pot of soup and my hunger would be appeased for a while. But the days before our arrival at Binabiburg were the worst. Four days without any food. The trains had stopped. The rails were destroyed. We were walking the muddy back roads until the wounded German soldier gave us a ride in his damaged truck. I remembered how my tummy hurt, growled and started to bloat. I remembered the look in my dad's eyes when all of us were experiencing hunger pains. In his eyes was a plea, a prayer, and despair. "Oh God, don't let Harij die. Help us to survive." Life is good now and it will get even better.

After supper Uncle Edis called me into his and Aunt Anna's room. "Finally I'm going to learn about cars and trucks," I thought. He sat on a white wooden chair and I sat on his bed.

"Harij," he said, "Tell me. What was the most memorable event in your travels with Uncle Rudis?"

"Uncle," I said, "you promised to teach me about cars and trucks and gears."

"Yes I did, and I will. But I want to hear from you first. Did anything happen that impressed you, scared you, or was extraordinary or different?"

I thought for a moment, wishing we would talk about cars, then I remembered our crossing of the Baltic Sea and said, "Uncle, yes there was. The night I spent on a German warship crossing the Baltic Sea."

"Okay, tell me about it. Your mother didn't like it. Right?"

"No, she didn't. She doesn't like to be on water. But I didn't like it either. We were attacked that night."

"Attacked?" asked Uncle. "Tell me from the beginning."

"Uncle Rudis got permission from the German Captain for us to board his… destroyer, I think it was. Mom was frightened at the thought. There were five German ships that were to sail from Liepaja to Germany. Uncle Rudis said we'd be safe onboard the German destroyer; a lot safer and faster than finding a way to Germany by land. But Mom was frantic."

"I'll bet she was," said Uncle Edis. "She's afraid of guns, boats and water, especially at the night."

"She wasn't going to board the ship. But finally we convinced her that it was safer and quicker to go to Germany by sea."

"You boarded the destroyer," commented Uncle.

"Yes, late in the afternoon. It was a cool and clear day with hardly any clouds. A light breeze was blowing. We followed a group of sailors boarding the ship. The sailors were carrying long crates. The crates seemed heavy. I could see panic on Mom's face as we walked by the rows of anti-aircraft guns. There were very big guns with long barrels in the stern and aft. We were led down a very steep metal ladder and shown a corner in a large room. There were some chairs, tables, a bar and bar stools, but no bunks or beds. That was our corner for the night. In the morning we would be in Germany."

"Sounds like they gave you a corner in the ship's dining hall," said Uncle.

"Yes, that's right. Sailors came to eat, three or four at a time. There was a kitchen at one end of the room with two sailors preparing food. They served us wiener schnitzel and sauerkraut with potatoes. Mom, Tinte and I got apple juice, Dad and Uncle Rudis, dark beer."

"You had a little party?" asked Uncle Edis.

"Yes, at first it seemed like that. I was surprised they let us walk around the deck. I was interested in the guns and the lifeboats. There was much to see, but as the ships were about to sail they asked us to stay in the dining hall. The ships were going to practice a maneuver."

"Did they?" asked Uncle.

"Yes, they did. We were in the dining hall as directed when I heard the sirens, sailors running above and commands over the intercom. I heard the big guns above us turn one way, then another. More commands and running.

I sensed the ship turning, accelerating and then slowing down. I heard another siren and the activities above us ceased and the ship's engines resumed a steady growl. We knew we were on the way to Germany."

"What's so frightening about that?" asked my uncle.

"Nothing, Uncle. After the maneuvers the cooks gave us more wiener schnitzels and sauerkraut and everything was fine for about two hours. Then chaos! I heard the sirens again and commands over loud speakers, "Battle stations! Battle stations! Enemy aircraft approaching from the North! Anti-aircraft batteries! Fire at will! Fire!"

We thought the drill was noisy but it was nothing compared to the firing of the anti-aircraft guns above us. Boom! Boom! Ka-boom! The ship was shaking like jelly on a plate. Then the lights went off. We were in total darkness. The worst thing was that we couldn't see what was happening outside. There were no portholes in the destroyer. Mom was crying. I was scared. I thought this was it. We had been issued life jackets, but couldn't find them in the darkness. Then a shock wave hit the starboard followed by a similar shock wave on port side of the ship. The ship careened some, first to the left, then to the right. I thought we were going to sink. The firing kept on through this left to right swaying of the ship, and it seemed to go on forever. Finally the ship steadied. The firing stopped and so did the ship's engines.

Mom cried out, 'We've been hit! The ship will sink!'

After what seemed like eternity the sirens sounded again and the lights came on. We were safe. The sailors were released from their battle stations. Some sailors came down the steep ladder to eat. I noticed their uniforms were tarnished, torn and some had blackened faces and hands."

"Did you ask the sailors what had happened?" inquired Uncle.

"Yes, Uncle Rudis did."

"And?" asked Uncle Edis.

"We were attacked by a squadron of British fighter planes followed by a formation of Lancasters. Three fighters were shot down and two German ships were damaged. Two bombs fell near our ship, one on the port and one on the starboard side. We stopped to rescue a British pilot who parachuted from his burning plane into the sea near our ship."

"Well, little rascal, you were in the war after all."

"I was, wasn't I. The German navy – but they didn't give me medals. No decorations."

"I wouldn't brag about the German navy part if I were you," advised my uncle, "nor do you get medals for sitting in darkness." We chuckled.

"Now will you tell me about cars and trucks, Uncle?"

"Wouldn't you rather learn why your mom is afraid of the water?"

"No, I want to learn about gears, cars and trucks. Cars and trucks - gears."

"But you simply must know about your mom, Harij."

"No. Cars and trucks - gears."

"About your mother, Harij."

"Okay, Okay." I gave in. "But then cars and trucks - gears."

"When your mother was a young girl, before she met your dad, my mother, that is your grandmother, sent her to buy fish from the fishermen across the River Daugava. She went to do that with a group of girls. The best way to get to the fish market was by a row boat, otherwise you had to walk to the pontoon bridge, and cross the river and back. A long walk. A man ferried people across the river for a few santims. The girls climbed in the row boat and the man took them across. They bought fish, other items as well, but on the way home the boat started to sink. Your mother didn't know how to swim."

"She almost drowned?" I interrupted.

"Yes. As the boat filled with water the other girls

jumped into the river and swam to shore. Your mother froze. She said the oarsman urged her to jump, but she couldn't do it. The oarsman stayed with her as the boat went under. Fortunately they were close to the shore. When the boat came to rest on the bottom of the river, your mother's head was above the water."

"That scared her," I interrupted again.

"Yes. The oarsman helped your mother out of the water and it turned out she was better off staying in the boat."

"How so, Uncle?"

"The girls who jumped into the river lost their purchases. When your mother came out of the water, her basket with the fish was firmly in her hands. She came home looking like a half-drowned rat. She said she'll never go in a boat again. Now you know, Harij."

"Uncle, are you going to publish a magazine?" Oops, I shouldn't have asked that. Now he'll really get going. How dumb of me, I thought.

"Harijs, who told you that?"

"Aunt Anna. This morning. She said you were talking with Americans about it. The UN something, people."

"The UNRRA people. Do you know who they are?"

"No, I don't." (Now I've done it. Goodbye cars, trucks and gears.)

"UNRRA is an international organization called United Nations Relief and Rehabilitation Administration. They are the people who're looking out for us. They have organized the D.P. camps in the American zone throughout Western Germany. Another camp is very near us – Hochfeld, on the other side of the Messerschmitt factory. One day we'll go see it."

"How did they organize these camps? Who lived here before?" (Why am I asking all these questions?)

"I believe the UNNRA asked the German people who worked at Messerschmitt to give up their apartments."

"That's not very fair," I said.

"It's not. But Messerschmitt planes shot down many American and British bombers. It's a penalty of sorts for working for Hitler."

"The people who were put out of their apartments will hate us, Uncle."

"They may. But this wasn't our doing. UNRRA has authority and the responsibility for our welfare. What UNNRA says, goes. Understand, Harij, that's why I must have permission from UNRRA to publish a magazine."

"You'll be a publisher then? The Editor?"

"As soon as I get permission."

"What are you going to name it?" (Rats! Why can't I stop.)

"I'm thinking *The Illustrated Word.* I have purchased a typewriter. Want to see?"

"Of course, Uncle." (No! No! No! A thousand times no!) "What's a typewriter?"

"It's a rather recent invention; a device, a machine for writing without a pen or pencil."

"A writing machine?" I'd never seen one.

"Look, Harij. In that corner, open the black case on the wooden crate."

I went to the corner and opened what looked like a black suitcase. Wow! A typing machine. So, that's what a typing machine looked like. In back it had a saddle with a black rubber rolling pin, like the one mom uses to flatten dough for baking cookies. An oval mouth with metal teeth on wires or spindles. A whole bunch of little round buttons with numbers and letters on them, attached to spindly metal legs.

"How does the writing machine work, Uncle?"

He came over to the wooden crate and took a sheet of white paper from a stack of papers on a shelf. I'd never seen so much paper before. He put the sheet of paper behind the black rubber rolling pin. He turned the pin and the machine ate the paper. No, the paper came up the front of the rolling pin. He pushed down a button with the index finger of his right hand and hit one of the buttons with his left index finger, and one of the metal teeth jumped up and bit the white paper, but not before a black ribbon jumped up to protect the paper from being attacked. The little saddle and rolling pin jumped to the left. When the tooth went back into the oval mouth, it left the letter "H" on the paper. He hit the letter "A". Everything happened just like before, except when the tooth went back into the mouth there was an "A" next the "H." Uncle Edis kept punching the buttons. Soon I saw my name, "HARIJS", on the paper.

"Your turn," said my uncle. "I'll help you. Stand in front of the typewriter. Now with one finger push down this 'shift' key, and with your right index finger briskly hit the key with the letter "K" on it."

I stood in front of the machine and was glad to know about typewriters. As directed, I struck the key with the "K" on it and it went – 'plek.'

"Not so hard, Harij. You'll bend the type-bar and damage the keyboard."

I looked at the very dark "K" on the paper. My uncle continued to direct me, and soon I saw "HARIJS KAPEIKIS" on the paper. I had actually typed on a typing machine, I mean a typewriter.

"Uncle, thank you. This is fun. I want to do more machine writing." I said.

"Typing," he corrected me. "You will when you get older. Typewriters are not toys, Harij."

"I know, Uncle. Please now teach me about cars, trucks and gears."

"You little rascal, what do you want to know and why?"

"I want to learn to drive. But I don't even know what those clock things are called, or all the gadgets behind the steering wheel under the front window."

"All right, little rascal, I can tell you about the instruments, the gauges and controls. We can talk about driving because I know how to drive. About gears and other engine parts I can't teach you. I'm a driver, not a mechanic nor an automotive engineer."

"Uncle, you don't know about gears?" I asked with surprise and disappointment.

"I actually do not know."

"Is that why you kept delaying the subject of cars, trucks and gears?"

"Little rascal, perhaps."

We talked more and my uncle explained about windshields, instrument clusters, speedometers and odometers, starter buttons and ignition keys, clutches, brakes, parking brakes and accelerators, gear shift levers, first, second, high and reverse, rear view mirrors, hand signals, headlights, brake-lights, license plates and driver's licenses.

"Someday I'll drive. Yes, I will."

eight

Haunstetten:
The Pre-School Days

IT WAS EXCITING TO EXPLORE OUR CAMP, to learn how big it was, where the boundaries were and who was living there. The camp had three sections. Latvians and Estonians were housed mostly in the two-story fourplexes, Lithuanians in two story row houses. North of the row houses as well as one block east of our street was German territory where only Germans lived.

The other two sides of the camp were exposed to open fields where we were allowed to play soccer, fly kites or just chase each other in pretend war games. Volleyball and stick and brick games were played between the houses or on the street. Beyond the Estonian section was an open area that was used for track and field events. Beyond that, our elementary school barrack, infirmary and an auditorium complete with stage and wooden plank dance floor. The camp also had a community dining hall and kitchen for people who chose to receive their rations fully cooked. Our choice was to do our own cooking and supplement our fare with food we could purchase in German stores – and once in a while, the black market.

Between Haunstetten and Hochfeld were the ruins of the Messerschmitt airplane factory complex. Many useful items could be found, especially in what appeared to be a dump that at one time may have been a storage yard. People would find pots and pans, boards, box springs, storage cabinets, tools, metal hoops and more. Imants introduced a game with a metal hoop which became very popular. Roll the hoop with a stick and run with it as fast as you can. Imants ran very fast. I couldn't keep up with him.

From my first day in Haunstetten, Imants and I spent much time together. Imants was two or three centimeters shorter than I, but in time he outgrew me. He was slender with strong legs and arms. Imants wore a perpetual smile and often ran with bare feet.

We loved the stick and brick game, and rolling the hoop, though he would outrun me every time. We kicked a soccer ball, but the walks to the river with his dad and sometimes also his mother, were the most enjoyable.

Imants and I became good friends in the pre-school days. He lived in the fourplex behind ours, which meant that my bedroom window and his kitchen window were about thirty meters apart. We could signal each other to open the windows and talk to each other. We devised a way of sending messages across the yard using a clothesline contraption; two empty thread spools and sixty meters of kite string. The windows were high enough that the kite string was about two meters above the heads of people. We called it our message machine. It was nice to wake up and see a message at my window: Harij, do you want to go swimming with us at Wertach River? We're going this afternoon. Signed, Imants.

Would my parents let me? Sure they would. Imants' parents were nice. Imants' dad was very interested in his boys. He did a lot with them, like take them to the river for the afternoon. Wertach was about an hour's walk west of our camp. The river was not deep and fast like the River Lech which was about one and a half hours walk east of camp.

Wertach was our favorite river for swimming. It had

many large pools were the water flowed very slowly over a sandy bed, deep enough to swim in and shallow enough to give peace of mind to our parents. Our parents had met and trusted each other to look after us. It was only a matter of protocol to ask if I could go to Wertach with Imants. They had consented before.

My mother was with Tinte and Aunt Anna in the kitchen. I quickly dressed and went to the kitchen to ask, "Mom, Imants' family is going to Wertach this afternoon. May I go with them?"

"I thought you wanted to play sticks and bricks this afternoon, and later make a kite," answered Mom.

"Yes, I do want to make a kite. I'll do that tonight. We can play sticks and bricks at the river, you know."

"Okay Harij, you can go."

"Oh, thank you, thank you," I said.

As I was attaching to our 'message machine' my 'yes' note onto which I had also scribbled a suggestion that we 'run the hoop', I noticed a group of older boys across the street. The boys were huddled around a bigger boy who seemed to be instructing them. I was curious. What was the big one telling the others? Were they friends playing a game? It would be nice to belong to a group, I thought. Then they broke the huddle and went their separate ways. What were they up to? I wondered.

When Imants got my note and read it, he opened his window all the way and shouted across the yard, "Okay, come out! I'll get my hoop and let's run!" He closed the window.

I went back to the kitchen and declared to my three mothers (that's how they thought of themselves), "Imants and I will run the hoop. Be back in about half an hour."

"You shouldn't," said my mom, "aren't you going swimming this afternoon? You'll get too tired."

"No, Mom, a half hour run will do me good."

"Okay, but before you go just look in Aunt Anna's

room."

I took a quick look. "Hey, where did you get the sewing machine, Aunt?"

"Uncle Edis brought it home last night after you went to bed."

"That's great," I said, "Will one of my three mothers sew me a new pair of pants for school when it starts?"

"School starts next week," said Aunt Anna.

"What!" I almost screamed, "Next week! It's still summer. June!"

"That's what the teachers decided. All D.P. children have missed a year of school. The building is available so they want to start right away," said Anna.

My three mothers: Tinte, Aunt Anna and Mom.
King Ludwig's castles were famous for their gardens. (1948)

"Harij," said my mom, "you should be happy to go back to school. In spite of the war and not much to eat, you're much stronger and healthier now than you were in Riga. You remember that not only did you miss a year of school, you were very sick during grade two in Riga. They didn't even give you marks for the second trimester. You missed fifty days of school and then had your tonsils out."

"Yeah, I remember. I was kind of a sick little kid then. That's why I want to run and jump and swim as much as I can. Okay. I'll be back in about half an hour. But I want new pants for school!" And I was out of there.

Imants was waiting for me by the front door of his building with a hoop in hand, ready to run.

"Let's go," I said.

"Where?"

"Around the camp twice, you first then me." (That was a mistake. Letting him take the lead from the start would leave me in his dust.)

We started to run. Imants, with the hoop, ahead of me. By the time we were to the end of the block he was already ten meters ahead of me. After once around the camp I was about fifty meters behind. He finished with over a hundred meter lead. Now my turn to roll the hoop. Imants had no trouble keeping up with me. I tried hard but couldn't pull away from him. He won.

Exhausted and breathing hard after a run of about three kilometers, we sat on the curb. We hadn't seen the young man walking toward us.

"Good morning, boys," he said. We should have stood and addressed the approaching adult with a proper greeting. Instead, he greeted us. "You both run very well. Track team material, no doubt," he said and added as he went, "See you next week in school."

We just sat there. We should have stood. We were impolite. When adults approached children it was expected that children stand up and greet the adult appropriately,

with a "Good morning, Sir" or "Good afternoon, Madam".
"Do you know who he is?" asked Imants.
"No, how would I?"
"Mr. Salins. Mr. Gunars Salins. A teacher."
We rested. Then I remembered my promise not to be gone longer than half an hour. But I had no watch. I told Imants I had to go in and I'd come over after lunch, ready to swim. We parted.

After lunch I put on my old worn-out brown cotton shorts, a shirt and wooden-soled sandals, said goodbye to my three moms, and went to Imants' place. His family was ready. We started to walk and, in about an hour, arrived at the River Wertach.

That day the river was exceptionally beautiful. The sun was bright and warm. The sky was decorated with beautifully sculpted clouds that seemed to change form endlessly. The foliage on the riverbanks was a deep green, interspersed with monolithic rocks in various shapes and shades from grey to black. All this beauty was doubled by the crisp reflections in the lazily flowing water as it made its way through elongated, kidney-shaped pools. Wild flowers, here and there, added their fragrance and color to the scene. Leaves, rustling in the breeze, added charm to the dry aroma of summer.

Into this paradise-like setting we descended; four boys and two adults. The adults sat on the shore, the boys plunged into the water. Laughter and splashes merged with the sounds of nature to compose a symphony of joy.

That was one day; a day to be repeated many times in summers to come. We played and jested in the water for about two hours, then returned home.

At home, Mom asked, "How did the swimming go?"
"Wonderful!"

Adults don't tell everything to children. This leads to the delightful feature of surprise in their lives, like the day when the Krauja's appeared at our front door. I knew they were coming to Haunstetten, but I had no idea when.

Aunt Marta answered the knock on the door, and when she opened it, in came strangers whom I soon learned were Aunt Hermine, Uncle Richards and Ojars Krauja. Mom and Aunt Anna exchanged hugs with the Kraujas. My dad, Uncles Rudis and Edis weren't home. There we stood, Ojars and me, looking at each other like two baby bulls. I didn't know him. I didn't remember meeting him. I knew he was my second cousin, but what do you say to a second cousin you don't know? I felt I had to say something, so I said, "Hi, welcome to Haunstetten."

He answered, "Hi, you're Harijs, aren't you."

"Yeah, Harijs, and you're Ojars. Mom told me about you."

"Yeah, and my mom about you." A moment of awkward silence.

"You lived downtown in Riga?" I said in a questioning tone.

"Yeah, above my mom's photo studio."

"Cool," I said. "Your mom's a photographer?"

"Yeah, she has lots of cameras."

"Like how many?" I asked.

"I don't know," he answered. "Five or six maybe. Big ones."

"Does she take lots of pictures?" I asked.

"Yeah, and charges for them." Another moment of awkward silence.

I noted the front door was still open. The silence was broken by Aunt Anna. "Close the door, Harij. Come in, Ojars. Harijs, Ojars, shake hands. You two remember each other, don't you? You're cousins."

"I don't remember Harijs," replied Ojars, to which I added, "I don't remember meeting Ojars, Aunt Anna." I closed the door.

"Oh, you have met," declared Aunt Anna. "You just

don't remember 'cause you were young boys then."

"Anna, I think the boys are right," said Aunt Hermine. "We were so busy in Riga. Poor Ojars didn't get to go with us very often. He had to stay home with a friend of mine."

"That's right, Mom," answered Ojars, "You didn't take me anyplace. This is the first time I've seen Harijs."

"Well then," Ojars' dad entered the conversation, "You two will have to get to know each other and become the best of friends. Right, Harijs?" he said slapping me lightly on the back.

"Right, Sir," I answered, "The best of friends."

The reunion went on for several hours. Coffee was served with jam and bread. Like us, the Krauja's didn't have much luggage. They did have a large, well packed container, where Aunt Hermine had packed her cameras with equipment to develop film and print photographs.

Ojars and I worked through our mutual awkwardness and were on our way to becoming friends, not just second cousins. He told me his story and I told him my travel story of escaping from Latvia. Our stories were similar, but the Kraujas had faired somewhat better than the Smits and us. Ojars told me they always got rides to where they wanted to go. They never had to walk, nor experience hunger like we did before we got to Binabiburg. There was more food in Austria than Germany at the end of the war.

Ojars' family was assigned a room in a fourplex like ours, one block away. Now the relatives who left Riga were reunited in Haunstetten, except for my father's sister, Emilija Zemrukis and her daughter Velta. We didn't know their whereabouts, nor fate. We hoped they were with the survivors yet to be registered as D.P.'s.

My mother also had a brother, Arvids, whose wife, Sasha and two daughters, Velta and Arija, stayed in Latvia. Aunt Sasha was petite, about one and a half meters tall, slender with black hair. She liked to dress nice in full flowing dresses. She liked to dance. Uncle Arvids was a big and strong man. He drove a Model T Ford truck for a brewery in Riga. When the truck would get a flat tire, he would lift the front or back of the truck all by himself, and have his assistant place a block of wood under the axle. He had no need for a jack.

He and his attractive wife were at a brewery sponsored party to which German soldiers were invited. Germans liked beer and so did Uncle Arvids. As the evening got livelier, a German officer tried to seduce Aunt Sasha, ignoring my uncle's many protests and warnings. Seeing that his words of protest were ignored repeatedly, strong Uncle Arvids grabbed the officer by the lapels of his uniform, lifted him off the floor and threw him backwards. They were too close to a stairway; the officer fell down the stairs and was injured. Uncle Arvids was immediately arrested and jailed. This happened in the summer of 1944. He did not come home from the jail. His body was not found.

nine

Haunstetten School Days

I HAD MIXED FEELINGS, looking out my bedroom window at Imants' fourplex as the sun was setting. School starts tomorrow. I'll be enrolled as a third grade student in the Haunstetten Latvian Elementary School. I should be pleased to have the opportunity to go to a Latvian school, I thought, fighting back feelings of apprehension. Will I be a better student here than in Latvia? Will I have an easier time? Kind teachers? At least I'll understand what they say, and not be embarrassed like I was in the German school.

I remembered the difficult time I had in grades one and two. My first seven years of life I lived as a loner. I didn't have friends except for Irene, who lived in the big house across the street, and Arija, my cousin, nicknamed Lule, who came to play from time to time. When my mom brought me into the first grade class room I was terrified. I didn't know there were so many girls and boys my age in the world. I didn't want to let Mom go. I cried and cried. No one could make me stop. My mom had to leave. When I saw her, through my tears, walk out the classroom door, the world I knew ended. I withdrew into myself and my anxieties, missing seventeen days of classes in the first trimester because of emotional stress and sore throats. I passed, but with poor grades. During the second trimester I did adjust, made some friends, and ended my first year of school with acceptable grades. I remember it as a difficult year. I was so glad I had already made friends in Haunstetten. I was determined my first grade experiences would not follow me.

During the second grade I developed severe tonsillitis, requiring a tonsillectomy. I missed fifty consecutive days of school during the second trimester and didn't get grades on my report card. I remembered the effort I had to make to catch up with the class when I returned. Math was the hardest, calligraphy a breeze. I remembered how proud and happy I was at the end of the school year when I passed grade two with good marks.

I'm in good health now, I thought, still staring at Imants' fourplex. I can run and jump. I don't have sore throats any more. I won't miss classes because of illness. I have a good friend. Bring on tomorrow! I went to bed.

One image came to mind before I fell asleep. The group of older boys I had seen again earlier in the day. I wondered if they would accept Imants and me into their group.

Morning came quickly. I dressed, had a good breakfast, and off to school I went. In Riga I had a backpack full of books, notebooks, pens and pencils. That morning I carried nothing, just a big smile on my face as I met Imants. I was so excited and nervous I lost track of what my parents were doing. Was I really going to school? Other kids were going too. Many children, adults with children, boys, girls. It felt like I was in a parade, a dream, a wish come true! School again – a Latvian school in exile. So much was happening all at once, and then the bell rang. School had begun.

I found myself in the third grade classroom sitting in the school bench assigned to me, gazing in turn at the empty ink well, fellow pupils and the teacher – the class advisor – Mr. Gunars Salins whom I had met on the street after a hard run with Imants. Will he remember I was impolite and scold me, or will he forgive me, I wondered. Maybe he'll forget the incident.

Mr. Salins told us that due to the lack of school supplies and facilities at the moment, we would have only five subjects – religion, grammar, English, math and literature. He would be our literature teacher.

He spoke about the lack of books and notebooks, impressing on us that even items like chalk must be used sparingly. In time supplies will come, he said, but in the meantime we had to do the best we could with what we had.

I liked Mr. Salins also his wife, the talented Mrs. Salins (Jautrite) for the way they explained these difficulties. They were not problems but challenges. From their words and how they spoke, I knew they cared about us. I was glad to be in their classes, listen to them and learn. I knew I had much work ahead of me. There was much for me to learn.

Later in the first trimester, as a result of his preparations to publish his magazine, Uncle Edis was able to locate a source of writing paper, notebooks and pencils for the school, enabling us to take notes of our teachers' presentations and black board illustrations. We now had notebooks with light blue covers, with lined paper or graphs for mathematics. There were very few text books for homework. Teachers wrote our assignments on the black board, and we copied. Sometimes the few available text books were shared, passed around for us to copy assignments. I remember copying by hand, like the scribes of old, a complete book, so that I would have a book of my own.

The teachers inspired us, setting an example of hard work, diligence and thrift. Nothing went to waste. A sheet of writing paper was precious. We wrote on both sides of the paper, with small letters and narrow margins. Copious supplies alone do not make a good school, but teachers who can motivate pupils, and pupils who want to learn so as to make a difference in their world in their future lives and contributions to society, do. I was in a good school, and when school started, time started to fly.

I was soon to learn not everyone can be trusted outside of school.

One day as I was coming home from school alone, I came upon the group of older boys I had noticed and thought about before. One of them beckoned me to approach them. I was eager to obey.

"What's your name?" asked the one I thought was the leader.

"Harijs," I answered, "What's yours?"

"None of your business, kid," he snapped back. "How old are you?"

"Ten," I answered. "Why do you ask?"

"I ask the questions and I give the orders here. Think you can catch that, kid, if you know what's good for you."

"What are you guys up to?" I asked and realized I shouldn't have.

"You have a hearing problem, kid," snapped the big one.

"Sorry," I backed off, "just that I've seen you around."

"Spying on us, are you," said another from the group.

"No, I'm not spying," I tried to answer calmly, "I just wondered if you all are friends. I like having friends."

"Do you, kid," said the big one, "have you made any friends?" he asked.

"Yes, I have a friend, I think two friends."

"Mind giving us their names," said the big boy as if he was giving me an order.

"No, I don't think so, not until I get to know you guys more."

"Hey, this runt has spunk," said the big one to the group, "even though he's a bit stupid and runs the risk of getting beat up."

"Sorry," I apologized.

"Listen carefully kid," said the big one, "if you want to

be part of this group you take orders from me. Got it, kid.? Me and nobody else."

"What kinds of orders?" I asked, "Like in the Army?"

"Yeah. You got the idea. I'll give you one," he said.

"Okay, give me one," I volunteered and immediately regretted the comment.

"See that post over there?" he asked.

"Yeah, what about it?"

"Okay kid, pick up a rock and see if you can hit it."

I found a nice little round rock about the size that would fill a tablespoon, took aim, wound up and threw it with all my strength. Smack! Beginners luck! It hit the post dead center.

"Not bad, kid," he complimented me, and some of the boys whistled. I was asked to do it once more and I threw and hit the post dead center again. Was I discovering a talent? I wondered, but kept my mouth shut.

"You could be of use to us, for our cause. Think about it, but don't talk to anyone about this. I'll give you a couple days, then we talk. Okay?" he asked.

"Okay," I said, "but what am I to think about?"

"Think about obeying my orders, that's all."

"Okay," I said again, anxious to end this confrontation.

We scattered. I went home rather distraught. The big guy said they had a cause. I began to wonder what it might be.

Kite flying was popular and I loved it. My dad had shown me how to make several kinds of kites, but I liked the rectangular ones best. They were simple and easy to construct and they flew steady and high. It wasn't easy to acquire a kite. You constructed it or asked a friend to build it for you. The most difficult job was to cut the sticks for the frame. There was a woodpile behind our school where D.P.'s could get logs if they had a legitimate need for them.

Some families had wood stoves for heat and cooking.

We had an improvised wood burning smoker to smoke fish. Therefore we had a legitimate need and could get the one meter logs. I liked that. The smoked fish was everyone's delicacy, but stocking the smoker was where I got the sticks for my kite frames. If I found a log with straight grains I wouldn't burn it, but set it aside and ask my dad to peel off about one centimeter wide and one half centimeter thick sticks. That wasn't an easy task. Most of them would break or be too thick or too thin at one end, triangular or crooked. Sometimes a whole log wouldn't produce a single usable stick for my kite frames. Oh well, we also needed kindling. But my dad was a good woodsman and most of the time, under his expert axe-man-ship, one log produced enough sticks to build several kites.

My first kites didn't perform very well. Some fell apart while others crashed or wouldn't fly at all, but soon I mastered the art and my kites flew steady and high. After finishing home work, I could make a kite in one evening.

I loved flying my kites. Sometimes there were three or four friends flying kites with me in the open field beyond the camp. We'd get our kites high in the air, until we'd come to the end of our strings. Then we'd start sending messages to our high flying kites by punching a little hole in the middle of a twenty centimeter square piece of paper and threading the kite string through it. It was fun to watch the paper sail up on the string to the kite. When I did this, I was careful to hang on to the end of the string. Kites were lost that way. There were kids downwind waiting for someone's kite to cut loose, especially when they saw the messages go up. I lost a few kites, and I also caught some. That wasn't stealing but taking a prisoner of war; repatriation if I got my own kite back.

One day in a fairly strong wind my kite was flying high. I had sent a dozen messages to it which made the kite descend some. The wind shifted, and my kite was flying over German territory. The wind also decreased and my kite was low over German houses, especially the string. Then I saw an arrow shoot up from behind a house and over my string. As it looped my kite string I saw the arrow had a string attached to it. The arrow fell and soon my string and kite were pulled down from behind a house. I tried to reel in my kite, but all in vain. I saw my kite cut loose as the string I was reeling-in lost all tension. The German boys had shot down my kite and taken it as a prisoner of war, stolen half of my string as well. I was alone, but even if Imants and Arnis were with me, the three of us wouldn't have dared to retrieve my kite from the Germans. We needed an army. The war hadn't ended, not among kids!

Arnis was my new friend who, like Imants, was also in the third grade. I got to know Arnis during breaks between classes. The weather continued to be sunny and warm well into the fall which allowed us to run outside as soon as the bell rang at the end of a class.

Arnis always dressed well, even on sports days when the school yard became our track and field park for races, high jump events, broad jump and shot put competitions. Not only did Arnis dress well, he was also a good student. He had his homework in good shape, memory work was easy for him, and he was quick to understand our lessons. During the breaks between classes he and I would review, mostly for my sake, what the teachers had tried to teach us. Mrs. Salins was an excellent teacher, but not always did I understand what she was teaching us. Arnis and I would talk about it, and by the time the bell would ring for our next class I'd understand what Mrs. Salins had taught.

Arnis and I had many interesting talks. He told me about his family's farm in Latvia and the notary public and community work his father was involved in. Arnis' father, whose first name was also Arvids, was the first chairman of our camp and well liked. He was fluent in German which helped improve our relationships with the surrounding population and in forming a smooth running camp organization. UNRRA and later IRO (International Refugee Organization) had the ultimate authority, but under them, the D.P. camps were self governing democracies.

Arnis had a horse in Latvia named Vika. He wrote the following in a class journal:

My magnificent Vika was a light brown stallion with pointed and always erect dark ears. It was the first spring for Vika to be harnessed to the plow, harrow and wagon and to do other tasks a grown horse must do. But that was not to the liking of my Vika. He did everything possible to get out of work, so he could gallop across the fields to the clover rich banks at the river bend.

Most of all Vika despised the metal bit in his mouth and resented a coachman or rider who dared to pull on the reins. That came to be my downfall which led Vika and I to become inseparable friends.

One afternoon I was asked to ride Vika out to a field and bring home a wagon. With delight I went into the stable and walked out with Vika, mounted him and pulled back on the reins. My magnificent Vika sensed the rider on his back was not a big one. Angered that I pulled on the reins, he reared on his hind legs and then, in full speed, raced for the clover covered bank at the river bend. He galloped so fast that I slid off his back and, with my arms firmly around his neck, hung on for dear life.

In a flash we were on the clover covered bank. Vika stopped and reared again. My strength had left me and I let go of his neck and fell backwards on the clover. Stunned by the fall, I lost consciousness. When I came to, smelling the fresh fragrance of the clover, I didn't know whether I had slept or been knocked unconscious, but I felt Vika's soft muzzle gently stroking my forehead. In fear I jumped to my feet, but Vika slowly approached me, winking his big eyes in a friendly way. He came very close to me, very gently placed his soft muzzle on my shoulder as if asking forgiveness. I stroked his nose, patted his neck with friendly strokes, and then mounted him. This time I did not touch the reins, but said, "Vika, go."

Now Vika, on his own, trotted to the field where the wagon was, stopped, allowed me to dismount and harness him to the wagon. Then I mounted him once more, and we rode home.

From that day I could ride Vika any time and anywhere, but I did not pick up the reins, I had no need to. Vika understood.

Vika and I had reached an understanding and we became inseparable friends."

"What happened to Vika?" I asked.

With tears in his eyes he replied with a question. "What happened to all we had in Latvia?"

"I know," with tears in my own eyes I answered, "You left Vika behind."

"Yes," he said.

On festival Sundays we worshipped in the Cathedral in Augsburg. The building was a large Gothic structure with beautiful stained glass windows. There were statues of saints along the sides of the nave. A central aisle with long oak pews on each side led to the chancel where an impressive altar with the Crucified Jesus, symbolized the presence of God. The lectern to the left of the altar, from which the Pastor read the Scripture, was of oak – a beautifully carved work of art. The pulpit on the right side of the altar was three meters above the people's heads, like in our church in Riga.

Why was the pulpit so high? In Riga, I thought perhaps that it was because everything the Pastor said went three meters above our heads. I didn't understand, nor remember the sermons I heard in Riga.

In Augsburg it was different. It seemed that Pastor Lamberts, who also taught religion in our school, spoke directly to me, and to the confusion and struggles I experienced in my everyday life. I thought about what he read and said as I walked home.

"Judge not and you will not be judged."

"Love your enemies and pray for them."

"Forgive and you will be forgiven."

"When someone strikes you on the cheek, turn to him the other also."

That's what we read in the Bible but what does it ask of me now? Do not judge the powers or the rulers of the world? How can I forgive the Communists, the Nazis, even the Americans for targeting me with their bombs? How can I forgive those who have destroyed Latvia and forced an evil, Godless, murderous regime on the land of my ancestors? How can I love those who torture, then kill?

But Jesus was tortured and killed, yet before He died, He prayed His Father to forgive those who had crucified Him because they didn't know what they were doing. Didn't the Russians know what they had done? The Germans? The British? The Americans? They were so adamant in telling us they knew exactly what they were doing. But did they? The crew in an airplane, dropping bombs on a city, then quickly returning to the safety of an airfield; did they know what they did? Did they think they were only following orders?

Did anyone else know the pain of leaving Vika behind besides my friend? Did anyone even care about pains like that or were such pains considered trivial. Perhaps no one even cared to know if their orders and actions inflicted suffering on millions of people.

During the war did the leaders or indeed, anyone, know what they were doing, or had the whole world simply gone mad, needing forgiveness for the pain they caused in the lives of billions of people. "Father, forgive them for they knew not what they did."

ten

School Days, Stamps & Windows

UNCLE RUDIS HAD BROUGHT WITH HIM some Latvian postage stamps when he left Riga. He showed them to me, telling me about their eventual value and suggested I begin my own stamp collection. Whole sets of German Third Reich stamps were readily available at reasonable prices in stamp collector stores. He promised to buy me a set if I was interested in starting my own collection. I was, and he did. It opened a window to a new world for me.

I learned most stamps are issued in commemoration of events, famous people, special places, celebrations or national and patriotic endeavors.

The Third Reich stamps Uncle Rudis bought for me commemorated Hitler's *Blitzkrieg*, the failed attempt to conquer the world. There were stamps bearing Hitler's portrait, German U-boats, destroyers like the one in which we crossed the Baltic Sea, the famous battle ship Bismarck, Panzer and Tiger tanks, fighter planes in steep dives, anti-aircraft guns and long range artillery in action. Collecting stamps was a lesson in world history.

Stamp collecting was also a lesson in geography, reinforcing my studies at school. Every country in the world issues stamps. As I bought more foreign stamps from friends and stamp collector stores in Augsburg, I examined and admired each stamp, stored them neatly in my stamp albums and then located the countries on world maps. Austria, Poland, Hungary, Romania, Portugal, Spain, Australia, United States of America, Canada, Mexico. China, Japan, India. Every stamp was a little piece of a country, and I held it in my hands.

Stamp collecting also led to some dubious social activities. The popularity of stamp collecting resulted in more and more new and young collectors like me, who were unsure of the value of stamps. I bought stamps from German retailers in value packages, giving me a reasonable price, but a lot of duplicates I needed to trade. This led to intense bargaining, cheating and even stealing. I don't remember the name of the fellow stamp collector, but only the bargaining session that went like this:

"I have three Hungarian stamps to trade from the Ezerp series picturing a horse and rider. What do you have?"

"I have some duplicates from Latvia. Want to see them, Harijs?"

"Yeah, I don't have many Latvian stamps. Let's see what you have."

He opened his collection book to his Latvian duplicate section, and my eyes popped wide open. "I'd like to get all of them," I said, "How many will you give me for the three Hungarian stamps?"

He looked at my stamps and said, "They're worthless, but you can have the 'Ulmanis head' for your three." (Ulmanis was a President of Latvia.)

"They are not worthless," I replied, "they're worth at least twenty-five pfennigs each."

"No, they're not," he insisted, "who told you that?"

"My Uncle." I told a little white lie, and we bargained more. Finally I made my closing and overwhelming offer, "Look, I'll take three Latvian stamps for my three Hungarian and give you two marks for these fifteen Latvian stamps," I pointed them out.

"Two marks and two packs of chewing gum," he replied.

"Two marks and one pack of gum," I counter offered.

"When do I get the money and the gum?" he asked.

"Tomorrow after school, I'll bring it to your house."

"It's a deal," he said, "You'll get the stamps when you bring the goods."

We shook hands. I made a good deal, I thought.

(The chewing gum and goodies like chocolate, preserves and cookies came in the American care packages distributed by UNRRA.)

My parents approved of my stamp collecting. They said it was a good investment. In time the stamps would go up in value, therefore they gave me money from time to time to buy more.

Bargaining over stamps didn't always go smoothly. There was an older man who had a large collection of stamps from all over the world. He was mean. He overcharged and cheated us boys when we traded with him. He knew the monetary value, and us young collectors valued more the design and shape of a stamp. If a stamp was a beautiful picture, triangular or large, we thought that added value. Not so. The value of a stamp depends more on its age and rarity. If a commemorative series was issued by a nation in limited numbers, it was more valuable. The young collectors didn't know that. It didn't go against the man's conscience to take from us a valuable series in exchange for a large, beautiful but worthless stamp. That's what he did to me. I had no more dealings with him after I found out. But there were some boys who tried to even the score. They stole from him and got away with it. They swarmed him in groups. While the old man was dealing with one boy, the others, out of his view, just helped themselves to some of his stamps from his other stock books. I didn't think that was right, but he had it coming.

I enjoyed collecting stamps and decided to make it a life

long hobby.

Coming home from school I ran into the older boy who had asked me to think about obeying his orders and becoming a member of his group.

"Harijs," he said, "have you thought about what I said?"

"Yeah I have," I answered, "depends on your cause."

"Ah, you want to know what we're about?"

"Yeah."

"You're a Latvian, right?" he said.

"Yeah, I'm a Latvian. A Latvian from Riga," I answered.

"Great," he said, "we're Latvians from Latvia. All in my army are Latvian patriots."

"You're an army?" I asked with surprise. "What do you do?"

"We train. We go on patrols. We protect our territory."

"You have a territory?"

"Yeah. This camp. The field where you lost your kite and more."

"You saw me lose my kite?" I asked in amazement.

"Not I, but one of my men. He told me and suggested we go help you get it back. But I said, 'No. Not until he's one of us.'"

"You can get my kite back? How?"

"Easy, man. Easy. I give the signal, we assemble and go get it."

"You'd go into German territory to get my kite back!" I exclaimed.

"Swiftly, like big cats. They see us coming in formation. They drop your kite and run. Man, they're afraid of us. We train for that sort of thing. That's why everyone in my army obeys my orders. We act together, man."

"Sounds impressive, man," I said.

"Well, you want to be in or what? We could use your rock throwing skill. How are you with a sling shot?" he asked.

"I had one in Latvia. I took a shot at a Russian platoon as they were marching near our house towards Zasulauks train station."

"You did what, you knuckle head?" he asked in surprise.

"Yeah, I took a shot at the Russians, in anger. I knew they were out of range of my slingshot. It felt good anyway," I explained.

"That's better. You do have some brains. Never attack anything you know you can't defeat," he said. "That's why we always win." Then he asked again, "You want to be in, then say so."

"Okay man, I want to be in," I said with goose bumps all over my body.

"You're in, Harijs. Be on the field where you lost your kite tonight at eighteen hundred hours for training. See you tonight." He left.

I was amazed how easy it was to get permission from my parents to participate in activities at the camp. I told them I wanted to go and play soccer, and they said, "Fine, just be home before dark." They didn't even ask with whom I'd be playing. They trusted me.

With some apprehension I walked to the field thinking that all the rough and tough talk must be a game; they're not a real Army, they're pretending, playing games like I did in Riga and Binabiburg.

In Riga I'd go to school early. Before classes started there were always enough boys to line up in platoon formation and march, imitating the German Army. The older boys knew the commands and the ways Germans marched. They'd teach us younger ones. We had fun marching and pretending we were soldiers.

As I came on the field, the leader was there and I counted six other boys, all bigger than me. I didn't know them.

"Hi," he greeted me as I approached them. "In my army

you will be known as Ha." Then, turning to the others, he introduced me.

"Men," he said, "meet Ha." They acknowledged me. Then he introduced his men to me.

"Ha meet Pe, Ka, Er, Je, etc." I was getting all mixed up and uneasy. I hadn't seen these big boys nor the leader in our school. That meant they were from the gymnasium (secondary or middle school) or from Hochfeld, the other camp nearby.

"In my army your civilian names are unimportant. You are new men, my men, and I give you new names. You obey my commands and we act as one man. Remember, and I say this for Ha's benefit, our motto is, 'All for one and one for all.'"

And the six shouted, "Bravo!"

"Armeee – fall in!" he commanded.

From my army games in Riga I knew that meant take your place in formation according to height. That's what they did. And I, the shortest, took my place at the end of the line, surprising the leader.

"Good Ha, you know!" he exclaimed, praising me, "You been in some army before?"

"Yes, Sir," I answered, briskly. "Riga, Sir." (Did I lie?)

"Good," he said and asked, "Ha, do you know how to march?"

"Yes, Sir," I snapped back.

"We shall see," he said with some sarcasm, then commanded, "Armeee – Teeen–Hut!" They snapped to attention, so did I. The leader was observing me.

"Armeee – Riiight – Face!" I did a snappy two count turn to the right.

"Forwaaard – Harch!" I stepped forward with my left foot in a German goose step and knew right away I had goofed.

"Ha, this is not the S.S.! March like an American soldier!" he shouted.

I started to walk in a normal way, and noticed the boys were marching like that. A normal step with arms swinging in a normal way. That was easy to catch on to. I was beginning to like this, pretending I'm an American soldier.

"To the Reaaar – Harch!" I did a perfect pivot to the rear, now I was the lead man.

"By the Riiight flank – Harch!" another two count pivot to the right. Now we were marching in a straight line side by side. Good alignment. We drilled for about twenty minutes. I enjoyed it. Then our drill commander shouted, "Armeee – Halt." One, two, and we stopped.

"At ease!" he commanded, and we dropped out of the upright, shoulders back, head straight forward position, and relaxed.

"Ha, you do know how to march," he complimented me. I was beginning to like him. He was a good drill sergeant.

"Ha, now we'll see how good you are at other army skills," he said.

It was turning out be an enjoyable evening. We did some target practice, throwing rocks at an old, beat up garbage can. I hit it every time. The big boys were impressed at my accuracy and power.

They had two sling shots, so we took our turns shooting at a tin can on top of a pole. I held my own also at this delightful army skill. My weakness was formation running. The others were bigger and older and I had a hard time keeping up with them. This was a maneuver the army employed to scare the enemy. We were in a V formation, running in step towards the enemy with a stick in right hand. I'm sure we looked like riot police.

The leader had a soccer ball. He divided us into two groups of four each, and we practiced penalty goal kicking. I liked to play soccer. I could kick just like the bigger boys. "So far, so good," I thought.

The leader gathered us around him, as I had seen

before, and said, "Men, we trained well tonight. "Ha" will be a good addition to our army. It's too bad that all of us weren't here tonight. With just eight of us, we won't go on patrol through German territory. When we go, we go in force. Scare them good. Remember men, Lithuanians are sloppy, but Germans are our enemies. The war isn't over until we even the score. Goodnight, men."

I started to leave, but the leader called me, "Ha, I want a word with you."

"Yes, Sir," I said.

"Ha," he said, "two blocks from your fourplex is a house with a red tile roof. Behind the house is a yard with rabbit cages. As your initiation into my army, I want you to sneak into the yard and release the rabbits. You have a week to do it."

"Sir, I had rabbits in Riga. I can't hurt rabbits. Please sir, ask me to do anything, but not to hurt rabbits."

"What, you love rabbits? You don't want to hurt rabbits? That's shameful for a soldier. Besides, no one refuses my orders."

"Please, sir, anything but that."

"I should give you a dishonorable discharge on the spot. No one says no to me, get it, Ha?" he was getting angry and annoyed with me.

"Okay, Ha, you have a good arm for throwing rocks and you're accurate. We need you. I'll think of something else, but don't you dare refuse again. Get it!"

"Yes, sir," I said.

"Okay, Ha, scram."

"Sir, can I think of something myself?" I asked.

"No, I do the thinking. Now scram!" he ordered angrily. I did, and how!

What have I gotten myself into? I wondered. I like the army idea, marching, target practicing, sling shots, soccer, but to hurt rabbits and to continue the war? No way! These boys are taking themselves too seriously. I didn't like that at all. This was so contrary to what we were learning at school. I was beginning to think of ways how to get out of that army without drawing the wrath of the bigger boys.

In school, the first trimester ended and I got my first report card from the Latvian Elementary School in Haunstetten. I did the best in religion where I got a five. Literature was a four, mathematics three, and a frightful three minus in grammar. A five in behavior and a shameful three in orderliness. Not bad, but not good. I resolved to do better, especially in mathematics and grammar. I liked to read and write. "I'm going to show Mr. and Mrs. Salins that I can write, even compose poetry. I will."

My army life was challenging in many ways. I liked being accepted into the group. I liked the training, and especially improving my soccer game. Soon I was able to keep up with the bigger boys in running games, and my rock throwing skill was improving. It was a thrill to go on patrol through the woods and the German territory and feel the strength and safety in our numbers. There were twelve, thirteen, sometimes fourteen of us. The German kids would watch us and stay away even when we foraged in the ruins of the Messerschmitt factory and found useful things.

But I didn't like that we were sworn to secrecy. I couldn't even tell Arnis and Imants about the army, nor my mom or dad. I couldn't understand why our allegiance to, and love for Latvia should lead us to dislike Lithuanians and hate Germans. This was contrary to what I was learning in school. Our longing for our native land ought not result in hate, but draw us closer to each other and God, who alone can restore Latvia to her former glory. Something was wrong with my army.

One afternoon "Je" and I were walking through the Lithuanian section and we heard yelling and shouting, and saw four boys running toward us with rocks in their hands. "Je", in his loud voice, shouted to them to leave us alone. We had done nothing to them and we didn't want trouble.

But they kept running toward us and, when we were in range, they started to throw the rocks at us. One hit "Je" in the leg, one rock came close to hitting me in the shoulder. That did it. "Je" and I bent down, picked up a rock in each hand, wound up like we had practiced many times and simultaneously threw as hard as we could. We didn't need to throw our second salvo. When the first hit the two leading Lithuanians in the chest with a thud, all four stopped, turned around and high-tailed back were they came from. Our training had paid off. We didn't aim at their heads to injure, but at the chest where a black and blue spot would remind them to leave us alone.

"Je" reported the incident to our leader together with a good description of the four Lithuanian boys. By our next training session the leader had located where the four lived and identified their bedroom windows. He didn't give any orders, just said that I knew what to do. The next morning in the Lithuanian section, four windows had round holes where a rock had gone through.

I heard rumors that German folk were complaining, accusing D.P. kids of releasing rabbits from their cages. No one in the army claimed responsibility. The false accusations made me angry, very angry when I thought about my stolen kite. I choose a target for myself in German territory. The war was on and I was in it.

One night as I was enroute to my firing point, I ran into Imants. I told him what I was up to and asked him to come along. He did. The next morning there were two round holes in a German window. We did this again with similar results. Imants was also good at throwing rocks. He had a strong arm, and his aim better than mine. Seconds after a salvo, we would hear the rocks penetrate a window pane. It sounded like a kilo of soft butter hitting the floor. Thud! The sound of shattering glass was diminished by the velocity of our pitch. The sound did not carry far. The two of us were in this together – our own little war on our own terms. I said nothing about the army to Imants.

Prior to a raid, we would survey the area and plan an escape route well hidden from view, close to buildings and shrubs, stopping at a hide out where we stayed until it was safe to go home. We didn't target windows where a light was on in the room, only dark ones. We didn't want to hurt people who might be in the room. A dark window meant no one was in there, giving us ample time for the getaway.

Then one night, after the sun had set and we took our firing positions, we heard several male voices shout, "Stop boys! Stop!" We dropped our rocks and ran for our lives. Imants ran home; a male voice followed him. The male voice was one of our camp police men.

My third grade report card shows the following inscription in beautifully handwritten calligraphy, "2nd trimester grade for behavior has been reduced to five minus for breaking windows."

eleven

Windows to Christmas

HOW MANY WINDOWS did we break? Imants and I were not the only freelance commandoes on the firing line. We were the two prisoners of war that night, I thought, and held morally responsible for all the damage done. But guilty, we were, for what we had done. I had made a big mistake. In less than three weeks I had ruined my reputation.

As banditos, we were inexperienced. It didn't take long for the newly formed camp police to discover our pattern. One half hour after sunset we hit Lithuanian targets, then the next night was a German target, then Lithuanian again. The night we were caught, the police had surveillance of all unmolested German windows within our range. We walked into their trap. They could see us. The moment we raised our arms to throw, we were caught in the act. I thought the newly appointed police were proud of themselves. They solved the first crime in the camp easily, proving their worth. One positive result from our misdeeds – job assurance for the police.

Our fiasco had deep reaching and profound effects on the people in our camp. There was scandalous disbelief – how could these quiet, otherwise well behaved boys do this? What got into them? Why did they do it?

My family was devastated. "How could Harijs do that?"

"We have been too trusty, too lax in our supervision, too permissive," they said to one another. My mom and Tinte cried. Dad and Uncle Rudis were speechless and shook their heads in disbelief. "Where did I go wrong?" Dad asked over and over again. Uncle Edis was very upset. He was concerned that my misbehavior would reflect negatively on his working relationship with UNNRA and consequently his as-yet unpublished magazine. He had a juvenile delinquent living with him who performed crimes of destruction under his nose. My family decided I deserved a thorough spanking, which Aunt Anna was more than willing to execute. Also, as recommended by the police and affirmed by my teachers, I was to come directly home from school and study for a month. No playing with friends, indoors or outdoors.

Directly home from school and study: Dad, Harijs, Mom.

It was my teachers who surprised me with their approach to, and treatment of, my acts of terrorism. They wanted to learn why I did it. What motivated me to depart so drastically from my normal behavior at school and become destructive in the evening? Our school principal, Mrs. Lapsina, and my teachers, Mr. and Mrs. Salins, listened intently as I spoke of my need to have friends and friendships that would last. All of my friendships had been terminated by frequent moves and changes in governments because of the war. Now that I had overcome my childhood fear of other children, I wanted to belong to a group and be accepted. Peer pressure to prove bravery was directing me.

Why did I break windows? In the case of Lithuanians, it was to show that I was not afraid of them. It was my way of saying, leave me alone on the streets, and don't intimidate me or chase and throw rocks at me. In the case of Germans, the goal was to retaliate and continue the war. They started the war that exiled me from Latvia. Now they stole my kites. What were a few broken windows compared to the damage adults had done to cities, and to the whole world. I was following their example of retaliation.

I didn't say anything about the army. I could have blamed them, but no one had ordered me to break windows. The idea, the responsibility was mine.

My teachers listened. Without approving of what I had done, they tried to understand why I had done it and how I felt about it. By what they said I realized that retaliation is not a sign of strength, but a weakness of character. The continuation of the war would not return to us our beloved country, but living in peace and striving for justice and harmony, just may. To be a loyal Latvian does not mean to hate Germans, nor any other people who have wronged us in the past. Knowing our history, living by our values and traditions, and upholding our virtues, makes us loyal Latvians. Latvia needs freedom through peaceful means and we strive, even sacrifice, for that.

My teachers turned the fiasco I had created into a life changing learning experience. They taught me nothing is gained through violence and destruction; there had been enough of that. Also that the world needs people who create, who value their heritage and are willing to work to improve themselves and the world. The world needs people who inspire others, not those who seek to hurt and destroy property. There had been enough hostilities.

I wanted to become that kind of a person, creative, kind and helpful. Mr. and Mrs. Salins became my role models, my heroes. They didn't just *tell* me how, they continued to *show* me, through creativity and loyalty to our heritage.

One more life changing experience came about because of the fiasco. To some adults I remained a delinquent, but to my peers, I became more like a hero whom they could taunt, especially the girls. They noticed me and said, "Hi Harijs." I noticed them. There were eleven girls in the third grade. I noticed also, they were very, very pretty, like angels among us nine boys who were trying to prove ourselves in our own macho ways.

The secret army quietly dissolved and would be remembered as a group of boys running, throwing rocks at old garbage cans, and playing war games and soccer. Soon I was hearing people talk about the need for organized after-school activities such as the International Brotherhood and Sisterhood of Boy Scouts and Girl Guides. I was interested and listened with both ears to such proposals. Had the secret army and my delinquency uncovered the need for a challenging and legitimate organization for boys as well as girls? I never found out.

Late in the fall of 1945, a Girl Guide and a Boy Scout group were organized, but my elders (uncles, aunts and parents) didn't allow me to join. I was still in the home-from-school, straight-to-homework, no-friends and no-play-time routine imposed on me two months earlier. My elders made certain I had learned my lesson.

There were eleven girls in the third grade.

Nine boys trying to prove themselves.
School barrack in background.
In back, left to right: Mrs. & Mr. Salins
Front row: Imants in front of Mrs. Salins.
Last two on right: Harijs, Arnis.

Christmas 1945 was coming and preparations were underway at school and at home. This would be my first Christmas in a time of peace; I was ten years old.

At school we were told there would be a full scale Christmas program with a party at our Community Hall, complete with a dance afterward. This was exciting. An upscale celebration of Christmas was all new to me. For political reasons, my school in Riga observed Christmas diminutively. National Socialism, Communism and Christianity didn't mix. Christians were at a disadvantage because, to the Communists, faith in God was the opiate of the people. National Socialism did not recognize any power higher than the state. Christ, to both political orientations, was a suspect figment of imagination in weak minds.

I remembered Christmas Eve, 1944, my family celebrated in an air raid shelter with three other families, none of whom had children. We were strangers thrown together by the need for shelter on a stormy night. There was no air raid, but there was also no other place to go. We sat by the walls in the light of a fifteen watt bulb. I sat on the floor, leaning against the wall, feeling the dampness of the underground bunker, inhaling the musty smell of damp soil. It felt like darkness had overcome the light. There was no Christmas tree, no presents for anybody, no Christmas dinner and no Santa. Late on Christmas Eve, one of the families lit a short, white candle, and we gathered around it and sang Christmas carols. I felt lonely, so small and insignificant among the tall adults.

One of the men, perhaps a pastor or an elder of a church, rose to speak. He recited the Christmas story. The dim glow of the fifteen watt bulb, augmenting the flickering light of the lone candle, made the bunker feel like the stable where Jesus was born. A sense of holiness overwhelmed me. The man concluded his speech with the song of the Angels:

"And suddenly there was with the angel a multitude of the heavenly host praising God and saying, 'Glory to God in the highest, and on earth peace among men with whom he is pleased.'" (Luke 2: 13-14)

Then he said, "There is no peace on earth, but let's pray for it." He prayed, "Father forgive them, for they know not what they do. Lord, we have been forced to leave our homes and our beloved country, forced to leave everything we have worked for. Now cities are being destroyed and people killed, soldiers and civilians alike. War, like cancer, has no respect for gender, age or race. Lord, we pray, heal your world of that fatal disease, restore your people to normalcy in thoughts, words, deeds and ambitions. Let there be light, Your light, in the world. We thank you for the Christ child, born so humbly among us, born in our hearts this Holy Night. May He bring us your peace that passes understanding, peace that does not vanish even in the face of death. Thank you Lord for the safety of this shelter, for our lives you have spared. Amen."

As the little white candle was about to expire, he invited us to sing Silent Night, Holy Night. He began in a beautiful tenor voice. We all joined him. Through my own tear filled eyes, I looked in the faces of the people gathered around, and saw the reflection of the burning candle in their eyes. There was not a single dry eye in the dimly lit shelter. It was, indeed, a Holy Night.

We were going to have a feast at our school's Christmas celebration. In the second trimester, as we were blessed with more books and writing paper, five new classes were added to our schedule of instruction: German, drawing, calligraphy, singing and handcrafts. In our handcraft class we were making cookie cutters from the metal of tin cans. We shaped them to look like stars, half moons, Christmas trees, Santa Clauses, sleighs and horses. The girls were mixing various types of dough and baking cookies and sweet breads.

We were also making Christmas tree ornaments – stars, half moons, and simple nativity scenes from colored paper. We constructed small colored cubes and wrapped home made Christmas candy to be hung on the Christmas tree. The older classes were building stage scenery and props for the Christmas plays and recitations each grade was practicing. In grade three we were given short verses from Christmas poems to memorize and recite individually onstage, and again for Santa, should he ask.

In music class we were learning Christmas hymns. We were expecting representatives from UNRRA , therefore the whole school learned a song in English entitled, "For He is a Jolly Good Fellow."

In physical education classes, older students were learning steps and patterns of traditional folk dances. Since the third grade didn't have physical education, some of our regular classes were cancelled allowing us to join grades four through seven for dance instruction. I got to dance with girls, including one lovely dance with the very popular and beautiful, blond pianist, diva and ballerina. My friends and I would sneak in and watch her practice ballet routines on our Community hall stage. She was a very attractive girl, tall and slender, with long blond hair draping over her gentle shoulders. She wore pretty dresses that allowed us to see her knees and nicely shaped legs when she practiced her magnificent leaps and enticing pirouettes.

Santa Claus was to visit the night of our program. That worried me. When I thought of it, goose bumps formed on my body and butterflies in my tummy. "What will Santa say to me? Santa knows everything. Everyone in Haunstetten knows I have been a bad boy." In Latvia bad boys got a bouquet of bound sticks used for spanking. "Maybe I should leave the Community Hall when Santa comes. Our program will be over by then. Nothing can be more humiliating than getting a bouquet of sticks. Yes, I will do that. But what will my parents think, and my friends, the whole school, when Santa calls my name and I'm not there. I must not be a coward. I must not leave. I shall face it bravely, like a man." I was much troubled, and found it hard to fall asleep at night. Had I ruined my first Christmas in peacetime by breaking windows?

Preparations for Christmas were also underway at home. Aunt Anna, Tinte and Mom, my three mothers, were baking my favorite cookies and piragi, small, half moon shaped buns with succulent chopped bacon in the middle. I liked them. Uncle Edis was elbow deep in fine flour, baking cakes and complaining he hadn't found the right ingredients to bake his layered cream and chocolate tortes he was famous for in Riga. Mom and Tinte were taking turns on Aunt Anna's sewing machine and Dad and I were ready to go and cut the Christmas tree which I had located earlier in the fall among the firs growing on the banks of the River Lech.

"Harij," Dad said, "It's time to get the Christmas tree you've been raving about. We have three hours before dark. Get your coat and brown leather hat, put on your boots and let's go."

Dad didn't have to say that twice. I was ready in two minutes, but not without some trepidation. I was running with the army when I had spotted the fir tree. No one from our family had asked me how I found the tree, and I didn't want my dad to ask now. Oh, the complication of being a boy!

"Dad, I'm ready," I said as I presented myself, dressed for the cold and trace of snow on the ground.

"Let's go," he said while opening the door.

"Bye everybody. Be back soon with a nice tree," I shouted, then slipped through the door ahead of Dad who was carrying a big axe under his arm. I led the way. We walked fast in the direction of the river. At that pace we should arrive where the tree was in less than sixty minutes. We walked in silence. "My dad is wearing me down with silence," I thought. "When is he going to ask me how I found the tree?" We kept on walking in silence: ten, fifteen, twenty minutes. I was getting frantic. When? When will he ask? All of sudden I heard him start to talk.

"Harij," (Here it comes, I thought.)

"Yes, dad. What?"

"Harij, Mom and I've been talking, wondering (Oh no. No! I stopped breathing. How will I explain?) …wondering if you have thought more about the Boy Scouts?"

"Yes," I gasped, regaining my breath.

"Harij, Mom and I think, and your uncles and aunts agree, we think it's time for you to join up. It seems you like to be with other boys, especially older ones, don't you, Harij?"

"Dad, didn't I say I wanted to join when they organized? I want to be a Boy Scout. I do. I do."

What a turn of events. Had Mom and Dad thought I didn't want to join because Scouts resembled the military? How little adults know about kids. I wanted to join precisely *because* of that. They hadn't allowed me to join because, yeah I knew…

"Then you will join, Harij?"

"Of course I will, Dad."

I hadn't realized we had stopped and were facing each other like two grown men.

"Good, Harij, now lead me to your tree."

I did an about face, army style, to resume our walk towards the tree. My dad didn't comment. He hadn't notice the military move.

In about five minutes we were standing in front of my tree admiring it. It was beautiful, cultivated by unseen hands, a gardener's prize, a perfect two meter Christmas tree. With three swings of the axe Dad harvested it, then placed the axe in his right hand and, with his left, picked up the tree at its base. We started for home. I followed and helped to carry the tree near its top. To go in the woods and harvest our Christmas tree had been a family tradition in Latvia. From now on, it will remain so forever and always.

Christmas festivities at our Elementary School in Haunstetten were to become a yearly highlight.

Under the American Military Government of Germany, we were free to celebrate Christian as well as National festivals in traditional and historic ways. We were free from the censorship we experienced under Communist and National Socialist authorities. As if to underscore this freedom there were no representatives from UNNRA at our first celebrations. Representatives did come later, not to spy or censor, but observe and learn about our culture and traditions.

However, there were two dark thunderclouds on the blue horizon of our future. Since the Russians were American allies, we couldn't speak freely about the injustices and cruelty of Communism all people experienced under Stalin's dictatorship.

The other cloud on our horizon was that adults, though they could be employed in the camp and work for the American military, could not seek employment in German industry. The growing concern around these two dark clouds led us to fear and wonder what might happen next to us. We can't work for the Germans, therefore we can't stay in Germany. We will not go back to a Latvia under the treacherous rule of the Communists. What does the future hold for us?

We celebrated Christmas in Haunstetten four times, 1945 through 1948, and memories of those celebrations blend as if the four were one grand event that happened just yesterday.

When the day and hour of our first Christmas program came, we were ready. I observed with amusement that my teachers seemed nervous, anxiously multi-tasking their activities. We had memorized our songs, recitations, pageants and dances. Why all the note books in the hands of our teachers? Why all the impromptu conferences and the shifting of props and furniture?

While our parents found their places in the rows of chairs in the auditorium, we assembled as directed for our grand entrance. Class by class we entered, first the girls, then the boys. We had been told this was serious. No one should talk, laugh or giggle. We sat down and exchanged glances, then little notes of provoking questions and jokes. I was slipped a note by the girl sitting behind me, "What does Santa have in common with bad boys?" The answer was on the other side, "Windows to Christmas." Didn't make sense. It was a bad joke, but I got the point and it hurt. I didn't pass the note. I crunched it.

The program was opened by the principal, Mrs. Lapsina. She greeted the parents and friends, and welcomed all to the program that we, her children, had worked hard to prepare. There were memorable expressions of gratefulness to the Americans for making it possible for us to have a school in exile, thanks to those who had helped acquire school supplies, and to all who had lent a helping hand. Our Lutheran pastor, Reverend Lamberts, addressed the assembly with the Christmas story from the Bible and words of spiritual encouragement. Following tradition, we stood and sang our national anthem: "God Bless Our Latvia, Precious For Our Father's Sake." The recitations and class presentations followed, starting with the first grade, then the second etc. After each recitation there was much applause by proud and happy parents whose son or daughter, of course, excelled everyone else on the stage.

We, the third graders, were called upon to recite our

verses. On our teacher's signal we stood and walked, in single file, to the front and up the steps onto the stage, forming two rows, with the girls in front of the boys. The girls did fine. The smiles on their parents' faces radiated like the sun on a cloudless day.

The boys were next. I was second in line. The classmate on my right recited his verse dramatically and was applauded. Now it was my turn. I went blank. I couldn't remember the first word of my verse much less what it was all about. I saw my teacher flipping through notes, mouthing something to me, but it meant nothing. My mouth went dry, palms became sweaty, knees started shaking and legs got weaker. My vision was blurred and I was losing my balance. But then, as if a bolt of lightening had dissolved the butterflies in my tummy, I remembered the verse and in a strong voice, recited:

> "Oh my girl! Oh my girl!
> Where has your one pigtail gone?
> Isn't it true, my fair friend
> It's behind the stove's black end."
> (Latvian folksong, translated and paraphrased.)

There was thunderous applause and roaring laughter. It was the wrong verse, and completely out of context, but I stole the moment. I had capitalized on my stage fright.

The program continued. From time to time our teachers had to use the notes in their hands as others, too, forgot parts of their verses. For me and many of us, this was our first onstage experience.

The highlight of the program for me was the performance of the pretty and popular blond girl I watched practicing ballet. She accompanied herself on the piano for a Christmas hymn and then, in silence, interpreted the mood of the song through professionally choreographed ballet. She captivated me with her angel-like stage presence.

She had me wrapped around her little finger.

The program ended with communal singing of Christmas hymns. Afterwards, the chairs were removed, turning the auditorium into a large dance floor. Several tables along the back wall disclosed the abundant and delicious results from the home economics and handcraft classes. Cookies, gingerbread, piragi and other sweet breads. It was chaotic and noisy as we mingled with friends and parents, all the while sampling the goodies and congratulating or kidding each other about our stage performances. Sampling a Christmas tree shaped gingerbread, I walked over to Mom and Dad at the piragi table. My dad looked at me, shook his head and said, "Harij, Harij, I don't know about you."

I didn't answer, just kept munching my delicious gingerbread and moved on to mingle with my schoolmates. I had mixed emotions. I enjoyed the comments, even the digs, but dreaded the yet to come event with Santa.

"Harijs, you're a joker," said a girl.

"You're a card," said another girl.

"The way to fly, Harijs," said a classmate.

"How could you forget your Christmas verse?" scolded a teacher, then added, "But you're a quick thinker on your feet, Harijs. Someday you may be a good public speaker, a statesman, actor or maybe just a circus clown."

Then I bumped into the beautiful, talented blond musician and dancer, still wearing the fairy white, knee length ballerina dress, and me around her finger. She looked at me and I looked at her, but I didn't dare look into her eyes for long. I said, "You play the piano, sing and dance very well."

"Why, thank you," she answered, and moved on.

What chance do I have to be friends with her? I wondered. She's not in my grade, and her parents are upper class while I'm working class. My dad is a foundry tradesman. There are no musicians or artists in my family.

No one has even gone to a university.

Three–quarter time rhythms of accordion music filled the auditorium, pleasing my ears and teasing my feet with folk dance melodies. Time for parents to leave the floor, and find a seat somewhere or go home and return at 11:00 p.m. for Santa's visit. Our gym teacher, turned dance teacher, quickly lined us up, boys at one end of the auditorium, girls at the other. In single file we walked toward each other along one side of the auditorium, meeting our partner for the first dance in the middle of the auditorium. We walked side by side across the auditorium to the other side, then along the outside walls forming an oval ring. Amazing how it worked out. There was a girl for every boy. No one was left out, nor had to dance with a same sex partner. Girls didn't mind to dance with another girl. Boys? No way! Not even Mrs. Lapsina could make a boy dance with another boy.

My partner for the first dance was a girl from the seventh grade. She was taller than me, but that was okay. She had dark brown hair tied in two long pig tails, brown eyes, a light complexion and freckles on her nicely shaped oval face. She wore a big smile on her ruby lips as she said, "Harij, you're an absolute clown, but I like you. You forgot your verse but out of the blue, you came up with a winner. You're great, Harij! You stole the show!"

"No, I was scared. I forgot the verse and I thought I was going to faint."

"It didn't show Harij. I thought you were great," she said, and added, "but don't even think about messing with my pig-tales. Pig-tales are a girl's pride."

The accordionist began the first dance. My first dance on a dance floor with an older girl at an actual event! A Christmas dance. Thanks to the folk-dance lessons at school, my pretty partner and I knew what to do and how to do it. I enjoyed it. I watched my partner swing smartly back and forth, then swiftly turn and curtsy, touching the hem of her dress, and smiling. I noticed how nice her full cut, knee length, brown cotton dress made her look. Nor did I miss seeing the gentle curves of fullness in her tight bodice. She was a pretty girl. The freckles added charm. She liked me.

We danced, changing partners, for about an hour when spontaneous shouts filled the auditorium.

"Santa, Santa Claus is coming!" Indeed he was. I could see his long, white beard. He was a big man. He looked old and tired, but he was strong. He carried a big sack on his back and pulled a cart loaded with more sacks. I didn't see any bundles of tied barren tree branches sticking out of a sack. They must be inside one.

He walked through the midst of us to the front of the stage, found a chair and sat down. We gathered around him. He told us to sit on the floor. This was the time when I could run and hide. No! I had decided to stay. Will I regret it? I moaned to myself.

Santa, the Dear Old Man of Christmas, as we thought of him, was very wise. He had lived a long time. He had much experience in the world. He knew much, especially about children. He was fair, yet unyielding. One didn't argue with 'The Wisdom of Christmas', endowed from on High. That was our Santa.

He told us what he had experienced during the past year. As for all of us, it had been a hard year, yet a year of answers to his prayers. We had survived the war-to-end-all-wars. The world now would live in peace forever. He was confident the people of the world had learned how terrible and costly a war is. People would not destroy or kill any more. The world had finally learned to settle differences through diplomacy, not on battle fields with bullets and bayonets, or with bombs destroying cities, indiscriminately killing innocent children. The United Nations would do this and ensure a lasting peace.

He spoke to us. He had our attention and we listened.

Santa knows! Then he said there were presents for those who have been good and had learned and grown in wisdom this year, obeyed parents, listened to their teachers and done their homework. Why did I stay? I thought, again. He knows about the windows. Why? Oh why, Oh why was I so dumb when I threw the rocks?

He was calling our names to come forward and receive our presents. Soon, I realized, he was calling in alphabetical order, class by class, starting with the first graders. Everyone so far had received praise, perhaps some suggestions for improvement next year, but no bouquets of bound spanking sticks. The gifts were very useful and needed. Pencils, pens, writing paper and bottles of ink, notebooks, everything we needed in school. And, oh! my! The top students were getting textbooks! Books! Wouldn't I love to own a book! I would share it with my friends, with anyone wanting to read it.

Then Santa, the wise, was in the K's of the third grade. "Harijs," he called, "will you come forward."

The blood drained from my head. My knees felt weak. Palms were sweaty, and my mouth was dry for the second time that night. I went blank again, but I went to Santa, the Wise Man of Christmas. I stood before him, trembling slightly.

"Harijs," he said, his blue eyes looking right through me, to the center of my being. I knew, he knew.

"Harijs," he said again, "you've had a difficult year, haven't you, Harijs?"

"Yes, Santa, a very difficult year," I admitted.

"Harijs, tell me, what have you learned from your difficulties?"

"Yes, Santa. War is wrong. It's wrong to break or destroy things. We should strive to be constructive and helpful, learn from one another, love one another."

"Very good Harijs. You'll remember that in the years to come, won't you?"

"Yes, I will."

"I have a little gift for you, not from me, but when you see it, you'll know who it is from." He reached into his sack and took out a small ream of white typing paper and, with a smile under his long beard, placed it in my outstretched hands.

"Harij, use it for its intended purpose. Learn to type," he said. "Go now and have a better year in 1946."

I was surprised and very, very happy. For me, that was the culmination of the Christmas program, dance and Santa's visit to our school! Truly, Santa is very wise and kind, I thought.

My Grade 6 class: 1948. I'm behind and a bit left of Mr. Salins.

Christmas Eve was spent at home, and it was as exciting as the program at school. My Christmas tree, adorning a corner in the kitchen, was decorated with our homemade ornaments. Colorful paper chains, like the tails on my kites, hung from its branches. Paper stars, half-moons, circles and make-believe Christmas candy (little cubes of wood wrapped in tinfoil with paper tassels at each end) which I had made, were distributed with geometric precision throughout the tree. There were twelve white paraffin Christmas candles placed symmetrically and fastened firmly with homemade wire candle holders, on the lush green branches of my tree. It was the most beautiful tree I had ever seen. Most of all it was my tree. I had found it on the banks of the River Lech. I rejoiced with anticipation. "Next year I'll explore the woods as a Boy Scout."

I wondered if mom would sew me a Scout uniform. She has to, I thought. A Scout must have a uniform to be proud of.

It was only four o'clock in the afternoon, and already turning dark and cold outside. It may even snow tonight, I thought, but that's alright. Tonight I'm warm inside. Warm with the happiness that comes with being forgiven. Warm in anticipation of a new start in school, at home and with my friends in Scouting, but most of all with my parents, aunts and uncles. They love me even though they may not approve of what I sometimes say or do. It's wonderful to be alive, wonderful to know forgiveness, wonderful to know I'm loved.

My three moms were in the final stages of setting the table for our Christmas Eve dinner. Meat this year! A big old rooster was simmering in a black cast iron pot, smothered in potatoes, sliced carrots and onions. A basket full of fragrant piragi rested on the table. Next to Uncle Edis' home-baked bread was a tempting dish of strawberry jam from an American Christmas care parcel. There was gingerbread, a pitcher of milk for cousin Ojars and me, and a large pitcher of dark German beer for the adults. I knew what beer tasted like. Everyone drank beer in Germany. Kids were allowed a little taste on special occasions, but when the adults weren't watching, Ojars and I would help ourselves to a full glass.

There was a knock on the door, and I heard the Krauja's voices outside, singing Merry Christmas wishes. It sounded like Uncle Richards had already downed a glass or two of the dark German beer he liked. My uncles also liked schnapps, the traditional Latvian fire water forbidden for kids to even taste.

My family enjoyed observing holidays and special occasions, such as baptisms, weddings, anniversaries, birthdays, and Name's Days, with elaborate parties. In the Latvian calendar there are two, three, and sometimes four names assigned to each day of the year, designating the day as one's Name's Day, making it a day more important than a birthday. How so? People don't know when your birthday is, unless you tell them. Everyone knows your Name's Day because your name is on the calendar. For example, Imants' Name's Day is July 1st, Arnis, June 6th, my mom's, Erna, September 12th, and mine, January 13th.

Mom opened the door and the Kraujas entered. Aunt Hermine and Uncle Richards went to the kitchen where dinner was about to be served.

"How nice, how nice!" I heard Aunt Hermine say.

Ojars came with me into the little bedroom I shared with my parents. Ojars was a year older and a grade ahead of me at school. We didn't spend much time with each other. Our interests were different. He played ping-pong and sometimes soccer but otherwise he wasn't interested in sports like Imants and I, nor did he seem interested in literature or world events, like Arnis and I. Ojars didn't collect stamps. He had his friends, and I had mine. (His parents were proud of him for not having been involved with me in breaking windows. They let that be known freely.) Our relationship consisted mainly of being biological cousins. But we got along. Our parents expected Ojars and I to spend Christmas Eve together in our family setting and that was okay with me.

"Harij," he said, using the endearment form of my name, "haven't seen you lately, what have you been up to since the Christmas program? Break any more windows lately?"

"Nooo. You know that. Straight home from school and into homework. Why do you keep bugging me about windows?"

"I'm not bugging you. Too bad you dummies got caught. Running home from the cops. Didn't you have a hideout to run to? Anyway, I can't see how you can take that 'home-from-school-and-into-homework' thing. Drive me crazy. How can you stand not having fun anymore?"

"I'm having fun. Yeah, it was hard at first, but now I like to study."

"You what?"

"Yeah, I like to study. Read. Borrowed a book from a friend, about little people. Labrencis and His Big Hemp Forest. I'm going to copy it."

"Don't make me laugh, Harij! My butt, little people. Copy it!"

"Don't you ever imagine things?"

"I imagine, yes, but not little people. Girls, Harij, hot girls. Kissing, that sort of stuff. You ever thought how they get babies?"

"Yes, I have. I bet I know more about girls than you do."

"Do you now?" he challenged me. "Prove it."

"Okay, but don't go repeating what I tell you all over Haunstetten. Not to our parents."

"There's nothing you can tell me that needs secrecy," he declared.

"There is, too! And if you can't promise not to repeat it, I won't tell you," I said, and sat down on my cot.

"See, I knew," he said triumphantly. "You don't know anything about girls. You're bluffing."

I continued to sit on my cot. I reached over my little desk and picked up the book about little people. Silence continued.

"Okay, Harij. You win. I promise."

"How can I trust you?"

"Harij, we're cousins."

"That hasn't meant all that much in the past."

"Having secrets between us will strengthen our friendship."

"Like how?" I asked. "I tell you a secret, and you can blackmail me?"

"Harij, I won't black mail you. Tell you what. I'll tell a secret about me," he offered.

"You really do want to find out what I know about girls?" I said.

"Yeah, I guess I do," Ojars confessed.

"Okay, Ojar," I dropped the "s" on his name, too. "You tell me your secret first."

"You really don't trust me, do you, Harij?"

"You said it, not I. So tell me your secret, Ojar."

"Okay, Harij. But you keep your mouth shut about it too."

"I promise," I said and meant it.

"Okay, I tried smoking a cigarette. I liked it. I think I'll start smoking."

"You're nuts, Ojar. Is that what you and your friends do? Smoke? Cigarettes cost a lot of money. How are you going to get them?" I asked, thinking he'd probably steal them from his dad or my uncles.

"Harij, that's all I'm going to tell you. It's a secret. You promised. Now what is it that you know about girls," he asked with curiousity.

"Ojar, you remember our cousin, Arija. In Riga we called her Lule?"

"No, actually I don't," he replied. "Who is she?"

(That's right. He wouldn't remember her. In Riga the Kraujas didn't visit much with us. They were business people and we were working class. But that was bygones. Now all of us are D.P.'s.)

"Arija is Uncle Arvid's youngest. She's a year younger than I am. She has an older sister, Velta. Anyway, she and her parents were visiting us, and after lunch Arija and I were playing hide-and-seek in our big yard. Lots of places to hide. Remember, Ojar."

"No, I don't," he replied in a matter of fact way. "So, what did the two of you do?" he asked, with a gleam in his eyes. "Did ya smootch?"

"We played hide-and-seek," I repeated.

"Is that all?" he asked, still with the gleam in his eyes.

"Listen Ojar, I'll tell you what happened that afternoon. Yeah, we had played hide-and-seek for a long time. After I found her during one of our rounds, she said, "Harij, I have to go to the bathroom."

"You want to go inside the house?" I asked.

"I don't think I can make it back that far," Arija moaned.

"Then go in the lilac bushes," I suggested, "I'll keep watch."

"I can't wait a second longer. I got to pee right now."

She was desperate. Then she lifted up the ruffled skirt of her pink dress, pulled down her pink panties, squatted down, and peed between her legs. I was amazed.

I said to her, "Is that how girls do it?"

"Isn't that how everybody does it?" she replied in surprise.

"I don't do it that way."

"You don't? How do you do it, Harij?" she asked with curiosity from her crouched position, looking up at me from just above her knees.

"I do it standing up," I replied in a matter of fact way.

"Standing up?" Arija was most perplexed. "It can't be

done that way. It would run down my legs and into my panties," she said with alarm, "and into my shoes."

"I don't wear panties," I said. "I just open the front of my pants, take him out and let it go. It works just fine."

"I can't believe it." She was shaking her head as she stood up, pulling up her panties, and lowering the skirt of her dress.

"I don't believe you. Can you show me how you do it?" she asked, grinning as if she knew I must be joking.

"You want to see?" I asked.

"Yes, show me," she said, with a smirk on her face.

By then I was also feeling the need to relieve myself. I thought, what the heck! She is my cousin. I didn't know how girls did it, nor did she know how boys do it. I undid my pants, took out my little penis and did the job. She was utterly shocked and amazed. Staring at my unzipped pants, she exclaimed, "What is that? Let me see that thing," she requested.

"That's my wee-wee," I said.

She lifted up her dress, and pulled down her panties once more, spreading her legs and pointing at what was between them and said, "I don't have a wee-wee yet, but I'm growing one. See this little lump right here."

Hearing this, Ojars laughed and shook his head, saying, "Harij, you don't know what you're talking about." He was right. I didn't.

The adults had seated themselves around the big table in the kitchen and we were summoned to join them.

"Okay, we're coming," I said.

On the way to the kitchen I said to Ojars, "Hope your dad makes a long speech tonight. Maybe he'll save us from having to recite verses by the Christmas tree."

"Right," he agreed.

To ensure we didn't talk, but listened to adult conversations, Ojars and I were directed to our places, next to our dads, on opposite ends of the table. That was alright with me. I wanted to eat, not talk. I was hungry. With succulent fragrance from the simmering rooster, freshly baked bread and gingerbread streaming up my nostrils, being hungry was divinely gratifying. Being hungry when there's nothing to eat, anywhere, drives one to prayers of despair. I'll never forget that kind of hunger, the hunger of famine, starvation and death. Food has a sacramental meaning for me. Food is a gift of life from God.

In thankfulness, we paused for a moment of silence before we helped ourselves to all the food we could eat. I remembered the empty tables, the lone slice of black bread topped with a thin layer of bacon grease for which we gladly returned thanks to God not long ago.

I ate and I ate. I didn't listen nor did I care what the adults were talking about. I ate until Ojars' dad rose from his seat, raised his mug of beer and proposed a toast, "To better days!" he said.

The adults raised their mugs, and I, my glass of milk, repeating, "To better days!"

That's when my dad surprised me. He turned to me and motioned for me to set my glass of milk on the table and handed me his mug of beer.

"Harij, have a sip," he said to me. I did. Bitter but good.

Ojars' dad remained on his feet to deliver, as always, his 'party speech'. "Resident family philosopher," my three mothers called him disrespectfully. I didn't understand why it was demeaning to be a philosopher. I thought it was an honor, not an insult, to be a philosopher. Philosophers are intelligent people. They understand what life is all about, and they write books, I thought. That's not dumb.

I listened to Uncle Richards' speech. It wasn't dumb at all. He started out by reminding us we were fortunate; we had survived the war. Fortunate that we found each other after hostilities ceased. Thankful we should be for the food we now had, even though in Latvia we had much better food and drinks. We were missing Edis' tortes, apple cakes and the very special black bread for which his bakery was famous. He spoke of their photo studio in Riga. They missed it much, he said. He even mentioned how good it was that Ojars and I were back in a Latvian school. I thought it was a good speech. At the end he raised his mug once more and said, "To better days." The adults raised theirs and repeated, "To better days!"

I just sat there and looked at my dad. He looked at me and gave me only a smile.

Uncle Edis rose to his feet. Uncle Edis as a rule didn't make speeches at our family parties but only when he had something very important to say. He, too, started by raising his mug and saying, "To better days!"

We all responded. I didn't even look at my dad, who never made speeches at parties.

Uncle Edis told us the first issue of his magazine, *The Illustrated Word* had gone to press. The January 1946 issue should be in our hands soon after the New Year. We applauded, giving him a standing ovation, and congratulated him. He was now an editor and a publisher. He had put it together in less than sixth months, in exile, working with the British and the Americans, whose language he didn't speak. He told us the magazine would be in two languages, Latvian and English. We had known he was working on its publication. The surprise was the relatively short time it took him to organize all aspects of its publication and distribution. An amazing Uncle I had. I was proud of him.

The time had come to light the Christmas tree. Since I had spotted it and my dad and I had brought it home from the forest, I was given the privilege of lighting the twelve candles, carefully secured on the branches so that the open flames would not ignite the branches above. Trees were freshly cut and decorated not sooner than the 22nd of December, as we had done. Traditionally Christmas trees were cut and decorated on Christmas Eve Day and taken down on January 7th, the day after Epiphany. The tree was burned, which was actually the lighting of the candles, twice – Christmas Eve and New Year's Eve.

"Harij," Dad called me, "get ready to burn the Christmas tree."

I got up and ran to the tree before Dad had finished calling. I placed a stool by the tree and climbed on it. Dad handed me a box of wooden matches. I took one out and, striking the side of the box, ignited it. I was thrilled to have a burning match in my hand. Stretching to my full height I lit the upper candles first. One, two, three, four. I almost lost my balance on the fourth. The middle candles were easy to reach. Five, six. seven and a little more to the right, made eight candles aglow. I climbed off the stool and, standing firmly on the floor, created four more little flames. Nine, ten, eleven, twelve! There were twelve little flames flickering before our wondering eyes, reflecting their light from the tinfoil on my Christmas candies. Mom turned out the overhead electric light and we sat adoring my beautiful tree. Then Tinte suggested, "Let's sing 'Silent Night, Holy Night'." We did. It must've been the light from our twelve candles that made our voices blend. I was hearing the harmony of angels from my family, though we were definitely not choir quality. I guess I was hearing with my heart.

We were together. This was my family, alive and well. The war finally felt over for me.

We sang other Christmas hymns. To our embarrassment, we discovered how few we knew beyond the first verse. We sang and laughed until the little candles burned down to about a centimeter of their bases. Ojars got the privilege of extinguishing them. The 60 watt electric bulb was turned on.

"Christmas present time," declared Aunt Anna.

From the Kraujas family, I received four black and white

photographs, one of each family. From Uncle Edis and Aunt Anna, the privilege to use Uncle Edis' typewriter, after proper instruction from Uncle Edis. Uncle Rudis and Tinte gave me a candle-powered thirty centimeter long metal boat that looked like a German U-boat; my first and only toy since leaving Latvia. From my mom and dad I received a light green shirt: the shirt of a Scout uniform. I was very, very happy. I would learn to type. I would have something to play with. I would be a Scout. A memorable first Christmas in peace and freedom.

"Christmas present time,"
said Aunt Anna.

twelve

Scouting Days

"MY REPUTATION PRECEDES ME," I thought. I was forgiven by family for breaking windows, but had anyone else forgotten? My cousin hadn't. He was ready to remind me, my friends and his, what a fool I had been for getting caught. The Scout leaders knew. Will they accept a hooligan as a member of the Scout Group?

Mom and Dad had promised to enroll me as soon as possible but now I dreaded the approaching enrolment like doomsday. What if the Scoutmaster says 'nix'. Scouts set good examples. They don't break windows. I had nightmares of rejection. They won't accept me, I thought again and again. They won't accept me because I was bad, stupid, a destructive ass.

The dreaded day came after New Year's Eve and New Year's Day, which I ruined with worries of rejection and self condemnation. January 2nd 1946, at 7:30 in the evening, the Boy Scout Group was scheduled to meet for outdoor games. Dad had spoken to Scoutmaster Strelis who had promised to interview me after the games. An interview? I hadn't heard of anyone having been interviewed before. He had invited Dad and me to come and observe the Scouts in action, to help me decide if I really wanted to join. Sure, I thought, he wants to humiliate me in front of the Scouts as a lesson for them not to behave as I had. Who doesn't want to be a Scout? It's an honor and a privilege for promising boys.

The hour came and Dad and I went. I was scared. The Scouts were meeting in front of my school. Familiar grounds were comforting. The Scouts looked sharp in their light green shirts over warm underwear. It was cold and dark; the moon and stars were dominating the clear, black sky, but there was no snow. I wondered if Scouts had frequent activities at night. The darkness made games more exciting. I wasn't allowed out after sunset since the dreaded night. Becoming a Scout will void that restriction. I wanted to join. Oh! How I hoped all would go well during the interview.

"Hey, Harij! Hey!" two boys greeted me. I knew them from school.

"You'll be joining?" they asked.

"Yes, I want to." I responded thanking the night for hiding my fears.

"Good," said the first. "We learn a lot and have fun. You're here to see what we do?"

"Yes," I said. "The Scoutmaster invited me." Oh yeah, I thought, invited me so he could embarrass me.

"Great. See you around," said the other and they wandered off.

The Scoutmaster came, greeted and welcomed Dad and me saying, "I'll talk to you after the games, Harijs. Come now and hear the rules of the game so you'll know what the Scouts are doing."

The Scouts were standing in two groups and chatting with each other.

They fell silent as the Scoutmaster approached, trailed by Dad and me.

"Be alert!" he greeted them.

"Be alert!" they replied in unison.

"Mr. Kapeikis and his son Harijs have come to watch us. Harijs is thinking about joining us. Should we let him join?" he asked.

"Sure. I know Harijs from school," a Scout replied.

"He's fast," said another.

"He's got a good arm," I heard, to my alarm.

"Good evening, Mr. Kapeikis," my dad was greeted. I knew I was being set up. The next comment would be "Sure, he can teach us how to throw rocks through windows."

"Scouts, did you have a good Christmas?" asked the Scoutmaster.

"Yes! Yes! Good Christmas! Very, very good," responded the Scouts one after another.

"How about New Year's? Had a good New Year's?" asked the Scoutmaster and the Scouts replied enthusiastically in near unison.

"Yeah, Yeah, Yeah!"

"How about you, Harijs?" he turned and looked at me. I hadn't answered.

"Oh, yes Mr. Strelis. A good New Year," I lied, and looked at my dusty shoes.

"Good," he said, then turned and addressed the group, "Tonight we'll repeat a favorite game, Messengers and Policemen. There was a murmur of delight from the Scouts.

"Yes, you know the rules and the out of bounds, but I'll go over them again. Listen now."

We stood in the large playground in front of the school, dimly illuminated by two electric lights and the full moon.

The Scoutmaster proceeded, "The playground is the battlefield. The messengers must carry a message across the battlefield one word at a time. The objective of the game is to decipher the full text of the message. The side that does that immediately wins the game. Each messenger will be given one word from the message to carry across the battlefield to his headquarters outside the battle field. The policemen cannot go beyond the boundaries of the battlefield but must intercept the messengers anywhere within the battlefield by touching his upper left arm or shoulder. No other body contact is allowed. When a messenger has been intercepted, he surrenders his word to the policeman who takes it to the police headquarters inside the battlefield. The deciphering of the message may be done by anyone at his respective headquarters. Write it out, show it to me at the starting point, and I'll tell you if it's right or not. After a messenger is intercepted or has safely brought his word to his headquarters, he goes back to the starting point for another word. If no side is able to decipher the message while the game is in process, the game will end when the last word has been sent and the messenger is either intercepted or brings it to his headquarters. Then you'll have ten minutes to decipher the message. After the ten minute period, if no side can decipher the message, the side with the most words will be declared the winner on a point per word basis. Alright Scouts, any questions?" asked the Scoutmaster.

I had lots of questions, but not the nerve to ask them. I didn't understand what was about to happen. There were no questions from the Scouts so I assumed they understood. I was eager to see action.

"Fine," said the Scoutmaster. "Patrol leaders, come forward to draw which patrol will be messengers and which policemen."

The patrol leaders came forward for the draw. The Scoutmaster had two straws, one slightly shorter. He said the shorter straw means messengers, the longer policemen. Who will draw? They both shrugged their shoulders. The taller boy said, "You draw."

"Okay," answered the shorter and drew. He drew the shorter straw.

"Determined," said the Scoutmaster. "The Lynx Patrol will be messengers, the Fox Patrol, policemen. You have ten minutes to decide on your strategies and to take your positions. When you hear three short bursts from my whistle, know the messengers have their first words and will try to cross the battlefield as they have planned. Let's play fair and clean. Remember, there's no body contact beyond touching the left arm or shoulder. Good luck, Scouts."

I had just learned the local Group of Scouts was organized into two patrols, the Lynx Patrol and the Fox Patrol.

The Scoutmaster explained to Dad and me that this was a very demanding game. The faster runners had some advantage, but it also required good strategy and teamwork. The policemen had to decide on a defense strategy to prevent the messengers from crossing the field. Messengers had to invent maneuvers to outsmart or confuse the policemen. The main challenge wasn't running and catching, but deciphering the message.

He excused himself saying he must go to the starting point to hand out the words to the Lynx Patrol.

Dad and I stood in semi darkness by my school, which was a remodeled army barrack. The Fox policemen were in the center of the battlefield talking and pointing this way and that. Suddenly one ran toward us, picked up an empty garbage can and brought it to the center of the field. Police headquarters, I thought. A couple of Lynxes ran across the field and positioned a garbage can on the other side of the field as their headquarters then ran back behind the school. The policemen spread out and took their positions, about twenty meters apart, in a straight line, facing the school and the starting point behind it. Then the battlefield fell ghostly silent.

"Harij," Dad broke the silence in a low voice. "You think you'll like being a Scout?"

"Sure I will, Dad. You think I'll be allowed to join?"

"What makes you ask that?"

"You know, Dad."

"Windows, right?"

"Yeah," I said. Just then we heard three sharp bursts

from the Scoutmaster's whistle.

I watched. Did the dim lights get dimmer? I listened. Not a sound anywhere. One minute, two, three. Silence everywhere. The policemen crouched down like sprinters on the mark. Still silence. Five minutes. At once, two messengers came dashing, full speed, from behind the school barrack; one ran straight, the other diagonally to the left. The whole line of policemen went into action, running as fast as they could after the two messengers. I noticed the two messengers were about my size but not as fast as me. The policemen were gaining on the two messengers, especially on the one running straight across the field towards the messenger headquarters. He changed direction to the left. The policemen followed. They were gaining on the two. Just then a whole group of messengers charged into the battlefield near the right border and were running fast. These were bigger boys. When the policemen saw they had been fooled, some turned to chase these bigger messengers, but in vain. They all made it across the battlefield and into the safe zone of their headquarters.

During this maneuver the policemen intercepted only one messenger, the one who started a diagonal run to the left. Even the smaller messenger running straight across got away. The Policemen who were closing in on him saw the pack of messengers on the right edge of the battlefield, changed direction to chase them, but didn't catch any. I wanted to be running on the battlefield with the Lynxes.

The messengers huddled around their headquarters, read each other's words and, in a restful pace, jogged back to the starting point while the policemen huddled by their garbage can over the one word they had captured, then quickly returned to their original guarding positions.

Once again silence fell over the battlefield. I tried to imagine what it would be like to be a messenger behind the school planning another maneuver. At once four messengers appeared, two at each end of the field. They weren't running, just standing. The policemen started drifting in their directions, creating an unprotected area in the center.

"Stay where you are!" shouted the policemen's leader, but a little too late as once more the rest of the messengers dashed through the center of the field toward their headquarters.

These boys are fast! But so were most of the policemen, who outflanked the larger group of messengers and intercepted most of them. The messengers on the ends of the battlefield were also intercepted. I watched with great interest how the messengers protected their left upper arms and shoulders. They turned, jumped and sometimes ran sideways so that their left arm and shoulder was away from a pursuing policeman. One messenger turned, ran backwards then suddenly stopped causing the pursuing policeman to run into him.

"Foul!" shouted an assistant leader. "No body contact! The messenger is free." The messenger took his word to his headquarters.

"Great mudbugs! One has to be agile and quick to avoid running into a messenger," I observed.

Soon there was continuous action on the battlefield as the messengers tried to surprise the policemen with a variety of maneuvers in groups, pairs and solo attempts to carry their words across the battlefield. The game lasted about forty minutes. No side had deciphered the message correctly though the messengers had tried. They tried again in the ten minute period, but were wrong, but won on the basis of points per word delivered. Lynx (messengers) thirty points, Fox (policemen) eleven. A number of the words were blank and had no point value.

The Scouts liked the game and someone suggested repeating it. They all agreed and the Scoutmaster set the repeat match for January 6th, the next outdoor night activity. To end the evening they sang a Scout song, "When Night

Enfolds Us". They sang very well. Good harmony, as some of the younger boys were still soprano. I was a bass, (tried to be), but wasn't very good at singing. Singing would be a problem for me in Scouting like it was at school. The song ended. The Scoutmaster greeted them, "Be alert!" "Be alert!" they answered in unison and were dismissed. The Scoutmaster approached me. I was standing by the school with Dad.

"Here it comes," I thought. "Thank goodness not in front of the Scouts. In front of Dad is bad enough."

"Mr. Kapeikis, Harij," he addressed us. "Tonight was a very typical outdoor Scout activity. This game has variations and is more exciting when played in the woods or on a larger field."

(In woods, at night! All right! Yeah but...)

"All our games require athletic endurance, teamwork, discipline and Scouting skills and knowledge. Tonight's message was a paragraph from Baden-Powell's last message to all Scouts as printed in the little booklet given the boys when they join. Had one or more of the Scouts read and memorized it, the game could have ended much sooner. We could have even played other games."

Looking directly at me, he said, "Well Harij, what do you think?"

"I want to join. I want to be a Scout." I wanted him to accept me right there and right away, and not go into...you know what.

"Scouts have rules, Harij. Scouts abide by them. (Here it comes, my knees were weakening, palms sweating. No! Please.) Do you know what our greeting 'Be Alert' means?"

"No, Sir."

"It means, Harij, that Scouts are honest, loyal to their country of birth, courteous and helpful, friendly, polite, fond of animals, obedient, brave in difficulties, thrifty, energetic, and clean in thoughts, words and deeds. Our salute 'Be Alert' reminds us of Scout Ideals and Laws. Can you accept such ideals, and live according to such laws, Harij?"

"Yes, Sir, I want to try, Sir."

"Are you sure, Harij?"

"Yes, sir."

"Do you give me your word of honor?"

"Yes, sir."

"Then say it. I give you my word of honor."

"I give you my word of honor, Sir." (I added the "Sir.")

"Okay, Harij, you can become a Scout. (I couldn't believe what I was hearing) When were you born? How old are you?"

"1935, July 22nd, I'm 10 years old."

"Oh, Harij. I'm sorry, Mr. Kapeikis. I thought your son was older than that. We'll have to put you in Junior Scouts for the time being."

"But, Sir," I started to plead.

"Junior Scouts, Harij. Rules are rules. Remember, Scouts and also Junior Scouts abide by them."

"Yes, Sir. Junior Scouts." I was elated and crushed.

"Yes, Sir. Junior Scouts."

Two days later I was wearing the Junior Scout uniform and insignias issued by UNRRA team No. 114. The light green shirt Mom had sewn was tucked away at the bottom of a box under my bed where I stored my clothing.

This Junior Scouting is temporary, I told myself. It wasn't all that bad. Upon making the Junior Scout Pledge of being "Faithful to God, obedient to my elders and Junior Scout Law, always striving to be helpful," I became a member of the Raven Patrol. Hey, I was the tallest and, before proving it in a competition, I knew I was the fastest Junior Scout in the little Junior Scout Group. Nothing wrong with that.

Junior Scouts met twice and sometimes three times a week for activities. Junior Scouts didn't have as many outdoor activities as the Scouts, nor were they as physically demanding as the many variations of messengers and policemen. Activities in Junior Scouts were mostly indoors where we learned to tie knots and signal using Morse code and whistles. We learned Junior Scout rules, the Ten Commandments and the Lord's Prayer from the Scriptures. We also learned about Latvian history, geography, our coat of arms and flag.

My favorite Junior Scout activity was woodworking where I learned to engrave and carve various folk symbols and designs on boards and plywood. I made a round sundial by darkening the engraved hour divisions with a pointed iron rod heated in the flame of a candle, a process we called wood burning.

We participated with Scouts and Girl Guides in many special events, such as the Division Rally in Haunstetten on January the 8th in memory of Lord Baden-Powell. That was my first major event in uniform. I was impressed by the number of Scouts and Guides in the two Augsburg D.P. camps; impressed also by our singing of Scout and Guide songs and impromptu presentations of skits.

At this Rally Pastor Lamberts, in his opening devotions, reminded us that following the example of Lord Baden-Powel, Scouts and Guides pledge their faithfulness not only to one's country but also to God.

January 20th, Junior Scouts were invited to participate in a Division Rally at Hochfeld. The Hochfeld Scouts helped us Juniors to improve our knot tying skills and later demonstrated to us their proficiency in sending and receiving messages by means of semaphores. Around the campfire each patrol was challenged to dramatize a folk song or a fairy tale. Then the Hochfeld Senior Scouts (Rovers) surprised us with fireworks. Five rockets shot high into the sky exploding loudly above our heads. I was thrilled. But some parents, when they heard about it, didn't like it, nor did the Hochfeld Scoutmaster like what these parents had to say.

My last activity as a Junior Scout in company with Scouts, Senior Scouts and Guides was on May the 6ᵗʰ, 1946 when Dr. Gulbis, our Camp physician, gave us first aid instruction.

"Check for breathing, stop the bleeding, then check for broken bones," she emphasized. She showed us how to apply pressure to a wound, use a tourniquet, and apply bandages and splints on different kinds of fractures. We practiced the first aid techniques with each other. Boys with boys, girls with girls. I wished the good doctor would let me practice with a girl. Tie a splint on her leg. Bandage her arm. Clean an imaginary scrape on her tummy. Then she could practice on me. When it came to resuscitation my imagination took over. Practicing with a guy was well..., with a girl it would've been heavenly. Yes, I was aware of the second Junior Scout rule, "Junior Scouts have self control" Not necessarily over their imagination, I concluded.

I did well in Junior Scout activities, and also managed to communicate to the Junior Scout leaders my desire for the company of older boys (and girls). I was ready for more demanding challenges. Soon after the first aid training I was offered the opportunity to become a (real) Scout. I was a Junior Scout for only a brief five and a half months.

May 14, 1946, I was transferred to the Scout Group and issued the *lilies*, our Scout insignia, to pin onto the light green shirt Mom had sewn me for Christmas. As a new Scout, I was considered a *tenderfoot* who had to demonstrate that one fits in before giving the Scout Oath and Promises. I was assigned to the Fox Patrol, where Arnis' older brother was the patrol leader. I was very happy about that.

Scout Harijs, wearing the shirt that Mom sewed.
Harijs, Dad and Mom, fourplexes in background.

This happened a day before a significant learning activity. On May 15th from 6:00 a.m. to 7:00 p.m. our group was instructed on program planning and overnight camping, a very important Scout activity.

We were given a typical Scout camp plan, including the layout of tents, central campfire, proper place for the flagpole, kitchen, outhouse and shower.

"Go to it," Scoutmaster commanded.

To the amazement of the Haunstettenites looking on, a perfectly laid out and constructed Scout camp was set up by noon, in the middle of the track and field park in front of our schoolhouse. The Scouts were sitting on the ground around an unlit campfire eating lunch.

Arnis' brother, my patrol leader, impressed me with his quick wit, quick comprehension of the instruction we were getting, and his ability to organize and direct us, his Foxes, teaching us how to set up our tents, build the outhouse and shower tent; our responsibility in the exercise.

After receiving instruction on activity planning for overnight camps, there was time for one game of messengers and policemen. My dream came true. Foxes were the policemen. There was one change from the game I watched. We wore paper ribbons attached with a rubber band to our upper left arm. To catch a messenger the policeman had to tear off the messenger's ribbon. This killed the messenger. But the messenger could fight back and kill the policeman by tearing off the policeman's ribbon. Not being the tallest and fastest any more, I was killed by the first messenger I tried to catch. That was okay. I was a Scout; besides, one could renew his life by getting another ribbon.

With delight I noted the increased outdoor activity in Scouts compared to Junior Scouts. We gathered for instruction, training, games, programs, and weekend camps and trips, three and often four times a week; sometimes three days in a row. For example, on May 30th, the Foxes gathered at ten in the morning for an hour of learning how to mark a path to enable others to follow you, and also to practice marching. The evening of May 31st, we participated with Estonian and Lithuanian Scouts and Guides in an all-Haunstetten D.P. Camp Fellowship Night. We overcame the language barrier with signs and body language. The following day, June 1st our group went on a ten kilometer obstacle course from 9:00 a.m. to 10:00 p.m. I loved it, but my parents were concerned that Scouting activities would affect my grades in school.

"Mom, Dad," I had to remind them, "Don't you know my teachers are involved in Scouting. My teachers know we're busy and they like it. It seems to me when big events are planned in Scouting, they give us less homework, and I like that."

With delight I noted the increased outdoor activity.
Squatting tenderfoot Harijs looking up at real Scouts.

My teachers are involved in Scouting. Mr. Salins in raincoat to
the left of Mr. Strelis. Harijs, far left, sitting on grass.

The principal of our school was also the Chief Guider for the Guide Group. Mr. Salins was active in Scouting events as was Pastor Lamberts who also taught religion at our school. The school, the Church and the Scout/Guide organizations were mutually supportive, strengthening the youth program in Haunstetten.

Table tennis and table tennis tournaments were popular. Arnis and I were practicing; not keeping score, just learning new serves and returns we had seen older boys do, when cousin Ojars came. Arnis was a Scout and so was Imants, but Ojars was not.

"Hey!" Ojars said, "Look at the Scouts play ping-pong. Anyone can beat a Scout."

"Oh yeah!" I replied, "You want to try later?"

"Not later. Now!"

"Can't you see Arnis and I are practicing now."

"I can see. I also see Scouts are afraid of a challenge."

"No, we're not. You want to take him on Arni?" Arnis was better than I. Actually, he was teaching me.

"No, Harij, you play. I need to do homework. I haven't finished the essay for Mr. Salins' class."

"Ha! Excuses. Excuses," laughed Ojars. "You don't want to lose."

"Listen, Ojars, I can beat you anytime and so can Harijs."

"Show me!" Ojars laughed.

Whenever table tennis was played, there were always spectators hoping to get a chance to play. The reason was one needed a ping-pong ball to play, and ping-pong balls were expensive, if available at all. I had two balls, both given me by Uncle Rudis for helping him. Being the owner of two ping-pong balls made me popular.

"Harij, take him on, I really should go," Arnis said.

"Ah, go on, bookworm, study. Give me the pleasure of skunking Harijs," Ojars said to Arnis.

Arnis put the paddle gently on the table and left. The

paddles also were mine, and they had a rubber facing. First class! More spectators gathered, among them two tall Guides, also Imants.

"Take him on, Harij!" shouted Imants.

"Take him on!" shouted the taller Guide. She was in uniform.

"Take him on!" shouted a fellow Scout. "Scouts versus non-Scouts!"

"Okay Ojars, let's play." I said. "I'll make you wish you were a Scout yourself."

"Oh yeah! You're gonna make me join?" Ojars replied.

"No. Just play. Okay."

"Non-Scouts versus Scouts," declared Ojars.

"Whatever. Just play," I said.

"If Harijs beats you, you'll have to join the Guides," needled the Guide in uniform.

I wasn't pleased how this was turning out or what it may lead to. Ojars wasn't a bad player. My estimate was that we were about even. It would kill me to let the Scouts down.

"Throw for the serve!" someone shouted.

I had the ball, so I said to Ojars, "Ready? I'll throw."

"Ready." He replied and picked up the paddle and banged the table with it.

"Don't do that," I said as I threw, thinking I don't want my expensive paddle damaged. The ball bounced high over the net and Ojars slammed a powerful backhand. I returned, high. He slammed again. I returned, but the ball went into the net. His serve.

He served. I expected his usual, powerful serve. I stepped back, but he bounced the ball just barely over the net and I missed the return. Point one for Ojars. This wasn't good. I had to get the serve back.

He served his usual serve. No problem, I returned it to his left court, low. He slammed a reserved backhand. I returned with a backhand to his right court, putting a spin on the ball. This was a move I had just learned from Arnis. Ojars missed the return. The serve was mine. I served my usual forehand serve, Ojars returned to my center, I returned to his right court, low. Ojars returned the ball to my right court just high enough for my back hand slam. I slammed and Ojars missed. The score: Ojars one, Harijs one.

We battled on, hearing cheers for Ojars and for me. Fellow Scouts were watching. The score was fifteen to sixteen, Ojars was one point ahead. Then I remembered the spin Arnis had shown me. It was my serve. I put that spin in the serve. Ojars missed. We were even again. Spin on the serve once more. Ojars missed. One more spin, and one more miss. Ojars wasn't catching on, he wasn't figuring out how to return a spinning ball. The score was twenty to fifteen. One point to go. Scouts were cheering wildly.

I served another spin ball, expecting Ojars to pop the ball into the net again. He returned it into my left court, but at a perfect height for a powerful forehand slam. I executed it with such a force I was afraid my ball might break. Ojars tried to return it but his return went wild and the ball missed the table. The game was over. The Scouts won. Twenty-one to fifteen.

"Well! Well, my cousin has been practicing!" said Ojars as he threw the paddle on the table and joined the little crowd.

"Thank you, Arni," I muttered to myself, hearing cheers and congratulations.

"Great game," Imants congratulated me. "That's a nasty spin you put on the ball."

"Yes, Harij. When did you learn that?" asked the uniformed Guide, as she touched my shoulder.

Golly, those uniforms are sharp, I thought, and noticed her blue A-line skirt and pretty blouse.

"Actually, just before this game," I replied with a smile.

"Oh you devil, you," she replied also with a smile. "You

want to bet you can't beat a Guide?"

"You mean you want to play?"

"Yes, shall we?"

"Okay," I said, and offered her the ball. "Let's practice."

"No! Play, play!" her friend demanded. "Guides versus Scouts!"

"Guides versus Scouts!" echoed the small crowd.

"No, not Guides versus Scouts." I protested. "How about Harijs versus....?"

And I looked in the blue eyes framed with long eye lashes, pretty eyes that were looking back at me. I saw ruby red lips smiling at me, and soft cheeks, partly covered with angel blond hair. The lips whispered her name, "Dzintra."[*]

"Nice to meet you, Dzintra. Let's play. How'd you know my name?"

She just smiled, took the ball from me, and went to the other end of the table, picking up the paddle and throwing for the serve.

We played. She was good, but she couldn't win. I played nice and easy, enjoying the game thoroughly. It was the first time I played ping-pong with a girl. I didn't slam hard, nor use the spin much, just enough to show that I respected her game. I did. I was hoping we would play again. When the score was twenty to twenty, the serve being mine, I put my paddle on the table and said, "Dzintra, let's call it a tie." Going over to her end of the table, and enjoying eye contact once more, I said, "That way we must play again." With a smile, she agreed.

It was about supper time. The little crowd of spectators began to disperse, but Ojars stayed and approached me.

"Harij, can I talk with you?"

"Sure. What about? Ping-pong? A re-match?"

"No, Scouts. You really do like Scouting."

"Yes I do, very much. Why?"

---

[*] not her real name

"My parents, mom in particular, want me to join."

"So, what's wrong with that?"

"Her reasons. I think she's jealous of you."

"That figures." (I knew her philosophy.)

"I don't want to join to keep up with you. I want to join for my own reasons. You know, Harij, I can't even tell her tonight that you won the silly ping pong-game. I hope she never finds out."

"I know, Ojar, but ping-pong isn't silly."

"I know, Harij, ping-pong is more important to you than me. (I was beginning to wonder if he had purposely let me win.) But it drives me nuts when she insists that I must always outdo you. That's probably why we don't seem to hit it off as friends."

"I have wondered about that, too, Ojar, but I can't change your mother."

"Nobody can, nor yours either, with all those fears of hers."

"At least we agree neither of us have perfect mothers."

"Harij, tell me more about Scouts."

I did. We talked like brothers who understood each other. He asked many questions and I answered the best I could.

When ready to leave, Ojars thanked me and rewarded me with his parting words, "Harij, I will join the Scouts."

He did. July 13th, 1946, both of us along with two other boys gave our Scout Promises before Scoutmaster Strelis and the assembled group.

> "Upon my honor and to the best of my
> Ability, I promise:
> to be faithful to God and Latvia
> to help my neighbor at all times and
> to live by Scout rules and statutes."

Ojars and I became members in good standing of the

62nd Scout Group Liepaja, of the Scout District Lielupe in Germany. Ojars, a member of the Lynx Patrol. I remained on the Fox Patrol.

Our memberships were celebrated the following day with an overnight campout on the bank of the River Lech where we were joined by Rovers (Senior Scouts.)

I had reached a milestone in life. Scouting became more and more important and natural to me. I enjoyed the new friendships and camaraderie of belonging; of working as a team, competing, learning new skills, learning new Scout and Folk songs, and meeting physical and mental challenges in an almost endless list of activities. Thirty kilometer hikes leaving at eight in the morning and returning late in the afternoon. Strength and agility-building Baden-Powell exercises. Memory enhancing exercises called Kim, where one observed thirty objects for sixty seconds, then wrote a list of the objects from memory. We learned to read maps and find our way to a given destination using the compass, even at night. We learned to estimate heights of trees by the length of shadows they cast, as well as by using trigonometric formulas. We gained proficiency in signaling, employing semaphores, Morse code, lights and whistles. We tied knots and erected structures with wooden poles held together with rope. We learned about animals, birds, the weather, environment and nature in general. We attended worship services as a group. And most of all we learned to appreciate our roots, our history, culture and traditions: though in exile and homeless, we were not defeated. Our leaders and teachers helped us look at life with a positive attitude. We trusted God.

Scouts and Guides served as ushers and helpers at events in the Community Hall, and at cultural events in Augsburg, such as the Song Festival and Latvian Independence Day, on the 18th of November at St. Anthony's Hall. Scouts and Guides welcomed celebrations as opportunities to proudly wear our uniforms.

October 19th, the first anniversary of our Scout/Guide Groups was celebrated with gusto: flag raising ceremony in the morning, competitive games in the afternoon, and a program in our school building at 7:00 in the evening. The portable walls were removed, making the school barrack into one large room, with a raised platform serving as a stage at one end.

The welcome by our Scoutmaster, singing of Scout/Guide songs, our young voices harmonizing, was inspiring. Recitations and skits reviewed the year's activities and accomplishments. The Fox Patrol had prepared a wild dance skit entitled "Hunt." I wore a goat's costume with an exceedingly large cardboard head. My fellow foxes were disguised, of course, as foxes. The foxes were hunting the goat in a choreographed dance. We were applauded and "ahhhh'ed." Suddenly my "head" fell off. Uncontrolled laughter seized the audience. Everyone saw that Harijs was the goat!

It took weeks to outlive my "Harijs is the Goat" days. My dear "friends" even renamed a tag game we played at school during intermissions to "Who's the Goat?" Everyone, especially the girls, wanted to tag me, saying, "Harijs is the Goat!" I didn't mind.

Losing my heart followed soon after losing my head in the program. A group of friends, including Dzintra, gathered around me to tease me and have some laughs. Amidst "Harijs is the Goat" chants, someone suggested we go for a walk in the field behind the school.

"Good idea, great idea!" exclaimed Dzintra, as she slid her left arm around me and nudged me out of the little crowd. I put my right arm around her. Another girl, Elita, hooked my left elbow with her right arm, while Arnis put his right arm around Elita's waist, and out into the dark night we went.

A slight wind cooled my face. The sky was black and

slightly overcast as on a haunted night. The full moon periodically hid behind a floating cloud, encouraging the girls to snuggle closer. A barking dog encouraged them to snuggle even closer.

I had never walked with my arm around one girl. The sensations of walking arm in arm with two girls was a pleasant discovery. Their shoulders touched my upper arms; hips would rub. I liked the way the girls' hips swayed from side to side. Their hair touched my neck. I wished they would lay their heads on my shoulder. Dzintra did. She was wearing perfume. Girls did that very rarely if at all. Perfume was far too expensive.

"Isn't this neat, Harij," she said quietly.

"Yes," I replied. "Neat."

"You like it, Harij?"

Of course I liked it. I hadn't known being close to a girl could feel so stimulating. But how does one answer a question like that? So I ventured, "Let me think about it."

"Harij!" she looked down and started to pull away. Instinctively I nudged her back. Closer, much closer.

"Harij," she whispered.

"Yes, Dzintra, I like it very much. Just don't know how to describe it."

"Don't describe it, just enjoy it."

"Are you enjoying it?"

"Very much, Harij. Even more than playing ping-pong with you."

"Glad you like ping-pong."

Now that was a subject I could talk about with some expertise. Serves, returns, spins, forehand, backhand, slams. This close-to-a-girl business was all new to me. I liked it. There was something very erotic, but it was embarrassing to talk about. There I was, between two girls, but aware only of Dzintra. Forgetting the group behind us completely. Nor was I hearing what Elita and Arnis were talking about. Aware only of Dzintra. Only Dzintra!

"Dzintra, would you play a few games with me tomorrow after school?"

She looked at me wide eyed and smiled and we made a date. We walked and talked about ping-pong, school, Scouting and her experiences as a Guide. She asked me what I wanted to be when I grew up. I told her I really wasn't sure. A writer, perhaps, as Mr. Salins seemed to be encouraging, or a journalist like my uncle. She told me she wanted to be a Guide leader and a teacher when she grew up. She wanted to go home to Riga. Riga! She was my home town girl. I should be seeing her more. Much more.

"Tomorrow after school's just fine," she said with a smile when we returned to the school barrack and parted for home. "We'll play after school, tomorrow."

As new residents arrived, Scouts were there to welcome them and help them move in. The Scout group grew and reorganizations of the patrols were frequent. One such happy change for me was on November 23rd when Arnis was transferred to the Fox Patrol. Soon the group grew to three patrols as the Wolf Patrol was organized. One month later the Squirrel Patrol was added to our group. The 62nd Scout Group in Haunstetten was four patrols strong.

As the Group grew in numbers the competition in games grew more intense. I wondered if the boys in the Squirrel Patrol felt they had to make up for their name; those (little) Squirrels, with ferocity, frequently defeated the Wolves, Fox and Lynx Patrols.

After one such group activity where the Squirrels outshined us Fox Patrollers in a soccer game, Arnis and I were reminiscing about the anniversary night we ended with the walk in the dark with the girls.

"Arni," I began with some trepidation, "wasn't it fun walking with the girls?"

"Yeah, sure," he answered, "You sure were hitting on Dzintra."

"No! What do you mean?"

"Well, the two of you were in another world."

"No! What do you mean?" I denied but remembered the exotic, hard to define feeling. Did Arnis know about such feelings? Oh, why did I bring up the walk?

"Harij, I talked to you. Elita asked you a question and you didn't answer. You looked sick. Leaning your head against Dzintra's."

"I was?" Darn it, he noticed, but I didn't care. It all felt right and wonderful.

"Yeah, and when the two of you weren't butting heads, you were staring in each other's eyes and walking like you had drank ten liters of beer."

He was right. The feeling was intoxicating. Does he know about it?

"Arni, you like Elita, don't you?"

"Why do you ask?"

"She's a nice girl. Petite and all."

"I see you've noticed."

"Yes, but hasn't everybody? But don't mind that. That's not what I really want to know."

"What do you want to know?"

"When you're with Elita, do you feel.... strange... urges?"

"What are you talking about, Harij?"

"Yeah, strange…desires… urges?"

"What?"

"Urges, like wanting to get real, real close… hug, kiss her?"

"Ha! Ha! Ha! Ha! Haaaaa! That's normal, Harij."

"That's normal?" Well, well. I was normal. That was good to know.

Normal like *that* normal, never felt better. Next time with Dzintra I'll be normal, normal. Perhaps even thrice normal. Wonderfully normal!

We got onto the subject of how to impress girls.

"Arni," I said, "when I get older I'm going to learn to drive a car."

"Yes, so will I."

"Then I'll buy a car, a fast one, a blue topless one."

"Yes, me too. Like an American jeep?"

"No, bigger, longer, something like Hitler rode in."

"Harij, they don't make those cars any more."

"I know. But someday they will. Even nicer ones with great big headlights on the fenders. A long nose and red seats, a red steering wheel and white tires."

"Yeah, then what?"

"I'll climb in, start the engine and drive off."

"Where to?"

"To where the girls live."

"Dzintra?"

"Yeah, Dzintra. I'll drive by her fourplex and she'll see me and my fast, sleek, blue, topless automobile."

"Then what?"

"She'll run out to see if it's really me."

"She will!" Arnis was going along with my fantasies.

"Yes. She'll be standing in the street. I'll drive around the block and back to her fourplex. I'll stop and ask, 'Dzintra, would you like to go for a ride?' And she'll answer, 'Why, of course Harij.' 'Then climb in and sit close to me, very close.'"

"And you'll get those… feelings?"

"Normal, Arni. Very normal. I'll drive off, put my arm around her and whistle a happy tune."

"Then what?"

"She'll lean over, kiss me on the cheek and tell me how surprised but pleased she is that I can drive so well, and how and where did I get this sporty no-roof automobile with white tires and a red steering wheel?"

"You know something Harij," Arnis said, "Your fantasies just may come true in your future and mine."

THE SCOUT FOREST

ON THE GENTLY SLOPING BANKS of the River Lech sat a five hectare expanse of pine forest, not dense, but with trees spaced as if someone had planted them, at perfect distances to support the center ropes of Scout A-frame tents. We knew that area interspersed with small, grassy meadows, as the Scout Forest. We went there often to camp over weekends, to practice our Scouting skills and engage in competitive games. The Scout Forest became familiar to us, and near and dear to our hearts. We knew the location of every shrub, stump and tree. We could run through it safely on a moonlit night.

We were there on the day of April 13, 1947. The small group of Rovers had joined us, likewise the Junior Scouts. From two o'clock in the afternoon until five, we listened to stories about Latvia, practiced sending and receiving messages by semaphores and defeated the Rovers and Junior Scouts in an outdoor game of finding hidden messages which told, in scrambled words, where to look for the next message. Easy for the Scout Patrols because we knew the area well. For example: "heT tumpS thaT ooksL ikeL earB" we knew exactly where "The Stump" was, ran there and found the next scrambled message, while the Rovers and Junior Scouts would run all over the forest looking for "The Stump That Looks Like Bear."

Suddenly we smelled smoke. It was drifting into our area from the north. At the edge of the nearby meadow was a tall pine tree with sturdy branches. The Scoutmaster sent two Scouts to climb it to see where the smoke was coming from. They had climbed no more than four meters when one of them shouted, "Smoke near the road by the bend in the river, about half a kilometer from us!"

"Do you see flames?" shouted the Scoutmaster.

"No. Just white smoke from an area about fifty meters wide."

"Thanks Scouts. Climb down," he called. "The fire is just starting," he said to all of us, now gathered around him. "Anybody here afraid of fire? Speak now," he paused. "We're going to put that fire out. Anyone afraid?"

No one spoke. We stood looking anxiously at our Scoutmaster as well as our patrol leaders. Did they know how to fight a forest fire? What will we do? How will we do it? We had five shovels and four axes.

"Good, since no one is afraid, we're going to that fire," affirmed the Scoutmaster, "Scouts! Be Alert!" he saluted us.

"Be Alert!" we saluted back.

"Pack our equipment into the wagons, put the axes and shovels on top. Quickly form a column of twos. Rovers in lead will pull the wagons. Scouts follow Rovers, then Junior Scouts. Quickly now! Move!" he commanded.

In less than five minutes our equipment was in our wagons, axes and shovels on top. Strong Rovers, in pairs, took our wagons (one per patrol) and their places in the lead, our patrols behind them, and Junior Scouts behind us. We were on our way, double time, to the fire. Running was a pleasure to us.

After one hundred meters, we ran out of our Scout Forest and onto a small dirt road. Our pace increased. The Junior Scouts were falling behind. That was okay. Their leaders knew our destination. We could see the smoke clearly. It was drifting towards us. This meant we must put out the fire or our Scout Forest was in danger. My apprehension was replaced with determination and trust in my leaders.

They'll know what must be done and I'll do exactly as I'm told. I'll be safe, I murmured to myself, running like a soldier amidst comrades into battle.

Our column of twos rounded a turn in the road. We could see flames through the sparse pine trees and, wonder of wonders, a fire wagon on the road in front of us plus a handful of firemen in the forest swinging axes and shovels, clearing the forest floor from fallen dry branches and underbrush. They looked up and cheered when they saw us running toward them. The fireman by the fire wagon was the chief. He knew what to do. In a minute all Rovers had an axe or shovel in hand and, interspersed between the firemen, were helping to clear the forest floor, creating a fire break. It was basically a brush fire to be contained downwind by cutting the lower branches of the pine trees and clearing the forest floor of flammable materials. The fire wagon had used up its water supply and the pump had run out of gasoline. It couldn't pump water from the river. Therefore the fire chief organized us Scouts and Juniors Scouts into a bucket brigade, hoisting water from the river to douse what he called hot spots. By seven-thirty in the evening the fire was contained, and a long column of wet, dirty, tired but exhilarated Rovers, Scouts and Junior Scouts were marching home in a column of twos, pulling their wagons and singing Scout songs.

A letter of thanks from the fire chief mentioned, "When we saw the column of Scouts running towards us, we thought they were an army of angels sent from heaven. Without the Scouts we would not have been able to put the fire out."

To equalize strength and make competitions more challenging in the fall of 1947, the patrols were reorganized. The Fox Patrol was terminated and I was assigned to the Wolf Patrol. Because of my interest in woodworking and handcrafts I was given the privilege of looking after the Wolf's Corner in our den. It was my responsibility to see that displays, trophies, instructional aids and other patrol properties were in good condition and attractively displayed. I kept the duty roster and had the authority to assign jobs and the joy of helping instruct *tenderfoot Scouts* in Scouting skills. I participated in planning social events such as campfire and Christmas programs. This gave me the opportunity to recite, at the 1947 Christmas program, a poem I had written about Christmas in Latvia.

After earning the Honor Student, Actor, Cyclist and Shoemaker badges, I was on my way to becoming an Explorer Scout.

Competition between patrols was intense but friendly, thus memorable. One such memorable competition took place in the Scout Forest on March 29, 1948.

The second day of Easter, at nine in the morning, three Scout patrols and three Guide patrols gathered outside their meeting places to prepare for a co-educational event in the Scout Forest. The Wolves were augmented by the 41st Guide Group's Daisy Patrol. The Lynx by the Crowfoots, and the mighty Squirrels by Dzintra's patrol, the Cornflowers. I didn't get a chance to talk with Dzintra beyond a mutual "Hi". I liked that she was keeping an eye on me as we were packing our patrol supply wagons. She looked attractive that morning in her sporting outfit of white blouse and shorts covering her gentle curves in the right places. Only attractive? More like a million marks, Yeah!

People passing by turned their heads our way as we marched in a column of fours, side by side; two Scouts, two sporty guides, singing in harmony like an accomplished choir, songs we loved and liked to sing. Soon we were in our familiar forest and anxious to get on with the game. Dzintra and I were on opposing teams. I knew she couldn't catch me, but she was quick and agile, a resplendent opponent.

The game was "Smugglers and Boarder Guards" in a three heat event. First heat, Wolves-Daisies versus Squirrels-Cornflowers. Second heat, Wolves-Daisies versus Lynx-Crowfoots. Third heat, Lynx-Crowfoots versus

Squirrels-Cornflowers.

We wore the paper ribbon, our renewable "life", attached to our upper left arm by a rubber band. "Guards" renewed their lives in "Latvia", the area across a safe line behind them. "Smugglers" renewed their lives in "Lithuania", the area beyond the safe line on the opposite side from "Latvia." The "Smugglers" were given a little white ball, worth five points, to smuggle into "Latvia".

For the first half of heat one, Wolves-Daisies were the smugglers, Squirrels-Cornflowers the guards. I attached my life to my left arm and carried the little white ball in my left hand. I took my starting position on the safe line, the Lithuanian border, and waited for the whistle to start the first half.

Across the battle field on the Latvian border three hundred meters away, I saw Dzintra run to her patrol leader who motioned to the Guide across from me to trade places with Dzintra.

Dzintra is after me, I thought. I'm going to show her.

"Wolves-Daisies – Smugglers! Are you ready?" shouted the referee, standing on the center line that divided the territories.

"Ready!" shouted our patrol leader.

A guard could kill a smuggler anywhere on the field, but a smuggler could kill a guard only in the smuggler's half of the field.

"Squirrels-Cornflowers – Guards! Are you ready?"

"Ready!" I heard from across the battle field.

A tense moment followed. The Lynx and Crowfoots, our next challenge, came out of the shade cast by the pine trees surrounding the battle field, and formed a sort of honor guard behind the out of bounds line on the east side.

The whistle. We sprang into action! I saw Dzintra running full speed, heading straight for me. "Nothing doing, girl," I murmured and changed my course to the left, behind my nearest Daisy, gaining on her 'to protect' her from a swiftly approaching big Squirrel.

"Go for Dzintra!" I shouted to her, "I'll take the guy."

She did, and changed her direction a little to her right. The big Squirrel seemed to approve of our maneuver and was running straight at me. Right at the center line he lunged for my life, but I jumped to my right, doing a three sixty turn, briefly noticing Dzintra jumping in circles with the Daisy. The big Squirrel tripped and almost fell. I had to get away from him and get my ball across the safe line into Latvia for five points. I would then battle to collect one point lives when my ball's safe. Having met the big Squirrel on the center line meant he wasn't faster than me. By the time he regained balance and turned around, I was steps ahead of him. Whoa! Blocking my way to Latvia were two Cornflowers. I had to alter course to the right. Oh no! Dzintra was running toward me from behind. She must've killed the Daisy and taken the ball, I thought. What's she doing coming after me with a ball when she should be carrying it back to Lithuania? She's nuts.

The two Cornflowers were running toward me, and Dzintra was closing in from behind. I couldn't run to the right because two Wolves were battling with two Squirrels. The big Squirrel that tripped was close behind Dzintra and gaining. There were four opponents closing in on me. I changed direction to my left, and ran toward the two Cornflowers. They separated. I went for the one on my right. She reached for my life, as I jumped and did a three-sixty again. She missed. I got away from her, but the big Squirrel and Dzintra were almost upon me. I ran flat out. The big Squirrel was close behind me. I heard his feet, but also cheers from the sidelines. Was he gaining on me? I didn't dare look back. A few more meters. More cheers. As I dashed across the safe line into Latvia, the big Squirrel grabbed my life and pulled it off.

We stopped, both out of breath. Then I heard the most uplifting words, greatly disappointing the big Squirrel. The umpire shouted, "The Wolf is SAFE! Squirrel, return the life to the Wolf!"

I placed my ball in the "safe" box. I had made five points for the Wolf-Daisy team. I was free to protect or come to the rescue of ball carrying Wolves or Daisies, if I could get back to smugglers territory. But how could I? There were three Cornflowers and the big Squirrel waiting to pounce on me the moment I entered their territory. I had five minutes to get back, or I would forfeit my life and be out of the game. But I realized it was a good gamble - there was one of me, neutralizing four dummies who could be catching Smugglers. I decided to stay until the umpire's warning, then enter the game and let them kill me. I didn't have to wait at all. Two Wolves and a Daisy had escaped their pursuing guards and were running towards Latvia. Except for Dzintra, her three guard comrades took off to intercept them. I took advantage of Dzintra's momentary distraction and ran by her. She shouted "Oh you!" and came after me. She couldn't catch me, but there were guards everywhere. A younger Squirrel was running to intercept me. I changed direction and sprinted directly toward him. We circled each other, reaching for each other's life. I ducked and pulled away but not before his life was in my hand. Just then Dzintra was upon me. We jumped, circled and reached for each other's life. I was having fun. I was jumping, ducking, dancing with Dzintra.

"I, I, I'm going to getcha!" she hissed through a smile. She was determined. Then, without thinking, instead of reaching for her life, I ducked and came up grabbing her in a firm bear hug and held her so close and tight that she couldn't move. Her heart was pounding. Tiny shiny crystalline beads of perspiration were forming on her forehead. She was breathing rapidly and struggling to break free. Her wide open blue eyes showed surprise but also pleasure. A desire to press my lips on her slightly open and inviting ones was growing stronger when three simultaneous umpire whistles pierced my ears, "Wolf! Wolf! Foul play! You are out of order! Wolf let go of Cornflower!"

I let go of Dzintra. She was holding back a laugh. Body contact wasn't allowed beyond right hand to opponent's left upper arm. Then a stern loud voice commanded and everyone heard, "Wolf! Give your life to Cornflower."

I pulled the paper ribbon from my upper left arm and gave it to Dzintra, thinking I'd rather give her my love.

"Wolf, you are out of the game for the rest of the first half." The stern voice of the umpire informed me.

I went to Lithuania sat on the grass and said to myself, "Oh what the heck. It was worth it."

As the smugglers the Wolf–Daisy team did well without me in the first half. We did even better as the guards in the second half. The rest of the afternoon Dzintra and I stayed away from each other. In our second heat with the Lynx and Crowfoots, we did very well.

Overall, we earned first place with forty-nine points. My misbehavior had cost us a three point penalty. The Lynx–Crowfoot team was second with thirty seven points, and the Squirrel–Cornflower team had thirty four-points.

In the evening, after a program where four *tenderfoots* gave their Scout pledge, Dzintra and I had a date. We sat on the wood pile behind our school, watched the moon and stars and talked about the good time we had playing smugglers and border guards. Dzintra didn't have the Daisies' ball when she came after me. After killing the Daisy she had run the ball back to Lithuania as required. My zigzagging to avoid the two Cornflowers was enough time for her to catch up with me. She was fast, agile, quick and pretty, yeah, very pretty.

Friday evening, July 31, 1948, at the home of our patrol leader, we packed our supply wagon for the next day's early departure to the Scout Forest. There were two new

Scouts in the Wolf Patrol for whom this was the first weekend camping experience. We showed them how to pack a supply wagon, and explained which supplies were essential and why; exciting for the new Scouts, even more so as all of us were apprehensive because rumors were circulating that some Guides, supported by Rovers, were planning to attack us during the weekend, knocking down our tents, stealing our food or dousing us with water. I tried to assure our patrol, especially the new Scouts, that this had never happened nor would it happen this weekend because the Guides were camping on the shores of River Wertach. Rovers won't attack us, I said. They were former Scouts. Nonetheless, I agreed with Scoutmaster, that this time, guarding our camp was not a formality, but a necessity. Everyone would have a chance to be a night watchman and at all times we needed to be alert, as the Scout salute prompted.

By seven o'clock Saturday morning the three patrols were at the Scout Den. The patrol leaders came with the wagons we had loaded the evening before and we were on our way in a column of twos. Front four Scouts were keeping a sharp lookout forward; last four were our rear guard, the rest on the right observed the right flank, and on the left observed the left flank. Were we followed by would-be aggressors? Yes! We were! Not far beyond our colony, as some had renamed our D.P. Camp, our rear guards observed some motion between buildings. "Stop!" one of them commanded, "Aggressors following! Two pairs of two! Over there by the buildings!" he pointed.

Our column stopped. We turned and looked where our rear guard pointed. Yes, there they were, crouched down and running between buildings. Hiding behind shrubs. Scoutmaster at once gave orders for twenty of the fastest Scouts to give chase, ten after each pair of aggressors. The rest were to guard the wagons. I was one of the twenty. In close formation we sprinted toward them. They began to flee. They separated. We separated, five chasing one back to our colony. The one I was chasing ran into his fourplex, (bringing back memories!) The five of us stopped and laughed. We knew who our aggressors were. Four Rovers, big brothers of four Guides.

"Harij," a fellow chaser questioned, "didn't I hear you tell our new Scouts we wouldn't be attacked?"

"You did, but wasn't this fun?" I replied with a question.

"This wasn't an attack," a fellow chaser came to my defense.

"I think we scared them," said another.

"I'd say we're in for new experiences. All of us," commented another. "Not just the new Scouts."

We resumed formation and proceeded to our destination. We were almost there when a right flank guard cried out, "I see movement in the bushes!"

"Me too! Me too! There they are, two guys!" a number of Scouts shouted.

"The same twenty!" Scoutmaster commanded, "After them!"

And we were! We spread out as we ran. We had discussed and practiced this maneuver in leadership training. Their need to look back, to look for places to hide will slow them down. We'll surround them and catch them. We didn't have to do that. One of them stopped and surrendered.

"Don't hurt me!" he pleaded. "We don't mean to harm you. Just wanted to see where you're going and what you do?"

"Oh yeah!" retorted our patrol leader. "Come with us peacefully and you'll know what we do and where."

"Who's the other guy?" asked another patrol leader.

"He's my kid brother. You guys scared us so much, he wet his pants. I surrendered, hoping you'd let him go."

"That's a Scout thing to do," I said. "You sacrificed

yourself to save your brother."

"You could be a good Scout," noted the first patrol leader.

"You mean it?" questioned our prisoner. "I'm not an athlete."

"Come. Let's go," the second patrol leader said with some impatience.

"We've been delayed enough today. We'll see how athletic you are."

"You're not going to make me run or jump or swim?" pleaded our prisoner. "Guys, please, I can't swim."

"We'll teach you," I said.

"But I'll drown!"

"No you won't," I said.

We took the prisoner to our group. The Scoutmaster inquired about his younger brother and, after ascertaining that he'd either run home or simply follow us to the camp and surrender after his pants dried, we moved on. We moved on, with the help of our prisoner! He pulled the biggest wagon. He helped unload, set up camp, and dig the latrine. He was cooperative. He'd never seen a Scout camp. After treating him to a late breakfast of black bread with margarine and coffee, we released him to join his brother who we knew was hiding behind a bush, having wet his pants again. They were free to go home.

By noon all amenities were set up, and we could enjoy a typical Scout lunch of cabbage with vegetable soup. The cook had forgotten the salt. We roasted him for that. Being a good Explorer Scout, he didn't mind.

Early in the afternoon we had swimming lessons with lots of practice time in a calm pool formed by the River Lech. There were Scouts training to earn the swimmers badge. They were serious about this, while the rest of us just had fun until Scoutmaster surprised us with a timely game.

Aggressors had torn up the text of an aggression plan

that outlined the attack and destruction of a Boy Scout camp. Wind had blown little bits and pieces of the plan into our area. We were to find the pieces and reconstruct the plan. No patrol was able to do so. Three patrols tied for last place and quietly enjoyed a supper of pancakes with strawberry jam.

At camp, Scouts always ended the day around a campfire. First with a treat of Scout bread, made from specially prepared dough wrapped around the end of a willow stick and baked above the flames of the open campfire. Ahhh... delicious. Then Scouts sit around the campfire and sing, listen to stories, act out funny skits, sometimes serious and sometimes spooky with Halloween-type content like the one the Squirrels presented the second night.

In this skit a warlock was casting a spell while walking around a blanket on the ground. He called for a devil in green pants to jump out from under the blanket and dance around the campfire. To our amazement that's exactly what happened. The blanket flew to one side and a green devil wearing tight green pants, jumped out from under it and danced around our campfire. He was an assistant Scoutmaster.

There was much laughter at camps, but also opportunities for learning. A Scout had been taking singing lessons and had qualified for the musician's badge. He sang three songs and was presented with the badge. Camps were an excellent time for us to demonstrate our skills and earn our badges. There was something special about receiving a badge at the conclusion of a campfire.

The flag was ceremoniously lowered, folded and put away. Each Scout drew his night watch time. Since there had been aggression already, this was serious. After some discussion, it was decided to trade times and relieve new Scouts from early night and morning hours as these were the more likely times for attacks. Along with two Explorer

Scouts, I ended up with the first watch, from ten to eleven.

The Scouts bedded down. After a day full of activities, they were asleep within minutes. The deep quiet of the night overshadowed the camp. I took my post in the center of the camp and the Explorers went to listening posts outside the camp. Every now and then I walked around the camp as quietly as possible, listening and watching for movement. The trees cast eerie shadows in the moonlight. It felt even more eerie when a cloud slid in front of the moon. The sky was ablaze with a million stars and the Milky Way was visible. The wind caused the leaves in the trees to whisper stories of approaching danger. I listened; my hearing was keen as a wolf's.

I heard something like feet crunching leaves, and a twig breaking. Did I see movement? Yes, movement! Something was moving through the bushes towards our camp and not from the direction of the listening posts. My heart started to pound. I put my Scout alarm whistle in my mouth, took a deep breath to sound the alarm, and then, into the clearing, hopped a little grey rabbit! I let out my breath, sat down on a rock and noticed that I was trembling. What if I had blown the whistle!

One more incident frightened me during the watch. A little garden snake slithered close across my path. I almost jumped out of my shorts. I was glad to turn over my night watchman duties to an older Explorer. I assured him as did the Scouts from the listening posts, that all was well, all was quiet. Under the open A-frame canvas tent, my old blue wool blanket never felt better!

Morning came soon and without incident. No attacks, no word about rabbits or snakes, Rovers nor Guides. We raised our flag knowing we would soon lower it. This was our last day. After breakfast our Scout leader surprised us announcing the morning was our opportunity to demonstrate skills towards earning a badge or a higher Scout rating. I earned one point towards becoming an

Explorer Scout by correctly naming all the trees and shrubs around our camp.

I watched others to learn from them as they demonstrated their skills.

After lunch we were sad to lower the flag, dismantle our tents and pack our gear into wagons. The leaders encouraged us, reassuring there would be many more camps. I believed them. I looked forward to camps. I loved camping.

Our wagons were loaded. We formed our usual column of twos and started for home. I hadn't noticed that the sky was overcast. In the morning it had been clear, but now low dark clouds had replaced the ethereal blue. Our column came out of the forest and onto the dirt road, approaching the burned area where we had labored with the firemen a year previously. I was startled when the dark sky was illuminated by a bolt of lightening followed by a crack of thunder equivalent to a salvo of a hundred nearby howitzers. Nature folded in upon itself, curling leaves and causing pine trees to drop needles in response to the ever increasing wind. Treetops bowed in anticipation of the attack by the approaching thunderstorm. The birds hushed their singing, branches swayed, and the tall grass in the meadow moved in waves like the deep ocean, as our column of Scouts marched on.

Scouts are brave. The lightning and thunder increased, as if to test and break our bravery, but to no avail. With straightened backs, pulled back shoulders and uplifted heads, the Scouts marched into the grey churning rain and hail illuminated continuously by bolts of lightning. And if someone could hear above the crashes of thunder, the Scouts were singing about a river in Latvia, the Daugava, foaming white in the stormy wind.

The little road leading us towards our colony in Haunstetten, our little Latvia in exile, turned into a little Daugava flowing against us. The wheels of our wagons were parting water like the keels of boats. We waded home singing, completely drenched but very happy. I was thinking about the Guides and Dzintra. Why couldn't they have camped with us? And marched home with us in the storm! I imagined protecting and calming her.

I loved my Scouting days. I learned much. I learned to make the best of any situation. I learned to be a team player, to get along with others, and to work with others and also on my own when that was necessary. I learned to accept, with dignity, who I am.

I qualified for Explorer Scout status, and later was appointed assistant patrol leader. As the patrol scribe I didn't do very well. I was told I didn't know how to summarize. I had recorded far too many details, earning zero points for the Wolf Patrol from the log auditor.

thirteen

Family Adventures

ICE CREAM

A GROUP OF BOYS WERE RUNNING down our street shouting, "Ice cream! Ice cream! There's an ice cream man on the road to Hochfeld! Ice cream in the square near Hochfeld! A man is selling ice cream!"

Two delicious words. Ice cream. I hadn't tasted ice cream since we left Riga in the fall of 1944. I didn't doubt the boys; they were all carrying a little bucket and in each little bucket was some ice cream. It was true! I knew the square where costermongers sold all kinds of merchandise; I had been there before to purchase postage stamps.

I found Mom downstairs in the storage area sweeping the floor, helping Tinte set up the little grocery store she and Uncle Rudis were planning to open soon, perhaps next week.

"Mom! Mom!" I shouted in my excitement, "Tinte! Someone is selling ice cream in the square by the stores near Hochfeld where I bought some postage stamps two weeks ago. Can I go to buy some ice cream? Can I? Please! Please!"

"How do you know that?" inquired Tinte.

"Who told you that?" asked Mom.

"Boys! On the street! Carrying buckets full of ice cream! Shouting! Someone's selling ice cream where costermongers

215

sell things, in the square on the road to Hochfeld. Mom! They had buckets full!"

"Calm down, Harij," Mom said, "some boys told you someone's selling ice cream?"

"Yes! Ice cream, Mom!" I was still shouting, "can I run and bring some home? It's not too far."

"That's too far, Harij, when Uncle Rudis gets home he can ride his bicycle and see if it's true," advised Tinte.

"No, Tinte, please no! It'll be too late. It's bound to be sold out soon. No one has sold ice cream here before," I pleaded.

"That's true, Harij," replied Tinte. "That's why it's hard to believe that someone actually has opened an ice cream store now."

"Who said anything about an ice cream store? You're the one opening a store; this is just someone selling ice cream on the street."

"Listen to Tinte," Mom said. "Wait till Uncle Rudis comes home."

"No, Mom! No, Tinte! You like ice cream, too. In Riga, both of you brought ice cream home in buckets just like that one in the corner over there, see."

I had spotted the perfect little bucket in which to bring home some ice cream. I wanted to taste ice cream so much I was starting to salivate. I wasn't going to take *no* for an answer. I pleaded for all I was worth, even reminding them of the incident in Liepaja, where my insistence to leave the railroad station had saved our lives. To eat some ice cream was a matter of life or death for me. Finally they consented.

"Alright Harij, if you want to eat ice cream that much, you can run to buy some," Mom said. "Take the little bucket and I'll give you money. But come right home."

Mom went upstairs. I took the little bucket, said goodbye to Tinte and followed Mom upstairs. I met her in the doorway of our bedroom. She gave me twenty German marks. After putting the money in my pants pocket, I shot off like a bullet out of a forty-five caliber revolver. I was after the treat of my life.

"Ice cream, ice cream. Ice cream," I whispered with every leap. "Ice cream. Ice cream. I'm going to eat ice cream."

I ran with the determination of a world class sprinter attempting to break a speed record. I knew the shortest way, but even so it was a long, long way to run. Finally the familiar buildings came into sight, and next to them the little medieval-like square where costermongers sold their merchandise. And yes, indeed, the ice cream man was standing by the roadside with his cart containing two large insulated cylinders of ice cream.

I wasn't running any more. Exhausted and breathless, I staggered up to the man. He looked at me and asked if I was okay. I told him I had run from Haunstetten to buy his ice cream. He suggested I sit down and rest awhile. He asked how much I wanted? I asked him how much I could get for twenty marks. He looked at my bucket and told me he would fill it to five centimeters from the top. Then he asked the most wonderful question in the world, "Son, would you like a taste?"

"Oh yes, please. I'd love that. I haven't eaten ice cream for many years." I exaggerated. He just smiled and replied, "I believe that, I do."

My eyes were about to pop out of my forehead when I saw him pick up a spoon and a little dish and put three big scoops of light yellow ice cream on it. As he offered the marvelous dish to me, I reached for it as a jeweler for three balls of pure Baltic amber. At once the spoon went into the ice cream and then into my mouth. Vanilla. Ooooooh the taste. Refreshingly grainy and cold. I was in heaven, eating ice cream with angels.

I took my time finishing that first bowl of ice cream. After about twenty minutes we completed our bargain. He filled my little bucket to within five centimeters of the top. I gave him the twenty marks, put the lid on my bucket and started for home. Like a bullet out of a forty-five caliber revolver zooming the distance in twenty maybe twenty five minutes in the heat of the afternoon? No way. Even after the three scoop rest all I could do was walk, and rather slowly at that.

I got home an hour and a half later and proudly presented my bucket to a smiling Mom for her to open ceremoniously. She did so, only to change her smile to a sad frown. My delicious vanilla ice cream had tuned to light yellow milk. I had made a mistake. I should have walked first and then, after buying the ice cream, run home like a bullet. I had done it backwards!

We didn't waste my ice cream-turned-milk. After supper, the Raudupes, Smits, Mom, Dad and I toasted each other and shared it as a dessert drink.

"Prosit!" we said. "Prosit, to better times!"

BETTER TIMES

THOUGH OUR FUTURE was uncertain, we experienced better times in our D.P. camp than the days when bombs were falling and our food supply was failing. Through those trying times my family had protected me and looked after my needs more than their own. Time and time again I observed Dad and Mom putting a larger piece of bacon fat on my slice of bread than on theirs.

In the days we spent living and traveling on trains, when soup time came and we lined up in queues with our tin soup bowls in hand, my parents would take the lone little square of meat in their soup and put it into mine. It was their silent way of saying, "Son, if any of us will survive the war and the famine, it must be you." In war, we feared for our lives; in camp, we feared our uncertain future. Where would destiny take us, in a world so much changed and damaged by the war?

MOTHER'S FEARS

MY MOTHER WAS AFRAID of many things. She was afraid of water, policemen, events she didn't understand, afraid to speak her mind in public, afraid she wasn't protecting me as well as she should. Who could blame her? What she had experienced in Latvia and during the war would make anyone fearful.

My mother loved me.

For example, toward the end of the year of Soviet occupation, June 17, 1940 to June 22, 1941, the authorities issued an edict ordering all children to attend a youth camp where they would be informed about the benefits of belonging to the Great Soviet Union. My mom didn't want me to go to this camp. It was fortunate I hadn't started grade school, therefore the Communist authorities had no record of my existence other than the registration of my birth and baptism, which they may not have been able to access as resistance to the occupation of Latvia was high.

To ensure the edict would be obeyed, the police were secretly ordered to canvass residential neighborhoods and round up children by force, if necessary. Fortunately our neighborhood was not the first to be "hit" and the word spread like wildfire.

"The Communists are taking children by force," we heard. My mom prepared a place in our root cellar to hide me under sacks of potatoes, carrots and other vegetables, until the search was over. I was five years old. She explained that mean men were coming to take me away from home. I must lie under the produce without making any noise whatsoever. It was like a game of hide-and-seek, but this wasn't a game. She explained that if they would find me, I would be taken away forever.

The day came when we knew our neighborhood was being searched by the police and into the cellar and under the sacks of produce I went quite willingly. She promised to look in on me frequently. She did. She looked after every one of my needs: food, milk, warmth, even potty. I had my friend, Peter, (a small rubber sailor doll) with me as well as my wood blocks. Other than my tricycle and garden tools, that was all the toys I had.

I didn't mind hiding at first, the cellar was a familiar place to me since I had helped with the harvests in the fall, but the second day and part of the third became extremely lonesome and boring. I was so glad to hear Mom, bounding down the stairs into the cellar singing, "Harij, Harij, you can come out now! The policemen came and believed that we have no children here!"

I didn't care to play hide-and-seek with my cousin Arija for quite some time after spending those hours in the musty cellar pretending I was a carrot, then a potato or rhubarb. Mom left the hatch to the cellar slightly open, allowing a slanting column of sunlight to lean against the rustic wall. I could see through the small ragged openings between the sacks.

I sat or lay down on the dirt floor. The wide planks of the ceiling supported potato sacks above; Mom or Dad would remove them and check on me frequently.

Tinte and Uncle Rudis lived opposite from us in the duplex, so the four adults took turns keeping constant surveillance of the street, likewise the neighbors behind and on both sides of our duplex, who were sympathetic to our cause. This allowed my dad or mom to be with me in the cellar when night came and I would fall asleep. I didn't know they carried me into the house in the evenings when it was safe and back into the cellar before dawn. Mom was with me in the cellar when I awoke those two mornings.

Uncle Arvids had taken my cousin, Arija, and her sister, Velta, to a farm in the country. Some families, even though they were not Communists, felt they had no choice but to send their children to the camp to be indoctrinated. After this I was not allowed to leave our big yard. I was told there were no children playing on the nearby sand hill anymore, nor seen on our street, the unpaved Basein Street in the suburb of Zasulauks, a residential area mainly for blue collar workers.

Indoctrination of the youth is one example of the terrorism used by the Soviets to intimidate and crush the will of the Latvian people. We never did learn whether this atrocity was orchestrated by higher Communist authorities or simply by our local Politburo against the middle and working class people in Zasulauks, Riga.

Not a single child taken in the roundup returned home. About three months later, in June 1941, when the Germans liberated Latvia from Russian occupation, not a trace of the Russian youth camps for Latvian children was found. What happened to the children? Perhaps they faced the same fate as the more than thirty-six thousand Latvians arbitrarily arrested and, on June 14, 1941, deported in cattle cars, as slaves, to Siberia. Most of them died of both exposure to freezing weather and starvation. Risking her life, my mother supported by Dad, Tinte and Uncle Rudis, saved mine.

THE DEMOLITION SQUAD

IN HAUNSTETTEN, there were ways in which my parents sought to provide extra opportunities for me that led to conflict between themselves, bringing the wrath of my uncles and aunts upon them; especially toward my dad.

I wondered, from time to time, where my parents got the money they gave me to buy postage stamps for my stamp collection; even the twenty marks for ice cream. My dad didn't smoke, so he sold the cigarettes allocated in our rations and the tobacco that came in the care packages from America. But we seemed to have more money than the sale of those items would produce.

One evening I found out. The funds came from the part-time job Dad had with the American Army. Dad didn't talk about this job. When asked about it, he would avoid talking by saying something like, "I help Americans load and unload trucks," or, "I sweep warehouses and clean yards." He was very evasive about the job until the day Uncle Edis came home looking distraught, and cornered my dad.

"Arvid," he said angrily. "What in the world are you trying to prove? You survived the war unscratched. Why do you want to blow yourself up now? Have you forgotten you have a son to raise?"

"Whoa, Edi, whoa," replied Dad, taken back. "What are you talking about? Why would I blow myself up?"

"The job you have with the Americans. You lied to us. I heard about it today! The captain in charge of bomb demolition bragged that Arvids Kapeikis is the bravest fuse setter and detonator he's ever seen. He said you go to the bombs, with fuses and detonators in hand, and set them like you've done it all your life. When you go back to the bunker and throw the switch, 'kabooom' goes all the bombs!"

Mom, Tinte, Uncle Rudis and I gathered around Edis

and Dad, bewilderment on our faces. I had wondered what my dad was doing for the Americans that he didn't talk about. He was blowing up unused German bombs and artillery ammunition. I remembered the trouble I was in when I blew up just one twenty-two caliber cartridge.

"Arvid, Arvid," was all Mom could say.

"Arvid you are crazy?" declared Uncle Rudis while Uncle Edis was glaring at my dad, standing so close to him I thought their noses would touch.

"Explain yourself!" demanded Uncle Edis.

"What's there to explain?" retorted Dad. "It's not at all dangerous."

"What? Not dangerous? Blowing up bombs isn't dangerous?" sneered Uncle Edis. "There's nothing more dangerous than that!"

"Edi," declared Dad, "publishing a magazine is far more dangerous than demolishing bombs."

"There is no comparison, Arvid. I make a mistake, I correct it. You make a mistake and there's nothing to correct. Nothing left even to bury. Think of your family! My sister, your wife! Think of Harijs!"

"I am thinking of them," said dad, "The job pays well."

It was as if my hearing failed. I didn't hear what anyone said after Dad said, "the job pays well." Once again he was risking his life for my benefit and Mom's. He was blowing up unused German bombs so I could buy stamps, eat ice cream and have a nice Scout uniform to wear. He was blowing up ammunition so we could go on a tour to Berchtesgarden in the Alps, or to a Latvian Song Festival. If that isn't love, then what is, I thought.

Stubbornly Dad held on to his job in the demolition crew until all unused German bombs and other munitions around Augsburg were destroyed. Besides earning extra money he was also philosophical about it, pointing out that while others were complaining they were being prevented from working, he had a job, and he felt very satisfied that the bombs and other ammunition he helped destroy would never be used against innocent people. For his bravery he received a commendation from the United States Army. I was proud of Dad.

My dad loved me.

HEADQUARTERS
88th ORDNANCE BOMB DISPOSAL SQUAD (SEP)
APO 9
United States Army

Augsburg 10 October 1946

To: WHOM IT MAY CONCERN.

This is to certify that.....Kapeikis Arnold..................
has been employed by this unit................................
from...............thru................The work he had to carry out was of a dangerous nature and his services were ....in every respect. He is released the job being completed.

JESSE J. BURBAGE, JR.
Capt. Ord. Dept.
Comdg.

WHAT WILL BECOME OF US?

"WHAT WILL BECOME OF US" was a grave concern of all
D.P.'s. We absolutely would not go back to a Soviet
occupied Latvia. The atrocities committed in Latvia by
Stalin's regime were burning in our minds and hearts. The
year of terror we had experienced: the year we would never
forget.

We knew D.P. camps were under the mandate of
UNRRA and, on February 12, 1946, would fall under IRO
(International Refugee Organization); a temporary solution
to the refugee problem. We also knew we couldn't stay and
work in Germany; we were D.P.'s and not allowed to join
the German work force.

But while the current situation of legislated
unemployment was a topic of many conversations, my
family was busy: dad was working, Uncle Edis was
spending long hours writing and directing the publication
of his magazine, and Uncle Rudis and Tinte were seeking
permission from IRO authorities to open a store in the
basement storage area of our fourplex.

My family was proactive. Did that make me more
fortunate or less fortunate than other children in the camp?
There were hidden blessings for all D.P. children when
their capable parents (and especially professional people)
were not allowed to work. They spent much time with their
children, their children's friends and the children of their
friends. They had time to share with us the knowledge and
skills of their professions, and most of all, there was time to
play with us. They had nothing to give us but their time.

We, the children, were fortunate and I, doubly so. Not
only did this broad spectrum of professional people take
interest in me, I also learned by the example of my
industrious family. Time was not wasted; it was an
amazing learning environment. Even greater dividends
would come later, in the form of motivation we received

throughout our childhood from the professional adult peers who gave us their full attention. There could be no better upbringing or education. A generation almost lost was enriched by their traumatic circumstances.

THE TYPEWRITER

UNCLE EDIS BRIEFLY SHOWED ME how to set up the typewriter; how to open the carrying case and set up the writing machine, insert paper, set margins, type capitals and find the punctuation. That was great. But he was too busy to teach me how to properly type, so when he told me to go at it and try to type, I felt like the editor-in-chief, myself.

I recognized the letters of the alphabet on the keys, but it took time to find the ones I wanted; I was frustrated that the keys weren't in alphabetical order. I used the middle finger of my right hand to hit the keys, one slow punch at a time, but at least I was typing. I was certain no other kid in camp had this privilege.

Soon my busy uncle and I were in serious trouble. Uncle Edis hadn't recently reminded me about the light touch of hitting the keys. He had left the room and, when he came back about half an hour later, he grabbed me by my ears and just about lifted me off the chair.

"Harij!" he said with concern in his voice, "you're bending the keys out of alignment. A typewriter isn't an anvil in a blacksmith shop to be pounded with a sledge hammer! This is how you touch the keys."

He showed me how, but a little too late. The typewriter needed repairs before he could use it again for his work. But he didn't revoke my typing privileges. I learned to type on my own when he wasn't using it. Eventually I borrowed a book from a friend and copied it on my uncle's wonderful repaired portable typewriter. *A House By the Hemp Forest* was a story about little people and small animals of the forest. Uncle Edis didn't punish me because I had bent the keys on his new typewriter.

THE STORE

YES. Uncle Rudis got permission from IRO to open a little store and sell non-rationed produce and other merchandise. Meat of any kind was strictly forbidden. Meat was rationed and in short supply. He could sell paper products, vegetables, fruit and other local farm produce the farmers were allowed to trade, barter or sell. Tinte ran the store and Uncle Rudis, on his bicycle, scouted the local area farms and people with large gardens, to see what he could bring into his store. When he was successful in making a deal, he'd load the produce in baskets on his bicycle and pedal home. Sometimes he'd make several trips to transport his purchases. From time to time a farmer would deliver larger purchases of potatoes, carrots and cabbage in a two wheeled cart and, after unloading, give me a ride around the block.

The store opened when the goods arrived; news was passed by word of mouth. This led to some complaints. Some people said, "The Smits are unfair about who they inform when the store opens and what they are selling. They're favoring some customers over others."

Generally, though, the little store was well received by fellow D.P.'s. It allowed people to supplement their menus and lifestyle with a better variety of fresh produce, bread, paper products, simple cooking utensils and, on rare occasions, even ice cream.

The store provided me my first paying job. Uncle Rudis hired me to make paper bags. He showed me how to measure, cut, fold and glue together various sizes of bags from the large rolls of brown wrapping paper he had purchased. He paid me two pfennigs per bag. My efficiency increased, and soon I was making fifty pfennigs an hour.

One day disaster struck. I was playing the sticks and bricks game in the yard with my friends when two American jeeps, each driven by a military policeman, stopped at our fourplex. The policemen quickly climbed out and, with firm steps, walked to the entrance of our fourplex. As they entered, I noted both had a sidearm. One had his hand on the gun as if ready to draw it. They didn't look at us playing. They looked serious. We stopped our game and chatter and watched with dismay. Why had they come? What will they do? What's the meaning of this? American soldiers didn't come among us armed any more. I got my answer fifteen minutes later. My heart skipped beats and there was sweat on my palms. I saw Tinte and Uncle Rudis, both handcuffed, led out the front door and into separate jeeps. They quickly sped away. The Military Police had arrested my aunt and uncle. Why?

Without saying goodbye to my friends, I ran inside, crying and pleading, "What happened? What happened? Why'd they take Tinte and Uncle Rudis away, handcuffed?"

"You wouldn't understand," said my dad.

"Tell me. Please," I pleaded in tears. "What did they do? What's going to happen to them? Will they shoot them?"

"No, no," said Dad. "They took them to jail."

"To jail? What for?" I asked, crying. "Why?"

"You wouldn't understand, Harij," Mom repeated Dad's words. "Yes I will," I pleaded. "Tell me, yes I will."

"Someone doesn't like them and reported to the Americans that they were selling rationed merchandise," Dad told me.

"They sold meat," I jumped to a conclusion.

"Harij, I don't know what it was they sold," said Dad. "Someone just reported them. The Americans came to close the store."

"Close the store? But why'd they take them to jail?" I asked.

"Probably to ask them some questions. They'll come home," Dad tried to assure me. "They'll come home."

"Can Uncle Edis help them? He knows Americans," I said, trying to calm myself. "He can get them out of jail, can't he?"

"You can ask Uncle Edis when he comes home tonight," said Mom, though she didn't sound very reassuring.

I had lost one Uncle, Mom's brother Arvids, just before we left Riga. He was arrested by the Germans, and didn't come home. Was I to lose another uncle and also Tinte. "God, please don't let the Americans shoot Tinte and Uncle Rudis," I prayed silently. Tinte and Uncle Rudis were like another mom and dad to me. We had grown close.

The rest of the afternoon my parents tried to calm my fears, but to no avail. I could feel through their many words of consolation, the fear and great concern in their own hearts. Dad tried to convince me Americans weren't like the Communists. He told me Americans didn't arbitrarily execute people; perhaps Uncle Rudis will have to see a judge or go on trial and be fined for breaking the law, but they will not hurt him physically. I listened to Dad's words, so did Mom, but I felt she was less convinced by Dad's assurances than I. All afternoon she was on the edge of tears. Mom loved her sister. We had depended on Uncle Rudis for advice the days we fled from the Russians. Were Tinte and Uncle Rudis gone too?

Aunt Anna and Uncle Edis came home late in the evening. They had gone to another D.P. camp to encourage writers to submit articles for publication in his magazine. There were two hundred ninety-four D.P. camps in Germany providing shelter and sustenance to more than one hundred twenty thousand people. Uncle Edis wanted to publish information about living conditions and cultural activities in as many of the camps as possible. There was a special camp, an orphanage in Unterschwarzach, where one hundred thirty children, babies to eighteen years of age, were provided for. Dad was right. Americans aren't like the Communists. They care for us. They will treat Tinte and Uncle Rudis justly.

Uncle Edis and Aunt Anna listened with alarm as Mom and Dad related what had taken place earlier in the afternoon. The Military Policemen had been very courteous, but spoke only English. Mom said she really didn't understand much of what they asked or said. The policemen had knocked on the door, Tinte had answered. They had asked Tinte if she was Mrs. Smits. Mom had understood that. Rudis went to the door and they asked him if he was Mr. Smits. Then they asked for their D.P. identification papers. Marta and Rudis showed the papers. The policemen then asked to see the store. Marta got the key and led them downstairs, while Rudis and my parents followed. Marta opened the door to the store, the policemen entered and allowed Rudis to enter, but not Mom nor Dad. They watched and listened from the hallway.

The policemen searched the store while conversing, but my parents couldn't understand what was said. They took nothing from the shelves. But after finding and examining the record of sales book, they asked something, but neither Marta nor Rudis answered. Then the policemen took Rudis and Marta's hands and handcuffed them. They took the sales book and said to Marta and Rudis, "Come with us." Mom also understood that. That's how Marta and Rudis were led away. My parents had assumed they were taken to jail.

"Edi, can you help them?" Aunt Anna asked.

"I don't know," Uncle Edis answered. "We don't know what the charges are. We don't know where they are."

"Don't you think they were taken to UNRRA's office for questioning? Oh, it's IRO now. Isn't that right, Edi?" said Aunt Anna.

"Please Edi, help them if you can," Mom pleaded. "You know some of the American officers. It's our sister. Help them."

"Darn that Rudis! Too ambitious, as I've said before. Opens the store and thinks he's above the law. Wants the money, I know," replied Uncle Edis. "Some brother-in-laws I have. One wants to blow himself up for money, the other risks blowing our chances with the Americans."

"Edi, leave me out of this," Dad said. "I know what I'm doing. My demolition job is about done, and I won't blow myself up."

"Don't start fighting now," pleaded Mom. "Edi, you've got to think of something to help Marta and Rudis. Please think of something."

The conversation went on late into the night. They were mostly speculating about what crime Rudis and Marta had committed in their store. If they had bought and sold meat, especially prime beef, then both my aunt and uncle, as well as the farmer who sold them the beef would be in serious trouble. For selling rationed merchandise there was a heavy fine with imprisonment for several months. But my parents and the Raudupes seemed to agree that the Smits weren't that stupid. What had they done?

Finally Uncle Edis agreed to visit the American offices next morning and see what he could find out. Then we went to bed. I didn't sleep much. Just as I would doze off, another concern about my imprisoned aunt and uncle would drive the sleep away.

The morning was tense. That Marta and Rudis weren't with us laid heavily on my heart. After a light breakfast of coffee and bread, Uncle Edis dressed in his black suit and went to the American offices.

Noon came. Uncle Edis hadn't returned. Not good.

Just before two in the afternoon, Uncle Edis came home with a smile on his face. I knew he'd done well.

Uncle Rudis and Tinte loved me.
December 10, 1947. Haunstetten.

Tinte and Uncle Rudis will be released, I thought. Uncle Edis wouldn't be smiling if he hadn't resolved the problem.

This was what happened. Someone had reported the Smits' store was selling meat. Beef. Prime beef. That's why the police were sent to investigate and, if necessary, arrest the Smits and close the store. The policemen had reported that they saw no evidence of beef in the store. They had found the record of sales book where some entries indicated the store had recently sold some pork rind, fat sausages and pork innards. They had tried to question the Smits about the fat sausages and the innards but they hadn't answered, due to the language barrier. To avoid further difficulties and a possible scene due to misunderstandings they handcuffed the Smits. As everyone knows, in any police language, that means you come with us without resistance.

Pork rind and fat were not rationed items. Sausages were rationed, but when it was explained the entry meant 'fat FOR cooking sausages' the Smits were not charged. There were some questions about innards like pork liver, kidneys, heart. The Americans, favoring free enterprise, decided it was alright to sell them. Uncle Rudis and Aunt Marta were released that afternoon and returned home to run their little private enterprise. We celebrated and ate fried pork liver that night and drank refreshing dark beer, the renowned German specialty. Even I got a small mug!

THE BICYCLE

TO EARN A CYCLIST'S BADGE in Scouting, besides learning how to ride a bicycle and pass a riding test, I had to disassemble and reassemble a bicycle in the presence of an adult Scout leader. Uncle Rudis had taught me how to ride on his bicycle and I had his permission to ride it anytime, but to take it apart? No way!

Ojars was in the same predicament. We had passed the riding test, but needed to demonstrate our mechanical skills. He proposed the solution. He had found a fairly decent bicycle frame, but it had no chain, wheels or tires. He suggested I buy the wheels and tires and he would purchase the chain, and we would become partners. We would assemble the bicycle and both of us use it to earn our cyclist badge. I couldn't refuse his offer.

I saw two used wheels in a store and bought them for twenty marks. I also purchased two new tires and tubes for forty marks. Ojars wasn't pleased I had bought used wheels. He had bought a new chain and he expected new wheels for the bicycle.

We assembled the bicycle. It performed alright, but was heavier than my uncle's because of the older, heavier frame and the heavier wheels. As agreed, both of us used it to demonstrate to the Scoutmasters that we could disassemble and assemble a bicycle. We got our cyclist badges. According to Ojars, that's where our partnership ended. We had earned the badges and from that point on the bicycle was his. It had cost me sixty marks to earn my cyclist badge!

I was riding my uncle's new bicycle and thinking about that and other unpleasant events: a friend had told me he saw Dzintra walking hand in hand with the big Squirrel, the tall Boy Scout who, with Dzintra as a Cornflower, was my chief rival in the Wolves-Daisies versus Squirrels-Cornflowers "Smugglers and Guards" game in the Scout Forest. Also, I had received a poor grade in a geography exam, I didn't get to go to the salt mines nor to Zugspitze, the high Alpine mountain, and I had played poorly in the last ping-pong tournament.

With such thoughts depressing my mood, I decided to see how fast I could make my uncle's bicycle go; maybe I could get rid of my negative state of mind. I was a good rider. I started to push the pedals faster and faster and faster. The wind brushing back my hair and whistling by my ears was exhilarating. The wind felt cool on my bare legs and face this hot summer day, but caused my eyes to water, blurring my vision.

A little too late, I saw a fire hydrant two meters in front of me. I couldn't turn, so I braked hard. My right leg and pedal smashed into the hydrant and I flew over the handlebars, striking the rough sidewalk with my knees and then my right elbow and shoulder. I came to rest on my left side in the dirt about four meters beyond the sidewalk.

What had I done to my uncle's new bicycle? He'll kill me if I wrecked it.

Then I felt fire in both my knees and right elbow. I looked at my right knee and saw blood oozing through grey dirt. There was blood on my right arm. I tried to sit up, but couldn't. I felt light headed and scared. Slowly I rolled onto my back and saw I was covered with dirt. Some people came. They spoke to me but I couldn't make sense of what they were saying. I felt like crying. I held back the tears. They helped me sit up. Two men lifted me to my feet by my armpits and slowly walked me three blocks to the first aid station in the colony. The painful fire in my knees and elbow spread throughout my body.

As I was being cleaned up I regained my senses and speech and was able to tell the nurse and assistant what happened. I confessed my thoughtlessness in racing the bicycle and the hollowness in the pit of my stomach regarding the condition of the bicycle. The nurse told me I was a lucky boy. I had only one badly scraped knee, with lots of minor cuts that would heal quickly, and she emphasized, "No broken bones. It could've been much worse, Harij." Small colony, she knew my name. "You could have broken your neck and died. Someone above was watching over you."

She cleaned and disinfected my wounds, put soothing ointment onto them, bandaged them and gave me two aspirin tablets with cool water. The pain was easing as Mom and Tinte walked in. Mom started to cry and Tinte said, "Oh Harij!" The nurse explained that I looked worse than I was. I was scraped all over. The bandages and band-aids on them made me look like an Egyptian mummy prepared for burial. The nurse was concerned only about my right knee and thought a doctor should examine that. Gravel had been embedded into the kneecap and there was some exposed bone.

My first word to Tinte was, "The bicycle. Is it home?"

"Yes," she answered.

"Did I wreck it?"

"No, Harij. The right pedal is bent but Rudi thinks he can fix it. The bicycle landed in sand and has only some scratches."

"Is Uncle mad at me?"

"No, Harij. All of us were concerned about you when the camp policeman brought the bicycle home and told us what had happened. He suggested we wait an hour or so before we come here."

"Harij, I was afraid you were crippled when he said you looked shaken and couldn't talk," Mom was still wiping tears.

"Mom, I was afraid I wrecked the bicycle."

Then turning to Tinte, I said, "Uncle Rudis won't let me ride anymore. Will he?"

"I think he will," she answered. "He knows you're a good rider and sensible – most of the time," she added.

After an hour's stay at the first aid station I was allowed to go home. An appointment was made for me to see the camp doctor the following day. Mom, Tinte and I walked home, slowly, and in silence.

I healed. The doctor took off some of the band-aids the next day. Most bandages came off in three days. In two weeks the minor scrapes were healed and in six weeks I was back in the game of life, but still limping a little.

"When you stop limping, Harij, you can ride the bicycle," Uncle Rudis had declared. About two months later I was riding my uncle's bicycle, but never again recklessly nor at full speed.

Harijs. August 16, 1946,
Haunstetten. Note the
condition of the knees!

OUR TOURS

THERE WERE SOME VERY SPECIAL DAYS that punctuated our lives with excitement and joy, and even encouraged the adults, who found life in D.P. camps monotonous and a waste of time because of the limitations on their work and creative opportunities.

Such special days included tours through the countryside to the Alpine Berchtesgarden, Garmisch-Partenkirchen and Oberammergau. The picturesque log farmhouses, the Baroque churches and the garden-like landscape of the Bavarian Alps impressed me. The sight of the resort town, Garmisch, overshadowed by the snow-capped 2963 meter Zugspitze, revised my concept of rugged beauty and magnificence. People lived and worked there, did they take it for granted? God forgive them if they did. But did I take for granted God's creation where I lived, the D.P. camp? The fourplexes we lived in were the homes of people who were forced to leave, providing shelter for me. God forgive me should I take that for granted.

Oberammergau, the town of the world famous Passion Play, was composed of rustic buildings, devotional paintings, and voluminous art from centuries ago. It was miraculously untouched by bombs and bullets during the war. I wondered if someday I would paint pictures like the ones I was seeing, and build beautiful buildings.

I had never seen a Passion Play, so I asked Mom what it was. She told me it was a realistic play about Jesus. That upset me and made me wonder if they really nailed an actor to the cross. I believed, even at that age, that Jesus died for us, and that the Bible's story is not a play, but reality. Should people, then, make a play of it? I didn't feel the need to see the Passion Play.

King Ludwig's castle stood on a craggy outcrop near Oberammergau, high above a reflective lake. It stood six stories high, topped by a steep roof dotted with dormers and surrounded by towers with turrets. It was called Neuschwanstein Castle. I tried to translate the word, "New-swan-stone castle." It didn't make sense, but it was impressive and it was grand. "Why did King Ludwig need all the rooms? His kids and wife must've had many friends," I concluded.

The Bavarian Alps, August 1946.
Aunt Anna (top left), Mom & Dad (extreme right).

SONG FESTIVALS

AMONG THE SPECIAL DAYS that thrilled both youngsters and adults alike, were our traditional "Song festivals." Latvians love to sing; songs and choral music play an important role in the culture. We are and always have been a singing nation, having accumulated songs since antiquity. Some of the folk songs are for special occasions, seasons and festivals.

The festival days surrounding the summer solstice are known as John's Days (Jana Dienas), an event celebrated colorfully on June 24th, the Name's Day for all Janis' - a popular Latvian name.

Men dress in traditional folk costumes, donning a wreath of oak branches, while women wear wreaths of local wildflowers. The custom is to gather in small neighborhood groups and go from house to house or farm to farm singing John's Songs, traditional folk songs ending with the refrain, "Ligo! Ligo!" which means to sway or rock back and forth.

Upon arriving at a neighbor's place, the singers address the hosts, in song, as "the Mother and Father of John," an honorary title even if they had no son with that name. They then sing requests for beer and cheese, usually home-made on the farm, and after some more singing and sometimes dancing, the group moves on to another neighbor.

As the sun slides towards the western horizon, bonfires are lit or a burning wooden barrel is raised on a pole. The singing and dancing continue around the crackling fire and can go on until the dawn of the next day, or until the beer and cheese failed, but an honored "Father and Mother of John" would never allow such a disgrace.

In the historic treasure chest of Latvia are folk songs that speak of love and others that are puns for teasing or just having fun. There are Christmas songs and songs of faith we share with other nations and a wealth of patriotic hymns and chorales, composed and arranged by Latvian musicians as well as translations of classic composers. Beethoven, Mozart, Bach and others are well known by our conductors and musicians.

The following is a translated and paraphrased excerpt from the program of the Latvian Song Festival at Augsburg, August 25, 1946.

RISE AND TAKE HEART

We cannot help but sing. Way back to our rural antiquity, Latvian ears have heard a singing voice in every step of life and work. Since long ago we have heard the song of the lark echoing over the waking, green fields in the early hours of cool mornings. Since antiquity we have heard the nightingale sing at the river bend. When the quiet peace of evening overshadows meadows in the fullness of summer, the scythe held in strong arms sings the harvest song at sunset. The plowshare hums the melody of the plower as it prepares the fertile soil to receive the seed. Together with these singers from nature, sings the man and woman who live among them and earn their livelihood with them. The young shepherd guides his herd and sings by the roadside, the plower sings and steps forward heavily behind his plow. The lovely blond maiden sings her song of love. In song the strong young man proposes to her. For centuries unnamed the songs we sang made us brave, gave us strength in heavy tasks, renewed our faith and hope, and gave us new courage to face the future.

A Latvian will say: "Singing I was born, singing I grew up, singing I lived all life through."

We cannot live without our songs. We sing not only in times of leisure but also in times of heavy labor.

We sing not just to exult and cheer with joy, but also in our deepest pain to console our soul. We sing not just among ourselves at home, but also in a far away land in exile, among people whom we do not know. Rise, take heart and sing. Behold the way to our home.

That memorable event began with a track and field competition, Saturday, August 24th at three o'clock in the afternoon. I wished Imants and I were a few years older and able to take part in the 50 meter dashes, relays and long distance runs. Imants would win. That day in August both of us sat on the bench and, with envy, watched the older boys and girls, Scouts and Guides we knew, compete.

Superimposed on the two hour sporting event was an hour long concert by a brass band. One had to make a choice. I stayed to watch the races.

Sunday morning at nine I had my chance to participate in the event when my Scout Group, together with our sharp-looking Guides, raised the flag in our colony. I had a chance to wear the uniform, march, stand at attention and honor the flag. This was all very meaningful to me.

Sunday, at eleven in the morning, the church was packed for the Worship Service, which was really a sacred concert. I preferred the beautiful singing over the pastor's sermon. Thankfully the sermon was short that Sunday.

The Festival Concert, the highlight of the afternoon, began at three o'clock with the grand entry of fourteen participating choirs from sixteen camps. I sat with my parents on the grass not far from the large, massive stone stage and watched, with amazement, the singers enter by the hundreds.

They were dressed in colorful traditional folk clothing which identified the region where a singer lived in Latvia. I spotted the thirty-member Haunstetten choir, and noted among them the parents of the attractive blond girl who played the piano and danced so well, also the father of the girl both Arnis and I liked. I also saw Arnis' dad, who was an Assistant to the Chairman of the Festival, sitting with the dignitaries. It was impressive. So many of us in exile, yet together; strength in unity, achieved through music.

The concert of twenty songs was impressive, especially the opening and closing songs, as well as others performed by the combined fourteen choirs. Two songs mystified me because I couldn't understand the words. I looked in my program. They weren't in the Latvian I knew, neither German nor English.

I watched the singers enter. August 26, 1946. Augsburg.

My favorite song, as it was for many, was a folk song about a sailor who is promised a maiden in the district of Kurzeme. The first verse, paraphrased:

Blow sweet winds, and sail my craft,
Sail me on to Kurzeme;
A mother of Kurzem's land
Promised me her miller girl.
Promised, promised but denied
Saying I'm a drinking man,
Saying I'm a drinking man,
An addicted horse race fan.

Throughout the festival I kept an eye on Imants. Both of us loved music, but we weren't good singers. Imants thought it hilarious when divas, especially well padded sopranos, opened their mouths wide to project high, forte notes. At one concert in our community hall a renowned soprano was performing an excerpt from a Christmas cantata; her voice was vibrant, and loud. Imants and I exchanged glances. I could see he was holding back upcoming laughter, his lips pursed shut, body shaking, hands protecting his ears. Then with her mouth wide open the soprano overpowered us with an extremely high and vibrant crescendo. Imants' hands slipped from covering his ears to cover his mouth, he jumped out of his seat and ran to the door. Fortunately, we were close to the back entrance. He barely got through the door into the foyer when he burst forth in flat out laughter. I joined him in the laugh.

"Boys, boys, what's going on?" an usher approached us in alarm.

"Somebody cracked a joke," I replied. Imants still laughing.

"Get out of here, calm down, then go back in, sit down and for heaven's sake, behave."

We followed his advice without objection.

There were four other Song Festivals the summer of

1946. Fishbach, Bayreuth, Ansbach and Eichstatt, altogether involving over eight hundred singers. I remember, from stories and pictures, the last Song Festival in Riga; two thousand singers gathered together in 1938.

Latvia Sings.

RABBIT RAPPI

IT WAS DECIDED that each family who wanted a vegetable garden could apply to the camp authorities. The available land between the sides of buildings in our D.P. camp was sectioned into equal parcels according to the number of families who applied. We were among the first to apply. Yes! We wanted a vegetable garden again. The nine meter square land we were apportioned was not as large as the garden we had in Riga, but the thought of growing our own vegetables here in our D.P. camp thrilled us beyond words. We would have fresh vegetables again right from our own garden.

That little garden will be our Latvia, I thought.

Early in the spring of 1946 we prepared the soil for planting. That's right, it was "we." No one could keep me from working with my dad again, digging and overturning the dark soil, raking it smooth and dividing it into beds for the various vegetables for which we had seeds; carrots, green onions, beets, peas, beans and some potatoes. But later I had a surprise for Mom. She had given me money to buy some stamps to add to my stamp collection, but I had come across someone selling little rose bushes. Knowing how much my mom liked roses, I bought and planted one little rose bush in our garden. Was she ever surprised and happy when she saw it. That was one time when it was fun to confess.

"Who planted the rose bush in our garden?" she asked with surprise and happiness in her voice as she ran into our apartment.

"I did!" I confessed with happiness in my voice, too.

Now our early spring labor-of-pleasure was bringing forth the awaited dividends. Everything we had planted was growing. Gladly I watered the plants by hand, and then, for enjoyment, laid down on the dark, almost black, fragrant soil, and observed at eye level the growing plants just like I had done in Riga. Boys don't get dirty lying on the ground, and if they do, the bath is worth the pleasure of sifting the productive soil through one's hands. It felt so cool, even soft, to scoop it up in my palms then let it trickle through my fingers, falling gently into little piles that I would imagine were castles where little people lived. What pleasure a little garden can give to a heart that thrills at the wonder of growing plants and loves the musty fragrance that brings back memories of gardens past.

I would lay there, day dream, and remember my big garden in Riga. I was six, soon to be seven years old, when I planted my first garden where the air raid shelter had been. What I remembered most vividly was the sunflower patch I had planted. It was a sunflower forest to me; an inhabited forest it was, populated by little people. It was a kingdom of my own which I ruled with love and concern for every one of my subjects. They came to me with their problems and squabbles and I would hold court and judge between them.

"King Harijs," little farmer Ned would accuse his neighbor Ped, "Ped stole my shovel and won't give it back," he said.

I would marshal my kingdoms' police and had Ped dragged out of his bed and brought before my court.

"Ped, did you steal your neighbor Ned's little shovel?" I'd ask.

"No, I just borrowed it and forgot to bring it back," said Ped.

"Ped, apologize to Ned,"

"Return the little shovel to your neighbor Ned
And then you may go back and sleep in your bed."
Then came farmer Ilk saying his cows wouldn't give him milk.

I told lazy Ilk to get off his ass, and feed his cows some good green grass.

I would solve all their troubles; just burst them like bubbles.

Their King I could be, that's easy to see.

Yes, I would sit or lie on the ground, my bare feet feeling the pleasing texture of the soil, the coolness of the earth beneath and, with the warmth of the sun on my back, I would make those moments rhyme with the passing of time.

I was fair and my little subjects liked me. But there was something that scared them. Besides the gardens we also had chickens and rabbits, for meat and eggs. But I preferred to think they were for my pleasure, to feed and play with. Rabbits I liked but I used to pull the chickens by their tails.

I adopted one special bunny as my pet. That alabaster white rabbit I had named Rappi. He could talk and become bigger than me; big enough that I could ride on him. That's what frightened my little people. Rappi would hop to me when I would lie on the ground daydreaming about my sunflower forest. So soft was he, a real pleasure to touch, to run my fingers through his silky white fur! Sometimes he would get knots in his fur and I would comb them out. I used to play with his big ears, look into his blue eyes, play with his wiggly nose and listen to his quick breathing. Then Rappi would say, "Time to go leaping." And in a flash he would become as big as a pony, just the right size for me to ride. The sunflowers would reach the height of the pines that grow along the Baltic sea. "Hop on my back," Rappi would say. I obeyed him with delight and, holding on to his ears, off we would go leaping and flying through the air above the lush, green forest of my giant sunflowers. That's what frightened my little subjects. They remained little, so little that ten of them could easily stand in the palm of my hand. They were afraid that Rappi wouldn't see them and squash them under his powerful leaping hind legs.

I spent much time alone in my garden in Riga, now again in Haunstetten, pondering what makes the plants grow, sampling their fragrance and enjoying my daydreams. I wanted to hang on to my fantasies and imagination. They gave me pleasure and they were fun.

Rabbits I liked, but chickens, I pulled by their tails.
May 5, 1938, Riga. Grandma and I in our yard.
Photo: Uncle Rudis.

fourteen

Trouble in the Colony

THE SCREENING

"DAD!" I EXCLAIMED, "What's going on? Where are these people going?" he didn't answer.

People from our colony were loading onto trucks, with all their belongings. Many onlookers had gathered to say goodbye. Some were crying; others, with looks of confusion on their faces, were shaking their heads. Some younger men were displaying anger, disgust. As one young man climbed into the back of the American two and one half ton truck, he was pale as a white sheet. He didn't look at us, but only at his feet. A young mother, climbing in, was crying. I saw her tears when she turned to take her baby, held by a friend. People of all ages, climbing into the two trucks.

"Harij, they have been expelled from our camp," Dad finally spoke.

"Why Dad? Why? Did they do something bad?"

"No, nothing, Harij, nothing bad at all."

"Then why do they have to leave?"

"The Americans say so," Dad answered.

"Why?" I asked again.

"Harij, you were so busy with Scouts and school. You didn't notice and we didn't tell you. Remember the screening we had to go through in Binabiburg?"

"Yes, and I thought the Americans arrested us. Ha! Ha!" I laughed and immediately felt out of place. No one was laughing.

"Yes, that's the one. We had another screening here."

"Another? Here?"

"Yes," said my dad, and I saw anger in his eyes.

"But why?"

"I think the Americans want us to go back to Latvia. If we didn't want to go back, they wanted to know the reason why."

"But we do want to go home to Latvia, don't we Dad?"

"We do, but we can't. You know that, Harij."

"Yeah, I know. The Communists. Damn the Bolsheviks."

"The Communists are allies, friends of Americans."

"The Americans don't believe us that Communism is bad, I know."

"So, Harij, what would you tell them if they asked you to go home to Riga?" Dad asked.

"I get it. These people are being kicked out because they gave the wrong answer."

"Yeah, something like that." I saw anger again.

"What did you tell them?"

"Do you remember what they asked us in Binabiburg?" Dad inquired instead of answering.

"Not really, but I remember better what they did not ask."

"What didn't they ask, Harij?"

"Why we left Latvia. Right, Dad?"

"Right."

"They asked that now, didn't they?"

"Yes."

"And what did you tell them?"

"The truth."

"That we fled from the Communists because they had tortured many Latvians, deported thousands to Siberia as slaves, and were going to take me away from you?"

"Harij, if I told them that, we'd be climbing into these trucks."

"What did you tell them?"

"That the Germans evacuated us."

"But that's only half the truth," I observed.

"But that's not a lie. You little interrogator. Are you giving me the third degree?"

"No, Dad, I just want to know what happened. Why are these people kicked out, really."

"I don't know, Harij. There is some talk about closing D.P. camps. This may be the first step. If anyone has something to go back to, they want them to go back. Americans won't look after us forever."

"These people are being sent back to Latvia, Dad?"

"I don't know. Probably."

"You told them we have nothing to go back to?"

"Yes."

"But that's not true, Dad."

"What do we have to go back to in Riga, Harij?"

"Our house, yard, rabbits, chickens, your job."

"Harij, the house and the yard weren't ours. We rented. I have no job–the factory was closed, probably destroyed."

"If we owned the house and yard, we would be on those trucks?"

"If we admitted it, that's if we did own the property."

"And we don't, I mean didn't"

"That's right, Harij. We weren't aristocrats."

"Then how did Uncle Edis get by? The Kraujas?"

"Harij, so long as Latvia is occupied and ruled by Stalin's Communistic regime, none of us has anything to go back to in Latvia."

"Dad, I hope some day Americans will find out how evil Stalin and his government are. They aren't friends of America, they have deceived America. They're just like Hitler, they want to rule the world. Oh, Dad I hope there'll never be another war."

"I hope so too, Harij."

The trucks were loaded. The motors started. The big wheels began to turn, throwing some dust into the air. We waved but they didn't wave back. I saw emptiness where the trucks had been parked. Emptiness, sadness, a tragic mistake, another day like Black June 14th, when thousands of Latvians were deported to Siberia just eight days short of the German invasion and liberation from Soviet tyranny.

THE HOPE

IN THE JUNE 1947 ISSUE of his magazine, Uncle Edis, in his editorial, wrote about President Truman having initiated legislation to allow the D.P.'s in Germany to emigrate to the United States. Good news! We hoped and prayed the legislation would become reality, allowing us to rebuild our lives in America. Also in the news were reports of UNRRA and IRO personnel returning to the U.S. and campaigning on our behalf. The American soldiers who had worked with us, were also affirming that D.P.'s in Germany were hard working people who understood democracy and yearned for peace and the opportunity to rebuild their lives; the opportunity to live again. When the captain in charge of bomb demolition returned home to America, I wondered what he said about my dad.

The answer to our question, "Where shall we go, what will become of us?" was taking a most unexpected but a wonderful turn. United States? Great Britain? Canada? Australia? One day we may become Latvian-Australians, Latvian-Canadians or Latvian-Americans.

THE ANKLE

TRACK AND FIELD EVENTS were frequent. If the races and chases organized during intermissions between classes at school would be recognized as sporting events, we had track and field events every day. In my class, Imants was the fastest, but for second place I had lots of competition, even from the girls, though I didn't admit that. In track and field events girls competed with girls and boys with boys. No one could prove a girl could outrun me. When she did in our chases, I would always say, "I let her."

A Latvian, Lithuanian and Estonian track and field event was organized in our colony and I was competing in the fifty and one hundred meter dashes, running broad jump, and high jump. Older girls and boys could also compete in pole vault, disc and javelin throwing, shot put, two hundred and four hundred meter relays and hurdles.

Fifty meter dash results–First place: Imants. Second: Harijs. Bravo for Latvia.

Hundred meter results–First place: Imants. Third: Harijs. Great for Latvia.

Broad jump results–First place: Imants. Second: Harijs. Bravo for Latvia.

The last event for me was high jump. I was third in the jumping sequence. The bar between the poles was set at one meter. The first jumper sprinted, and jumped, pushing off with his left foot, neatly clearing the bar. The second jumper sprinted, approached the bar head on, jumped and cleared the bar.

My turn. I sprinted and approached from the right and sailed high above the bar. Some applause! "Show off!" someone ribbed me. All competitors cleared the bar at the one meter height. The bar was set at 110 centimeters. First jumper cleared, second didn't. I sprinted and approached the bar from the right, jumped and sailed over the bar. After all competitors had their chance, the jumper before me who knocked down the bar had his second chance. He didn't make it on his second nor on his third try. He was out. Understandable, as he was a head shorter than me. There was a boy considerably taller than me. "He'll win," I thought, "height helps."

The bar was set at 120 centimeters. I cleared it on my first try. The tall boy cleared it. Two more were out.

The bar was now at 125 centimeters. No one except the tall boy cleared it on the first try. I cleared it on my second try. Two more were out.

The bar loomed at me from 130 centimeters, at my eye level. No one had cleared it as my turn came. That was a challenge. I sprinted, approached again from the right and sailed up and over, cleared the bar on my first try. I heard some cheers. After their second and third tries only the tall boy and I were left.

The bar went up to the 135 centimeter mark. That was above my eye level. The tall boy jumped and knocked down the bar. I jumped and the bar went down. Tall boy jumped and the bar went down. I had to meet the challenge. I took a deep breath, sprinted and gave it all I had, jumped and sailed into the air, and I cleared the bar. So did the tall boy on his third try.

If the bar was raised to 145 centimeters, a record would be broken if either of us cleared it. One more level to go; the bar now stood at 140 centimeters, way above my eye level.

The tall boy sprinted and jumped, and the bar went down. My turn, and the bar went down. His turn, and the bar went down. My turn, and the bar went down.

It was his last turn. He looked at me, took a deep breath, exhaled, sprinted, jumped and the bar went down. There were cheers for me now. "Harij! Harij! Go, Harij, Go!" I took my position, closed my eyes and relaxed, opened my eyes, took a deep breath and, with determination, sprinted. I approached again from the right; the liftoff was from my right foot. I sailed up, I didn't feel the bar! I had cleared it!

As I landed I saw the bar in place between the poles. But the landing was painful, so painful I couldn't get up. Cheering people helped me get up but I couldn't put weight on my left ankle. It hurt. Oh, how it hurt! Another trip to the first aid station ended with a jeep ride to the hospital in Augsburg. I won the event and sprained my ankle. I was brought home late at night with a plaster cast from my big toe to just below the knee. Was it worth the jeep ride? No! Attention from girls? Yes!

Another six weeks of limping. But the feeling was heavenly when the cast was removed. I could finally put on both of my shoes and walk, walk, walk a wonderful walk!

At the track and field event in Haunstetten.
Left to right: Mom, Dad, Uncle Edis, Aunts Anna & Hermina.

THE ROSES

MY MOM'S BIRTHDAY, the 8th of August, was just two days away. The rosebush I planted last year in the spring had developed ten beautiful red roses in three clusters. Two clusters of three and one cluster of four dark red roses. A perfect gift for my mom. People had commented on how well the rosebush had done. Of course it should, as I watered it every other day, and fertilized and trimmed it as necessary, removing dead leaves and branches. The aroma around the bush was wonderful to inhale. The thorns, however, were sharp and could draw blood easily. The botanist living in our fourplex said the rosebush was "Red Pinocchio" of the "Floribundas" variety, one of the easiest to care for. (He had to say that, didn't he.)

The morning of the 8th I planned to get up early, cut the roses, arrange them nicely in the potato soup can, and surprise Mom at breakfast. I knew she liked roses. She wasn't a perfect Mom with all her fears, but I loved her very much. She sewed clothes for me and cooked. I knew she loved me. It'll be a happy moment for me when she delights at the sight of the red roses, I thought.

The evening of the 7th, I inspected the roses once more. Yes, they were beautiful and they were fragrant. Mom would love them.

The morning of the 8th, before anyone was up, I sneaked out of our room. If Mom or Dad heard me leave the room, they'd assume I had gone to the bathroom. I went to the kitchen, found the sharp knife, then quietly out the front door and to our garden. My dark red roses were gone!

Someone had cut them, stolen them during the night. I was angry. I thought of finding the thief. I thought of revenge, but I remembered the windows and the lessons I had learned. I snuck back quietly to our room and into my cot.

During breakfast I wished Mom a happy birthday. I told

her about the roses. There were some wet eyes: mine, Dad's and hers. She said to me quietly, "I love you, Harij."

THE FIRE

IT WAS A CLOUDY AND DARK LATE AUTUMN EVENING. The wind was whistling outside the single widow pane that separated me from the cold. Dad was reading my uncle's magazine, Mom was knitting and I was about to finish homework for my arithmetic class when I heard sirens, reminding me of past air raid warnings. The three of us impulsively stood and exchanged anxious glances.

"What's that all about?" I asked.

"A fire alarm, I think," said Dad.

I went to the window. In the dark I saw only the light in the window of Imants' apartment kitchen. Imants' dad came to the window. I saw the alarm on his face as he pointed beyond the corner of our fourplex and, turning his head, said something to whomever was in the kitchen with him. He quickly went away from the window but almost instantly appeared on the porch outside the front door of their fourplex. Now I could hear him through our closed window as he shouted, "Fire!"

My dad had also run outside, seen the fire and shouted, "Fire!" All of us ran outside, joining the stampede of people emerging from the doors of other apartments. There was a red glow above and beyond the roofs of the fourplexes, in the direction of the ruins of the Messerschmitt factory. Sparks were racing towards the moving clouds above, creating a scene reminiscent of days gone by. A nearby building was on fire in our colony. The crackling of the flames told it was a wooden building, one of the army barracks.

A former officer of the Latvian army, living opposite us

in the fourplex, took charge saying, "Gentlemen, we must go and help the firemen, ladies please stay and watch over our children. Don't let them come to the fire."

Without hesitation the men from our building joined others rushing in the direction of the glowing sky, but I was offended by what the man had said. That's a fine how-do-you-do, I thought. One and a half years ago I was old enough to help firemen put out a forest fire, but at home I'm not old enough to help save one of our buildings!

I was all the more annoyed when I saw older Scouts joining the stampede to the fire, while my mom had her arms on my shoulders, making certain I stayed put, by her skirts. Then something I hadn't expected happened, relieving my hurt feelings. Most of the men, including my fellow Scouts, my dad and uncles, were sent back. The fire chief had kept only the ones who had fire fighting experience, the rest he had begged to go away and stay away. I had fire fighting experience, I thought. He would've let me help.

We lost our Community Hall. Regardless of all the efforts to extinguish the blaze, the wooden building burned to the ground. Where we had listened to concerts, danced, and presented programs as students and Scouts, now was a ruin of black ashes and tangled electrical wire. The twisted wood burning stove stood atop stained concrete blocks which had once been the firm foundation of our social hall.

It bothered me to look at the pitiful remains of our hall, the monument of our social life, the emblem of our community. Why? I had seen the ruins of an uncountable number of buildings, edifices compared to this minor army barrack. Why did my heart feel so drawn towards these black ashes? Were the ashes telling me that everything must end?

THE STRIKE

THE ELEMENTARY SCHOOL in Haunstetten was near and dear to my heart. I went to classes not because I had to, but because I wanted to. Books were a rare treasure, and to read and study, a privilege. I didn't know what I wanted to be when I grew up, but the direction I wanted to follow was emerging. To discern it more clearly, I knew I must learn. In this I wasn't the exception among my peers, but the norm. We all wanted to learn and be ready to accept responsibility in the world as our turn came.

We loved and respected our teachers but, motivated to learn like young adults, we discovered that all teachers were not equal. There was a teacher from whom we had problems learning. The teacher either didn't know how to teach or didn't want to teach. This teacher, in place of encouraging us to learn, as the others did, confused us. If we didn't listen to this teacher and just read the text book, we did better in exams. What were we, young elementary pupils, to do? It was "we" the whole class, not just me and some of my friends. We brainstormed for weeks during intermissions, after school and during the times the teacher came late to class.

One day it exploded. The bell rang, we were in our desks with text books on top of our desks and notebooks open, but no teacher in front of the class. A girl suggested, "We have talked about this. The teacher isn't teaching. Let's go on strike and walk out."

"Yeah! Yeah! Good idea! Let's walk out!" were some of the responses from members of the class.

"Let's go," someone said.

Instinctively, a student went to the blackboard and chalked in big letters, "Class on Strike." I picked up my notebook and textbook, put them in my black briefcase and, with all my classmates, walked out. Since this was the last class of the day, we went around the back of the school and home, avoiding the teachers in the staff room.

The following morning the bell rang for the first period to begin and in walked not our teacher for the first period, but Mrs. Lapsina, our principal, followed by Mr. Salins, our class advisor, who was liked by everyone. We stood, as was customary. After the teachers were seated we kept on standing, which was not customary. The principal told us to sit. We did and the classroom fell gravely silent. I knew; we knew, what was coming.

The principal began with a scolding, telling us how unprecedented, inappropriate, rude, deplorable, unacceptable and severely punishable our behavior the day before had been. She wanted to know whose idea it was. There was absolute silence. Whose was it? Was it all of us who had brooded for weeks, or it was no one's at all? She wanted to know why we did it. No one volunteered to say anything. It was too complicated to answer or explain. Then, in alphabetical order, she started to ask us individually, "Why did you walk out of class yesterday?"

One after another my classmates answered, "Because everyone else was walking out."

She came to the K's and asked, "Harijs, why did you walk out, yesterday?"

I foolishly answered, "Because the teacher is not teaching us, but confusing us."

"Does anyone else think that?" she asked.

Again that grave silence in the classroom. The interrogation was over and I went with the principal and our class advisor to the teacher's room.

I was in serious trouble once more. In the teacher's room I tried to explain our grievances with the teacher we walked out on. Our grievances, the grievances of the whole class, not just mine. They listened but suspected I was the instigator. My parents were called to the school. They were shocked to hear the teachers suspecting I was the instigator of a strike in elementary school.

I spent days trying to explain to the powers that this particular teacher was confusing us, and that it was not just me but the whole class who thought so, and that no one in particular had schemed and organized the others to go on strike. I made no progress.

Uncle Edis got involved in the scandal. Through his magazine he was a benefactor of the school, enabling the school to acquire supplies, notebooks and textbooks. Some teachers couldn't understand how his little nephew could be such a rebel in a school he supported. Uncle Edis asked me for my explanation, but my credibility in this event was waning with him, as it was with everyone else.

The class was interrogated several times. Inspired by my honesty and feeling some guilt, my classmates eventually backed my story of a mutual dissatisfaction with the teacher's way of teaching. The teachers eventually accepted that there were no instigators of the strike and also that there was some basis for our dissatisfaction. They also believed that our strike or walkout was spontaneous.

From fearing I may be expelled from my beloved school for inciting a wildcat strike, I had the delight and happiness of seeing on my report card a perfect grade of 5 under the category of Behavior.

THE PARTING

THE SUMMER OF 1948 brought news that the hoped-for legislation to relocate D.P.'s. to the United States, Canada, Australia, Great Britain, Argentina and other countries, had passed.

To accomplish this massive effort, organizations like the Lutheran World Federation were established, with local offices in the countries accepting us.

News this good was loaded with a sense of unreality. Could this really be happening? We will all be leaving Haunstetten. My parents will establish themselves in a country much further from Latvia than Germany; we'll be scattered all over the world. It will be goodbye, again, to my friends, school and Scouts. Good news, though bittersweet news, mixing anticipation with anxiety, certainty with uncertainty. IRO was to close all D.P. camps by July 1, 1950. Where will I be two years from now?

We were asked to list three countries of preference. Dad's sister, Emilija and her daughter, Velta, came to visit, hoping to influence us on our choices. They were going to Australia. Aunt Emilija had met an Australian soldier who was sponsoring both her and Velta. Their immigration process to Australia was underway.

I listened to the intense discussions during her visit. Dad, influenced by his sister, argued for Australia to be our first choice. The Smits preferred Canada, arguing Canada had a more European flavor through the nation's relationships with Great Britain and France. The Raudupes, having worked with Americans, preferred the U.S. The one point they agreed on was that we all choose the same country as our first choice. This put Dad in a position of strength since his sister was going to Australia.

"We're in this situation because we had to get away from Russians," said Dad, "Let's get as far away as we can."

Sure, I thought, but it's also the furthest from Latvia.

As a family, we decided Australia was our first choice, Canada, second, and the U.S., third. We were informed there was no guarantee a family would get their first choice.

The country a family was called to, was determined by job availability for the head of the family. Refugee resettlement organizations in the respective countries located employers guaranteeing employment in a given trade. Then, a tradesman who was qualified for the job would be called to accept it. Dad was a machine molder in a foundry, Uncle Edis was a baker and Uncle Rudis learned chicken farming since professional or white collar work was not available to D.P.'s. Medical doctors learned to be orderlies; businessmen and pastors learned to be janitors, farm hands, construction workers or some other trade. (Professionals, such as doctors, nurses, architects and lawyers cannot practice their profession without being licensed by respective boards through examinations and interviews.)

Since our choices were English speaking countries, my parents enrolled in an English language course. I had taken English in school for almost four years and could ask, for example, "Where is the bathroom?" or "How much does it cost?" Though I was far from being fluent in English, a new phase had begun in my life: I was tutoring my parents.

Every morning I would wake up, wondering, "Will the call come today?" Every day there were conversations about life in Australia, Canada and the U.S. I studied maps of the three countries, and read all I could about their climates, vegetation and animals.

The kangaroo and the smaller wallaby fascinated me. Big rabbit hoppies, they were, hopping on two legs, carrying their babies. I liked the koala. The duck nosed platypus would make a funny pet, I thought. There were crocodiles in Northern Australia, also in Florida, in the U.S.

An excited Imants caught up to me one evening, saying breathlessly, "We got our call, we did!"

"To where?" I asked, matching his excitement.

"To America, to Iowa."

"Where?"

"To the United States. Iowa is a state. Here, I wrote it down:

Pochahontas, Iowa, United States of America."

Imants' family was the first family to leave our camp, others soon followed. We said our farewells to Imants' family in the fall of 1948, two or three months after receiving the news. It was happening, again. Friendships formed, and then dissolved. I waved to him as he sat in the back of a departing two and one half ton American Army truck. Through the tears in my eyes I saw Imants waving back.

"Write to me when you get there!" I shouted after him.

"I will," I heard him promise.

He did, and an exchange of letters was started that was to last for years.

After saying goodbye to Imants, returning to school was difficult. I couldn't concentrate. I could only think about Imants and the fun we had together; the trouble we got into. When I looked at his unoccupied desk, tears formed in my eyes. Would I ever see him again, run with him? Swim with him?

Christmas 1948 was around the corner. On Wednesday, December 16th, I woke with the usual question in mind, "Will we get the call today?" Yes, we did!

We had exchanged several letters with Aunt Emilija, who was happily settled in Melbourne, Australia. She wrote about the good life and many opportunities in Melbourne and wished we were there to rebuild our lives together. Wedding plans with the Australian soldier were in the making. She was enjoying, once again, the bright side of life. I was looking forward to moving to Australia and catching my "Australian Rappi", this time a kangaroo.

But on December 16, 1948 the IRO office informed my parents that a job was waiting for Dad at Atlas Foundry in Tacoma, Washington, United States of America. Our medical examination was scheduled for January 12th, 1949. After receiving the medical clearance, and we foresaw no problems there, we were to pack our bags and be ready to go, as the resettlement program was moving quickly. It seemed unreal, but it was true. We were going to America. America! What we feared may happen, did happen.

Goodbye Aunt Emilija. The family will be separated once more when we immigrate to the United States

But of course we were excited and happy in spite of that. The United States was one of our choices. The protocol was to accept the arranged-for call to one of the three countries chosen. Dad had a job with a guaranteed salary in the land that flowed with milk and honey. What more could one ask for? From his letters, I knew Imants liked America, and I knew I would too. I wrote to Imants immediately. I told Arnis, and everyone I met on the streets. Next day when I entered the classroom, I didn't say mundane words like "Hi" or "Good morning," I shouted. "I'm going to America!"

"Where? Where?" asked the classmates.

"To America! America!" I repeated, reaching up with my arms. "To Tacoma, Washington State."

"Where," they asked again, "is that?"

Christmas 1948 was filled with excitement and expectation. My aunts and uncles celebrated with many toasts to, "The future Americans!" There was no end to the advice and speculation during our after dinner discussions. The faraway Pacific Coast of America in a city called Tacoma; the name Tacoma sounded so strange to our ears.

"Erna will live in a luxurious apartment," said Aunt Anna. "She'll sew herself new silk, or velvet or soft wool dresses."

"Erna will buy white leather shoes, nylon stockings and purses to match her dresses. She'll wear a fur coat and have lots of hats," said Tinte.

"Erna will sleep until noon and have her work done by machines," said Aunt Hermina, "washing machines, dust sucking machines, ice boxes."

"Arvids will wear a top hat, a tux and white spats on his shoes," said Uncle Richards. "Too bad he doesn't wear glasses …he might smoke a Cuban cigar."

"Arvids will get fat eating pork roasts, ham, wiener

schnitzels and caviar," said Uncle Rudis adding, "and cream puffs for dessert."

"Arvids will be a millionaire," declared Uncle Edis. "He'll save his money and won't strive to buy a car."

That did it. Enough of this adult ultra foolishness. I had to say something sensible, something that would come true.

"Uncle Edi, my dad may not strive to buy a car, but I will. Uncle Edi, after I buy a typewriter and a phonograph, a big car with a red steering wheel, no roof and white tires, is exactly what I'll buy in America, I will."

"Ah you little runt of a Zepher," was all my uncle could think of in response to my self-fulfilling prophecy.

Right, I thought, I will buy a blue car with a red steering wheel.

After the medical exams on January 12th, we were cleared for emigration. Our appointment with the Consul at the American Consulate in Augsburg was February 15th. In our case the meeting was a formality, as we had been screened some time ago. The Consul checked and verified our papers, and asked if we had questions about America. We had many questions but dared not ask even one. He asked us, "Are you happy to emigrate to America?"

"Yes, we are," replied Dad through an interpreter. "Very happy."

Then, looking at me, he inquired about my name, "Harijs. Would that be Harry in English? That's a presidential name. Our president, Harry Truman."

"Yes," I said, speaking English for the first time in public. "In English it is Harry and in America I shall be your next President."

Mom gave me a look of horror, when the Consul said, "Very good, President Harry, very good indeed. You speak with a presidential accent already," and he puffed his big cigar a couple times.

As soon as we knew we were going to America, instruction in key subjects was accelerated for me, together with end of the year exams. I wrote them and completed the sixth grade. I was thirteen years old.

Mom and Tinte made a list of our belongings for customs and packed our earthly treasures in wooden crates to be picked up the 23rd of February. The driver of the truck, checking the list of contents, couldn't help but smile and laugh at a translation Tinte had written on the box containing my two suits. He read aloud, "2 boys dress."

My last day in Haunstetten was a day of paradoxes; a day of joy and sorrow, anticipation and remembrance, fulfillment and emptiness. The ever nagging question, "What will become of us?" was being answered. The new world powers had heard our pleas for an opportunity to forge a new life and granted them to us. Will we make the best of it? Will I?

Lessons or not, my parents didn't speak English, nor did I, really. My English was barely good enough to get by on the street. Nonetheless, I would have to take over as interpreter for my parents.

We knew little about life in America. In theory I understood what it was like to live with equal opportunity under a democratic government. My experience, however, had only been a police state under ruthless dictators. Haunstetten was familiar, even Germany. But the United States – a world power that had overthrown Hitler by destroying Germany, and then chosen the Communists as Allies, didn't make any sense to me.

I'll make new friends in America, but once again, I must part with the friends that I have. Ojars and I didn't become the best of friends, but I must also leave him behind, along with my beloved aunts and uncles. I'll miss them all very much, especially Tinte who had been so understanding and generous to me.

I was going to America, but where will my aunts and uncles, and the Kraujas go? America? Not necessarily. Our call to America had no bearing on where their call will come from. The first choice, Australia, stood as firmly as ever on their applications. Were we parting forever?

I said goodbye to Mr. & Mrs. Salins. They assured me I would do well in America and once more urged me not to forget my heritage, but be proud of it, as well as a credit to it.

I said goodbye to Arnis. We shed a tear, but we also laughed. Now he had the girls all to himself. I bequeathed him that! When we first came to Haunstetten, we agreed, we weren't sure if we wanted to be seen with a girl, but now we didn't want to be seen without one. Yes, I said goodbye to the girls, even Dzintra. How did I say it? Of course, like a man who's going to be a big fourteen this year. I looked right into their lovely eyes.

Our departure. Harijs and Dad in hats; Mom, Aunt Anna and Uncle Edis looking onto, and behind, Harijs.

Since most of our belongings were sent ahead to Bremen, Tinte lent us sheets and blankets for the night. It wasn't easy to fall asleep, but the morning came quickly. We dressed, shared a breakfast of coffee with bread and jam, then we hugged and hugged and hugged. We knew our first ride would take us to an assembly area on the American Army Base in Augsburg. Tinte and Aunt Anna said they'd follow us there. The time had come to go. The trucks that would take us to the Army Base were waiting.

I saw the trucks. They were surrounded by a large crowd of people. All my teachers were there, my friends, girls from my class, people we had known in the camp. Tears were flowing everywhere. Once more I made the rounds, saying my goodbyes and hearing well wishes. Then, like in dream, I climbed into the truck. I got to sit by the gate. People cheered and waved and I waved back. Is this really happening? Overwhelmed by a sense of unreality I was aware only of myself. The familiar people inside the truck and those who were waving goodbyes became like shadows moving in moonlight, like mists of the sea. The motor started and I sensed the forward motion.

We departed Haunstetten on the morning of February 25, 1949.

Waving goodbye to our friends.

fifteen

Across the Atlantic to America

IT WAS A SHORT RIDE to the American Infantry Base in Augsburg, where America-bound families from the Hochfeld D.P. Colony joined us in the designated assembly area, a large central field surrounded by long barracks. American soldiers were coming and going. Across the field a platoon of soldiers were exercising. I noticed Vija*, a girl from my class, and her parents, Mr. & Mrs. Grinvalds, also her older brother, Vitauts, climbing out of the other truck. Vija was medium height and slender, with dark brown hair draping to her shoulders. She was wearing a tan coat reaching just below her knees. She had nicely shaped legs, tan shoes. Why hadn't I noticed her before? She was very attractive. She was also going to America.

"Vija," I said, going to her. "What a surprise."

"Surprise indeed, Harijs. You finally noticed me."

"Sorry, Vija, really sorry." I tried to apologize, thinking how blind I had been.

"Sorry you should be. We were in the same class almost four years and you didn't even know I existed."

"That's not so," I tried to protest, then realized the

---

* Vija appears in the Grade 6 class photo on page 164, on the extreme right hand side in the front row. Pronounced "Vee-ya".

uselessness.

"I know, Harij, you had your eye on other girls."

"Vija, I'm sorry, really sorry," and I was.

"You were so taken up with going to America, you didn't even hear when I said that I was, too."

"Sorry, I'm sorry."

"Sorry. Really! Is that all you can say?"

"No, Vija, but that's how I feel."

"I know, Harij. We both are excited about going to America but also frightened, sometimes I don't know what I'm doing, saying or feeling. I'm going to America but I think more about what I'm leaving."

"I know, Vija. It hurt when Imants left, now I'm leaving Arnis, others too."

"Yes. By now we should be used to saying goodbye, we've done it so many times."

"So many times we've been hurt," I said.

"It must be hard for you to leave your aunts and uncles."

"Yes, especially Aunt Marta. How about you?"

"I have relatives, too," she said. "Friends."

"So we hurt and are excited at the same time."

"Yes. I have mixed feelings."

"Vija, can I ask you something?"

"What?"

"Can we be friends on this trip?"

"Harij, we don't even know if we'll be on the same ship."

"Vija, let's chance it. Shall we?"

She didn't answer, only looked in my eyes. Smiling, she started to walk and motioned with her head for me to follow. Our parents were milling around, talking with one another. It had been announced the bus taking us to the train station would leave at four in the afternoon. We had time, so Vija and I walked slowly, side by side in silence, crisscrossing the large field several times before we rejoined our parents.

Tinte, Aunt Anna, Uncle Edis and Rudis came to see us at the assembly area as they had promised. They had ridden on the electric trolley. I wanted to hug and hang on to them as long as possible. I didn't want to let go. The long, cold fingers of the pain of separation were reaching for my heart. At times I thought my confused emotions were spinning me into an ethereal world of unreality. Were the goodbyes I was about to say to my friends and family real, for keeps, forever?

To add another dimension to my sense of unreality, Zaiga, another girl from my class, came looking for me. She told me she had a hard time finding me in the crowd, but she wanted to see me just once more. She told me she would miss me. She asked me why I didn't "ring her" the years we lived in Haunstetten. I wasn't sure what she meant by "ring her" and thought better of asking. I noticed she, too, was very attractive with long blond hair in two neat pigtails, blue eyes, and fair complexion.

How blind I was, sitting in that desk at school, I thought. You fool. You missed it all, and now it's too late.

Was I looking at girls with different eyes now, seeing in them something very special, unique and attractive?

Vija joined us and the three of us reminisced about incidents that had happened at school, especially the strike, and the chases during breaks between classes. Both girls said they liked to catch me, because then I'd be the "dog," and catch them back. Our conversation shifted to Vija's and my "future life together" in Bremen and the journey across the Pacific to America .

"Lucky for you two," Zaiga concluded. "You get to be travel companions across the wide ocean."

I explained we didn't know if we would be on the same ship. Zaiga just looked at me and then at Vija and smiled as if to say that I was now Vija's problem.

The three of us went for a slow walk around the field,

thinking aloud about our destinies. Talking also about how painful it was to say goodbye, and how much more painful when the goodbyes disclosed missed opportunities of more intimate friendships. Unreal, unreal, unreal! My insides hurt and my heart was sinking in a pond of swirling emotions as I walked between those two attractive girls, having an honest heart to heart talk about our feelings. How long can I hold back the torrent of upwelling tears?

Arnis and Hermanis, two more from my class, rode on their bicycles to see Vija and me once more. Soon the whole class arrived on a flat bed truck. I was overwhelmed. There was a lump in my throat as I saw Vija turning pale. I went to her and put my arm around her, but she pulled away, tears in her eyes. The whole class had come, for the second time that day, to send us off to America. We were hugged and slapped on the back. A friend gave me a swift but easy kick in the butt.

"Farewell. Take care. Good luck. Be good. Be brave. Remember us and send us some chewing gum. Candies. Chocolate. Farewell."

Tears were rolling down my cheeks. I was leaving such good friends behind. Goodbye my friends.

The buses to take us to the train station rolled into the field at ten minutes to four. I hugged my aunts and uncles again. They would follow us to the station, but my friends I would see no more. Vija's family boarded the bus, and we followed. Vija and I took window seats so we could wave to our classmates for the last time. The buses left the field as scheduled at 4:00 p.m. There was a large round clock on one of the barracks.

My aunts and uncles were already at the station. How their American taxi got ahead of us, I never found out. The train we were to board was at the station, the locomotive steaming, the conductor shouting, "All aboard for Bremen and Bremerhaven. All aboard!"

We had about five minutes to linger, to hug, to hold

each other in our arms, to wish good luck, good health, and God's loving protection. We boarded. I sat by the window, looking at Tinte standing on the platform. She was crying, Aunt Anna was wiping her eyes and so were my two uncles. I heard the clang of the iron bumpers and felt the gentle pull as the train began to move. I heard the muffled puffs of the steam-powered locomotive. The train began to roll faster and faster taking me away from my aunts and uncles. Soon their silhouettes slipped out of my view. I saw them no more. The lump in my throat rolled into my eyes, and a flood of tears cascaded down my cheeks. I cried and cried and cried like a baby, with heart, and soul and voice.

Everyone in the day coach was crying, sobbing and wiping tears from their eyes. All of us had left relatives and dear friends behind, with no assurance of ever seeing them again. I was aware only of the people I had left. Deep within I felt the pain, the sorrow, the emptiness of separation. In my sorrow, America didn't exist, but only images of friends and loved ones left behind.

The rhythmic clatter of steel against steel, the frequent whistles from the locomotive at road crossings, the rush of wind and louder clatter when the conductor opened the door at the end of the coach, all spoke of the increasing distance between me and my aunts and uncles, my friends. The clattering wheels were ruthlessly taking me further and further away. My heart was at war with the probability that I would never see them again.

A porter came with coffee and chicken sandwiches for supper. I ate, but the sandwiches were tasteless, the coffee, bitter. Tinte had given me a loaf of shortbread she had baked. I broke a piece from the little loaf and ate it. It tasted good but the taste intensified the grief of separation from my dear aunt.

Night was falling and darkness overshadowed the landscape, hiding cities that lay in ruins. It was a cloudy night, no stars, no moon, only an occasional raindrop striking the window, a tear from clouds I couldn't see.

I went to sit with Vija. We looked at each other with reddened eyes. We talked about Scouts, Guides and school, our memories. She said she was sleepy. I wished her good night; tomorrow will be a better day. I went back to sit with my parents, and soon fell asleep.

A porter woke me, with a breakfast of coffee and a chicken sandwich. I tasted it. Not bad. I waved good morning to Vija. She smiled and waved for me to come over. I took the sandwich and coffee and walked to sit with her. We ate our sandwiches and speculated what the transition camp in Bremen would be like. Gunars, a boy from our class had gone there earlier. We wondered if he might still be there. We didn't know how long we would stay there. Both of us hoped we would be on the same ship. We'd like that very much. We talked all morning until the porter came with lunch. Coffee and sauerkraut sandwiches. Not bad at all. Actually, very good. I ate with Vija, then went back to sit with Mom and Dad. Soon the train would stop in Bremen and we would be taken to the transition camp for final processing. Then, as ships became available, we would board one and sail to America.

The train came to a stop. Dad picked up the brown suitcase containing our personal belongings and I picked up the paper sack I had made for Uncle Rudis' store, containing Tinte's shortbread. Two large buses were waiting for us. This time I managed to sit with Vija, behind her parents. The sense of her consoling presence by my side made the ride to the transition camp seem short.

We disembarked and were told to stay in family groups and have our papers in hand. We would be assigned quarters and later given access to our belongings that were shipped earlier. As our papers were checked, a military police officer asked what was in my brown paper sack. I showed him Tinte's shortbread. He took it from me. I was close to tears again. Tinte had baked it for me. I wanted it.

Was that how people were treated in America? Then, as if to add to the heaviness in my heart, Dad and I were separated from Mom. Men and women had separate quarters. In this large and imposing camp, I didn't like that at all.

Dad and I were assigned a large room to share with other men in a multi-storey brick building. Our cots were side by side along a windowless wall. The common latrine and shower were at the end of the hall.

The women fared better. They were housed in a building with small rooms occupied by two or three women. Vija and her mom shared a room. My mom was assigned a room to share with Mrs. Rozental, a widow who soon became a friend of our family.

The separation was perplexing. The war hadn't separated my mom from me, not even for a single day, but now the Americans have, and they took the shortbread Tinte baked for me. Germans never did that. What am I to think? But bunking with men reminded me of camping with the Scouts. I would look forward to that even if there wasn't a boy my age in the large room.

The first night we had meat for supper: pork roast, potatoes, gravy and vegetable soup. Great. There was even milk and cookies on the table. Mom joined us for supper in the large dining hall. The camp may be okay after all, especially if I could eat with Vija sometimes!

Next day I met Gunars over a breakfast of "burned white bread" (toast), jam, bacon and scrambled eggs. American cooking was great! Vija joined Gunars and me at the table. Yeah! It felt like a Haunstetten reunion. We were allowed to eat as much as we wanted, so we took our time and enjoyed our new standard of living to the fullest. Gunars told us he was boarding ship tomorrow, February 27th. His family was packed and ready to board, allowing the three of us a fun day together. We explored the camp under Gunars' guidance, reminisced, played games pretending it was the break between classes at school and speculated about life in America.

"What do you think America is like?" asked Gunars.

"It's a big country," I said, "and we're going to cross it on trains, all the way to the Pacific Coast. I'll really get to see what America's like."

"We're staying in New York. It's a big city," noted Vija.

"Do you think you'll like that?" I asked Vija.

"Oh yes!" she exclaimed. "I'll be a big city girl. Wear pretty dresses, go to movies, concerts. There must be good ballet teachers in New York. I'll dance on a real stage with hundreds of people watching. I heard girls wear makeup in America all the time, not just on stage."

Vija was so right that in Haunstetten I had my eye on other girls. In some group numbers Vija had danced alongside the girl I had watched and admired, the girl that didn't know I existed. I should have watched Vija. So much I had missed. So short was the time to make it up.

"I wonder what American girls are like," commented Gunars.

"Oh Gunars, you'll see. They're not as pretty as Latvian girls. You see, they need makeup to be pretty," Vija teased.

"You're right, Vija," I said, enjoying the eye contact with her, "You're pretty without any of that."

"Oh Harij, don't be so…" she turned away. "So what do you think American boys are like?" She looked at me and I enjoyed our re-entry into eye contact.

"They're ugly but they drive cars. Big ones," I answered.

"How do you know? Are you going to have a car?" she asked.

"Certainly. A blue one with a red steering wheel, open to the sky!"

"Really Harij. Will you take me for a ride?"

"Of course, Vija. Anytime."

"Really?" Vija smiled, looked away and giggled.

"Cut that out, you two!" Gunars laughed.

After a fun day, Vija and I said farewell to Gunars, this time without tears. He sailed for America early the next day.

I was looking forward to a day with Vija all to myself. But where was she? I didn't see her at breakfast, neither at lunch nor supper. I looked for her all day and didn't find her. It upset me.

In the evening Mom, Dad and I went to a Lutheran Worship Service led by a Latvian Pastor also going to America.

The morning of February 28th we had an appointment with the American Consul. However, Dad thought we should get our vaccinations before we saw him. We went to the clinic, got in the queue, but the queue was moving very slowly, allowing me the opportunity to look, though unsuccessfully, for Vija. Where was she? Finally Dad decided we had better go see the Consul and come back for our shots another time.

Our meeting with the Consul went very smoothly. Our D.P. identification, call certification papers and travel vouchers were in order. We were reminded to get vaccinated, and once we were notified of our boarding date, an appointment would be made for a final physical examination.

The rest of the morning I spent looking for Vija.

Where is she? I wondered, and wandered all over the camp. I thought it improper to knock on the door of her room.

Why isn't she coming out? Where is she?

At noon, Mom, Dad and I were waiting for the dining room doors to open, when Vija came, accompanied by her parents and brother.

"Where were you?" I asked. "I've been looking for you all over."

"Really!" she answered with a pleasant smile.

Miracles happen. Mom, Dad, Vija's mom and dad, Vitauts and Vija and I ate lunch at the same table. Our parents and Vitauts had a lively conversation going. From time to time they looked at Vija and me as if to ask, "Hey, what's going on there?" But they kept on talking, giving me an opportunity to lean close to Vija and whisper in her ear, "Vija, do you want to go to a movie tonight?" Movies were free.

"Yes," she whispered, nodding her lovely head.

"Second showing?" I whispered.

"Okay, It's a date," she replied.

"Where were you yesterday?" I asked again, and she just smiled again. At least she didn't say she was with another boy. Was I getting possessive? I liked Vija and I hoped her brother didn't mind. He was bigger than me, and much stronger. It would be awkward if he thought he must protect his sister from me. I would never hurt her.

Second showing started at 7:30 in the evening, the perfect time for an after-dinner date. I was excited all afternoon. Dad had challenged me to a game of chess; that afternoon was one of the few times he beat me. Why think chess when you can think Vija?

Evening came and I was ready. By 7:15 I was waiting near the open doors of the movie theatre. 7:16, 7:20, 7:25, 7:29, 7:30. The doors closed. Then came Vija, accompanied by our mothers. A most unexpected and unacceptable turn of events for me. We missed the show. I missed a date. What made them late? Did someone take too much time deciding what to wear?

I felt lonely trying to fall asleep that night. Feeling a little cheated, I thought about Tinte and the good times in Haunstetten. Those were the days. School, Scouting, friends, good teachers. Yeah, but being with Vija was also good. A nice thought to fall asleep on.

Next day, March 1st, Dad woke me early, and we were first in line for breakfast and first in line for our shots in spite of gale force winds blowing tiles off the roofs, toppling garbage cans and tearing at women's skirts. I wasn't comfortable with the idea of being "shot," but it didn't hurt.

Mom was on kitchen duty, peeling potatoes until noon, and with the wind storm raging, I didn't expect Vija would come out, so Dad and I played cards in the morning. In the afternoon when Mom was done with the potatoes, we all went to the movies. It was an awful movie about black men working in a coal mine and fighting among themselves using knives and bats as weapons. This was a movie Mom shouldn't have seen. It upset her very much. Afterwards in the foyer, we had words. "I told you black men are savages," Mom attacked Dad and me.

"Mom, No! Black people aren't any different from us. This was just a movie, a fictional story about coal miners. The men could've been any color. They could've been white. Remember when Uncle Rudis was Lager Fuhrer, and a Latvian man attacked him; other men had to stop him from hitting Uncle with his fists."

"That was different, that man was jealous of…"

"No, Mom," I cut her off, "not different at all."

"Harij, that man wanted Rudis' job and…"

"The same, Mom," I cut in, "jealousy doesn't respect skin color, Mom."

"Harijs is right, Erna. Have any of the black soldiers here tried to hurt you?"

"No, but I've stayed away from them."

"Mom, black men are athletic and great drivers. When we get to America, I'm going to have a black friend and his dad will teach me to drive a big truck."

"Now, now, Harij. We'll see about that," said Dad.

"I won't let any black boys in my house. I'm afraid of them."

"Mom! They're good people. I like their smiles."

"Harij, you don't know what they do!" exclaimed Mom.

"Mom, if I have a black friend, he's coming in our house and if his dad can teach me how to drive, teach me he will."

"Harij," said Dad, "we don't have a house or a car."

But we will, Dad. We'll have a car. I'll work. I'll save, Dad."

"Maybe you will..." Mom started to say but Dad cut her off saying,

"Let's talk about something else."

"About what, Dad?"

"About the wind storm."

Just then I saw Vija, her mom and dad and brother, outside, struggling in the wind, heading for the dining hall.

"Let's go eat!" I exclaimed, watching Vija's coat and skirt flutter wildly.

I didn't get to eat with Vija, but after supper she came to me, saying her parents had suggested, since there was a wind storm raging, she and I should go to the big games room and play ping-pong, shuffleboard, or some other game this evening. Her dad would come and walk her home if the wind persisted.

Hey, this is my day, I thought. Thank you, wind.

"Oh, that's a wonderful idea, Vija," I said, moving a little closer to her.

"Let's go right away. And afterwards, I'll walk you to your room."

To which she firmly replied, "Harij, my daddy will."

Vija and I had a wonderful time in the games room. We played ping-pong, and she skipped rope while I watched and admired her gracefulness. I liked the way her hair was swinging. I wondered if she knew her skirt was floating up, way above her knees. She was beautiful. People will love her on the stage.

We talked, laughed and made a movie date for the following day. We played checkers on a very small table. I leaned a little over the table. Our foreheads were close. I could feel her breath. It felt wonderful! Wonderful! She asked what I was doing tomorrow morning. I told her we were going to the marketplace with Mom's roommate. Hearing those plans, she looked a bit sad. She smiled when I told her I would be back in the afternoon in time to go to the movies with her.

"I'll be ready," she promised.

Her dad came to walk her to her room. I said goodnight to her and also to her dad. A wonderful windy day to remember.

Next day, March 2nd, Mom, Dad, Mrs. Rosental and I went to explore the nearby marketplace. We couldn't buy anything to add to our luggage since our customs declarations were finalized and we were allowed to carry on board only necessary clothing and items of personal hygiene. But Mom said she had to buy something. We were skipping lunch at camp, so she bought four smoked flounders, one for each of us, and a small loaf of white bread. Mom said we hadn't eaten the flat smoked fish since Riga. We ate them and the bread while sitting on a low concrete wall. The fish tasted good but mine was a bit smelly. As we were walking around the marketplace, looking at this and that, my tummy began to hurt. It growled and bloated. I tried the bathroom, but no relief. I begged to go back to camp, realizing I had a movie date with Vija.

In the dormitory I tried the bathroom once more, but with no results. The time for the afternoon matinee was drawing near. I pulled up my pants but could hardly button them, as my tummy had bloated to an enormous size. I went to summon Vija, and on the way, knocked on my mom's door, telling her what I was up to. That was a mistake. Mom told me she was coming with me.

"See you at the theatre door, Mom," I suggested. That way at least I'll walk alone with Vija to the theatre.

Mom agreed, "See you at the door of the theatre, Harij."

I knocked on Vija's door. No answer. I knocked again.

No answer. I knocked once more. No answer. I tried the door. It opened. I peeked in. No one was home, but I saw a note pad and a pencil. I sneaked in, feeling like a prowling thief, and wrote a little note. "Vija, I'm back. Did you forget? I'm at the movies with my mom. She invited herself to come with us." I put the note on her bed and got out of there, stomach growling and mind wondering, "Is she playing the disappearing game again?"

Mom was waiting for me at the theatre door. "Where's Vija?" she asked.

"She wasn't in her room."

"You said you had a movie date."

"Yeah. She must've gone someplace with her mother or brother and got delayed or something."

"You like her, don't you."

"Yeah Mom, I do. Let's go in before the doors close." We still had plenty of time. I just didn't like the direction of the conversation.

The auditorium was not crowded. I saw an empty section about the middle of the auditorium and directed Mom toward it. I didn't want to sit close to other people because of my tummy. It kept on growling, though it wasn't hurting as much anymore.

The first film was a short one. A Charlie Chaplin movie. Mom and I laughed a lot. I decided it wasn't all that bad to have Mom as a movie date. The short movie ended, the lights came on, doors opened and in walked Vija and her mom. Vija saw us right away, ran and sat next to me, her mom sat next to her. We had a Mom on both sides. My tummy did a summersault and thundered. Vija looked at me, but said nothing.

The feature started; it was an American cowboy film. The galloping horses and the shooting will camouflage my problem, I thought. No such luck. It was a love story set in the American wilderness with lots of singing, dancing, hugging and kissing. Vija kept stealing glances at me, and sat as close to me as the seats permitted, but my stomach was louder than the film, embarrassing me greatly. Finally Vija leaned toward my ear and whispered, "Do you need to go to the bathroom?"

"No. Yes, I wish I could. I ate a spoiled fish."

"A spoiled fish?"

"Yeah, at the marketplace."

"Does your tummy hurt?"

"Some. It's so bloated."

"Oh, Harij."

"Ssshh." A soft hiss from my mom, with a finger to her lips.

Besides embarrassed, I felt miserable. My stomach growled and growled. After the movie ended my problem was obvious not just to Vija and our moms, but to most people in the auditorium. I said to Vija and Moms, "I have to go for a walk. I need some fresh air." (Well said.)

Vija wanted to go with me. To my surprise she was allowed. I assured our moms we wouldn't be walking very far from a bathroom. Quite true! We had walked about five minutes and I had to let Vija in on a secret, "I have to go."

We hurried to my imposing red brick dormitory. At the door Vija told me she would wait for me. I was glad. I ran straight to the room at the end of the hall and five minutes later, emerged at least fifteen centimeters smaller around the waistline, feeling immensely better.

Vija was waiting outside the door. I went to her, looked into her sparkling eyes, and put my arms around her shoulders, wanting to say, "Vija, you're beautiful." But the words got choked in my throat. Puzzled, Vija just looked at me.

We walked another half hour, in silence. I enjoyed her presence very much. We walked to her building. Once again I held her shoulders and looked in her eyes, again I tried to say, "Vija, you're beautiful," but I couldn't get the words out. All I could say was, "Good night, Vija."

"Good night, Harij," she replied with a puzzled look and we parted for the night. I never felt about a girl the way I felt about Vija. Her presence made me feel so complete.

I skipped supper and went to bed early hoping I would wake up with more confidence after the pleasant dreams I was sure to have. Mom and Dad went to Vespers. Was it to pray for their son?

The morning of the 3rd of March, I skipped breakfast. I was still feeling the effects of the spoiled fish. About ten in the morning, my parents, Mrs. Rosental and I walked to town where mom, feeling sorry for me, bought a box of ten waffles and a small piece of smoked sausage for herself. I ate one waffle, and that was enough. It tasted like the spoiled fish. Mom ate her sausage. Dad stuffed the remaining nine waffles under his shirt and smuggled them into the camp.

In the afternoon I went to the movie theatre, only to discover it was an adult movie and the doorman denied me entry because I wasn't sixteen. Dejected, I was drifting towards Vija's building, hoping she'd come out and we could spend the afternoon walking hand in hand, talking, watching the drifting clouds and laughing at the birds. To my delight she did come out, and I told her what had happened at the cinema doors. She wittingly advised me that she would fix that. I was to wait outside her building patiently imagining what she had in mind. She skipped inside, and about fifteen minutes of eternity later, appeared in the doorway, a stunning young woman, no less than an eighteen year old beauty. She took me under arm and we walked back to the theatre. When the big doors opened after the short cartoon, we simply walked in. No one questioned us. The young male doorman stared only at Vija.

After the movie we went for a walk and Vija told me how she had cut her left thigh running through brush near the Scout forest. She showed me the scar. I had a hard time concentrating just on the scar, but I felt sorry for her. I told her girls should be careful and not injure themselves. She insisted girls aren't different from boys when it comes to trying thrilling things; sometimes there are accidents. I should know all about that. What's so thrilling about running through the brushes, I thought.

Vija invited me to her room. After the temptation of the scar, I was hesitant about going into her room. She must've sensed that. Without me saying anything she reminded me that I had been in her room before, leaving notes on her bed. I accepted her invitation, fearing my own anticipations. She led me into her room.

Her mother wasn't home. The room was neat, beds nicely made, quite unlike my bunk. The few items of girl's stuff were nicely arranged on a shelf. The closet door was closed.

She motioned for me to sit on her bed, and she sat next to me. This was the first time I had sat on a girl's bed, with the girl beside me. We talked, joked and laughed. I wanted to hold her shoulders again, tell her how beautiful she was, then do like they did in the movie, put my arms around her and kiss her again and again. She might kiss back like in the movie. But that wouldn't be right. Her mom might walk in.

Vija showed me her collection of programs from the many movies she had seen. It took us some time to see and talk about them. She asked me who my favorite movie stars were. To hide my ignorance I told her all of them. She named a few of her favorite stars and showed me who they were in the programs. Clark Gable in *It Happened One Night*. Gary Cooper in *Sergeant York*. Bing Crosby in *Going My Way*. Seeing one of her programs, I pointed to Ginger Rogers in *Kitty Foyle*.

"She can dance. She is pretty," Vija said.

"So are you, Vija, so are you." I finally got it out, though only partially. Her eyes sparkled and smile widened as she leaned toward me and I towards her. Then I heard footsteps in the hall. It was Vija's mom.

Friday morning, March 4th was my turn to take a morning shower. Whatever the building was built for, it wasn't to house many people. There were only two showers. Showering in the afternoon or evening was on a first come, first serve basis, but morning showers were scheduled.

After showering I went to visit Mom. She hadn't felt well last night. She felt better now and said she would come to lunch with Dad and me.

In the afternoon Mom and Mrs. Rosental decided to go to town, so Dad and I went to the afternoon matinee. I expected to see Vija, but to my disappointment she wasn't there. We saw many movies in the Bremen camp; they were free and there wasn't much else to do.

After the movie Dad and I left to explore the fisherman's harbor, about a kilometer from the camp. While we walked I made Dad promise he wouldn't buy more smoked fish. It was a cool day so we walked quite fast and soon were at the harbor. Seeing the many varieties of boats, yachts, row boats and cabin cruisers, I fell in love with the harbor. There wasn't enough time to look at all the boats before sunset, so I pleaded with Dad to come back in the morning and spend the whole day at the harbor, hoping Vija would come with us.

Time passed quickly watching the activity in the harbor. Just before sunset, the fishermen returned, anchored their little ships, sorted and unloaded their catch. A nearby fisherman saw us watching him. He waved to us, then pointed to a pile of fish, then to us. Dad shook his head, meaning, "We don't want to buy fish."- Thank goodness, I thought.

In the evening I met Vija and invited her to come with my dad and me to the harbor. She said she'd like to but her family was going sightseeing in Bremen. I was glad she didn't invite me to go with her. I would've been torn between Vija and the boats. She was a pretty girl and I was a boy who liked pretty girls *and* boats.

In the morning, Dad and I returned to the harbor and admired the many boats as we walked up and down the wooden plank docks. We got to board two vessels. The three young fishermen, attired in red waterproof jackets, black baggy trousers and black rubber boots, were proud of their vessel and glad to show us around. They even allowed me to stand by the helm, turning it back and forth by the round knobs on the big wheel, and blow the boat's loud horn.

Dad and I walked beyond the opening in the breakwater where vessels entered the fisherman's harbor from the River Wesser, flowing north through Bremen to the North Sea, about 64 kilometers away. The river was wide and deep, allowing ocean-going ships to dock at the Port of Bremen. The sandy, tan banks of the wide Wesser, or Bremen Canal, as we called it, reminded me of the Baltic seashore near Riga where I had spent many happy days playing in the sand and wading far out into the gulf.

Here on the bank of the wide Wesser, watching the waves created by passing ships break on the shore, I was thinking about Latvia and Vija. Soon we would be aboard a ship making such waves as it sailed further away from Latvia and the loved ones we left behind. Would there be waves on a distant shore when Vija and I must part?

When we got back to the entrance to the fisherman's harbor, Dad spotted a large freighter wrapped in its own black smoke, coming our way.

"Dad, that freighter will make big waves wash up on the shore. We better go up higher or we'll get wet."

"Just wait and you'll see."

As the big freighter was getting closer, I wasn't sure I wanted to stay so close to the water. I liked getting wet in summer, but not in March. I was soon relieved. As the freighter approached the entrance to the fisherman's harbor, it slowed to a snail's crawl. It made no waves at all. No waves at all.

Sunday, March 6th, we woke to heavy wet snow. It snowed all day; nevertheless Dad took me to a small circus that had come to Bremen. I'd never been to a circus like that before. I remembered a circus where animals did tricks, but there, before my eyes, I saw a man's head cut off, strange creatures crawl out of boxes, and people flying through the air. I knew it wasn't real, but how did they do those tricks, I wondered?

It was still snowing when we walked home. I realized I hadn't seen Vija for two whole days. I hoped I hadn't offended her. I'd been insensitive; ignored her. Will she forgive me? As Dad and I walked past her building, I wanted to go in and knock on her door, but I was afraid of what she might say.

On Monday morning, March 7th, the snow was melting and Dad and I were playing cards when the news came. A new list of departure dates had been posted on the bulletin board by the warehouse where our luggage was stored. Down on the table went our cards. With long steps Dad and I rushed straight to the warehouse. Many people were crowding around the bulletin board, stretching their necks, trying to read the long lists. Finally I worked myself to the front where I could read. At once I saw Vija's name listed under *U.S. Troopship General Muir*, departing Friday, March 11, 1600 hours. I skipped on to the K's. Yes! Kapeikis, Arvids, Erna, Harijs under *General Muir*.

I took off like a bullet shouting, "I'll tell Mom!"

I saw Vija and her mom coming out of their building. She ran to meet me and I ran to meet her.

"Harij!" she shouted, wide-eyed, as we met.

I didn't care if her mom saw. I caught both of her hands and shouted, "We're on the same ship!"

I pulled her closer, we held on to each other's hands, dancing in circles. "We're crossing the Atlantic together.

We're not parting! No, not yet!" Vija and I had enjoyed each other's company fourteen memorable days, exploring the camp and getting to know each other, and now we would deepen our friendship during a trip over the Atlantic.

There wasn't much to pack, so Vija and I had the next three days to ourselves. We ate meals together. We went to movies, played games in the big games room, walked to town where I bought two ice cream cones and paid only for one. (That's what the ice cream man charged me.) We talked, laughed, and reminisced about Haunstetten and Latvia, in search of a way to deal with our ambivalence. We were about to sail away from our roots, but we were sailing into our future. Encouraged by our confidence in each other, we could face the ambivalence looking forward. "We can do it!" "We can do it!" we said to each other.

Friday, the 11th of March, Dad woke me at 5:30 a.m. Departing families could eat an early breakfast and be ready to leave by 7:30 a.m. I ate breakfast with Mom and Dad. Vija ate with her mom and dad and brother across the dining room from us. We looked at each other for what seemed long periods of time. There were no smiles on our faces. We were leaving. We were leaving on the same ship, but we were leaving Europe, it seemed, forever. My thoughts and emotions were focused on leaving, not on where I was going; on the loss and not the gain.

Hundreds of people had gathered at the warehouse. Vija and I stood side by side in silence. The skies were cloudy, a modest wind cooling our faces; it was threatening to rain. Consistent with the perplexity gripping my heart, my hands were cold. Our belongings were already taken to the ship. Incoherent thoughts were racing through my mind: Haunstetten. Tinte. Scouts. Vija. Latvia. America. The Army buses came at 9:00 a.m. As in a strange dream, I followed Vija into the olive-drab bus and sat next to her. Mom and Dad sat behind us. To break the silence someone said, "Ready or not, America, here we come!"

There was some laughter. Vija looked at me and I said, "It's going to be alright." She nodded as the bus began to move, taking us to the same railroad station in Bremen where we had arrived from Haunstetten, February 26th, two weeks ago. We boarded a train again for the short ride to Bremerhaven, where we transferred to an army truck that took us to the port. At the gate, a military policeman came around the truck, stood tall on the rear bumper and looked us over. He said something, but I didn't understand it. He was smiling. I took that to mean all was okay. The truck proceeded into the port and we disembarked on a pier.

Wow! There it was! A huge bluish-grey troop ship with the inscription, *General Muir*, on the bow. We had to wait, but I didn't mind. I stole a glance at Vija and saw her eyes were focused on the ship, wide open in amazement. There was the ship that would sail us to New York, to America. I looked at the size of the steaming smoke stacks. Each one was bigger than the fishing boats in the fisherman's harbor. I noticed the lifeboats, strung in a row along the edge of the deck high above me. They looked like ships themselves.

I glanced at Mom. Her eyes were fixed on the lifeboats, her face serious and her lips tightly drawn. I should know her fears of water; memories of the German destroyer, attacked as it sailed us across the Baltic sea, the mighty Bismarck, the Titanic and her frightful experience as a girl crossing River Daugava in a rowboat that sank near the shore. Yes, she was afraid.

General Muir fascinated me. The two hours we waited were shortened by excitement. Everyone was talking. Near us stood a man who seemed to know about ships. He pointed to the features of the ship and explained what they were and what they did. Imitating him I explained to Vija why there were no anti-aircraft guns on the ship. "The war is over," I told her. She called me silly.

We boarded at 1:00 p.m. Again, I was separated from my mom. We were assigned to large rooms with bunk beds, four levels high. Women towards the front and men near the middle of the ship. Dad and I were assigned to a large dormitory-like room on the starboard side. I was lucky to claim a third level bunk by a port hole, Dad was below me and a younger man above me and an older man on the first level.

This was how American soldiers sailed to war, some never to return, I thought. I'm sailing to peace and new opportunities, but it feels like I'm heading to war and uncertainty.

After settling in, Dad and I went up to the open deck to see if we could connect with Mom and Vija. There were many people on the deck, but none we were looking for. Dad and I worked our way to the railing. There were some workmen on the pier, but no one else. All were aboard and there was no one on the pier to wave goodbye to. I thought of my aunts and uncles. The ship's whistles blew. I noted it was 4:01 p.m. on the big round clock above the door leading to my bunk room. The heavy ropes securing the ship to the pier were released and wound onto huge metal spools on the deck of the ship. Pulled by a tugboat, the grey *General Muir* was moving away from the pier. We were on the way to America. Ever to return?

Dad and I stood in silence, watching first the pier slip away, then the ships anchored at other piers, the port, and finally, in the distance, the ruins of Bremerhaven. And then the shoreline grew distant. The ship slowed and the tugboat was released. Soon the ship started to accelerate. I heard its powerful engines and saw the black smoke rise from the three slanted smoke stacks, diffusing into the dark overcast sky.

Mom found us on the deck, standing by the rail.

"Mom," I said, "you missed our departure."

"I know, Harij, I didn't want to see it."

"Why, Mom?"

"I didn't want to cry again."

My dad put his arms around her and held her close. They both were crying silently and so was I. Was Vija crying too, I wondered?

Supper time came and Dad, Mom and I entered the dining hall. There was a long table with succulently arranged food. I couldn't believe my eyes. I didn't know there was that much food in the world. At the end of the long table a chef was carving a turkey. There were five kinds of sausages on big, elongated silver plates, two varieties of soup, both mashed potatoes and baked potatoes, carrots, breads, fruits, some of which I had never seen before, sweet breads and cookies.

I indulged in the meal of my life: two different delicious sausages, a slice of dark turkey meat with gravy, a slice of white bread with butter and jam, a big helping of various vegetables, an apple, some cookies, real coffee made from freshly ground coffee beans, with lots of condensed milk and two big fig bars. I had thought the food in Bremen was fabulous. This surpassed anything I had ever seen, even before the war in Latvia.

We had been warned to not eat too much when we boarded the ship, as American food is richer than our simple D.P. camp cuisine. One should get used to it slowly, besides something else happens on ocean going ships that a land-lopper mustn't take for granted. The eyes of a thirteen year old had forgotten the warning, but the tummy soon experienced the consequences. It started to hurt, growl and bloat. The wind had picked up and at about 8:00 p.m. the ship began to rock in the rising waves. I was seasick on an overly full stomach. To the men's room I staggered as the ship rocked. I stayed there a long time; I held on and didn't throw up. I did manage to communicate through sign language and my limited English with a sailor. He gave me two tablets to swallow with good tasting carbonated water. I went to bed and slept well on a stomach that hadn't been so full for many years, maybe never, with such delicious food.

The morning of March 12th came soon. As I was bringing my diary up to date, the ship's alarm sounded and we were instructed to don our life jackets and go to the open deck. That was an exercise to familiarize us with emergency procedures and the area on the deck we were to report to in case of a real emergency. We were shown how to board the lifeboats in the event the ship was on fire or sinking. I thought of Mom and how frightened she must be. Later she told me she had been dizzy and almost fainted. During the exercise I saw Vija, and through long distance sign language we agreed to meet on deck after the emergency exercise.

I went down to my floating dormitory, took off the life jacket and stored it in its designated container, put on my coat and went back on deck to meet Vija. She was already there waiting for me in the bow, hair dancing in the crisp wind. She wore a dark blue jacket and a light blue skirt which flapped gently to one side. She looked lovely against the background of the foaming sea.

She told me about her dormitory. Her bunk was near the bow of the ship. She, too, was on the third level and by a porthole. I told her about overeating and getting seasick last night. She laughed and said I seemed to have those kinds of tummy problems. We walked the deck exploring the ship, looking at the lifeboats, imagining what it would be like having to board them. The wind was getting stronger and the sea rougher. The ship was swaying a little but we liked it. We weren't allowed to run on the deck, so the swaying just made life more interesting.

In the afternoon the coast of England came into sight. We were near Brighton. Our ship slowed, coming to a complete stop to receive a delivery from a motorboat. The coast of England, as far as I could see from the distance, reminded me of a medieval fortress, with steep, high cliffs like the weather-sculpted rocky crags of the Alps.

The *General Muir* turned her bow to the southwest and began to pick up speed, heading directly for the Atlantic Ocean. From the stern we watched the coast of England recede into the distance. At 3:12 p.m. the cliffs of England, the westernmost coast of Europe, slipped behind the horizon. We were on the Atlantic Ocean. The *General Muir* was plowing full speed through choppy waters toward America.

Vija and I, in the company of our parents, supped together. Vija made sure I didn't overeat again. Little did I know how wise it was to observe one's limits and listen to good advice.

The ship was rocking and swaying mildly as we dined, but soon after supper we were advised, through the ship's intercom, that we were entering a major rain storm with gale force winds. For the next two days, children younger than sixteen weren't allowed on the open deck without adult supervision. I went to bed heartsick; how would I see Vija? There were solid bulkheads separating the bow, middle and aft sections of the ship.

Sunday, March 16th I awoke in a rocking ship. My bunk was going up and down, up and down. I could see the floor of the large cabin tilt up and then tilt down like a teeter-totter. When the floor under my bed went up, the contents of my stomach were forced towards my lower back, but with the downward motion, the contents were pushed upward and toward my throat. A man was trying to get to the door of the latrine, holding a hand over his mouth. When the floor went down, he ran, when it went up, he stopped and would try to hold on to anything he could grab. There was also some side to side motion that would make him stagger. He wasn't drunk, but looked comical.

"Dad, you up?" I called, and looked down over the side of my bunk, bumping my nose on the edge of the bunk when it came up to meet me.

"Yeah. You all right up there?" he inquired.

"Yeah, so far. How do you think Mom's doing?" I inquired, but I was thinking about Vija.

"Don't know. She's strong you know."

"But easily scared. You think she's afraid the ship may sink?"

"I don't know, Harij, I don't know."

"What time is it, Dad?"

"Five to eight."

"Did you remember to turn your watch back an hour yesterday."

"Shoot, I didn't. Thanks, I'll do it now."

"Then it's only seven. When do we meet Mom for breakfast?" I really should have asked, "When do I get to see Vija?"

"Eight thirty."

"Then we can sleep longer; doesn't take us long to get dressed."

"Sleep, Harij. I'll get up, shave and see if I remember how to walk a teeter-totter."

"Dad, I don't feel so good."

"We'll get used to this. We'll be sailors by the time we get to America."

I watched Dad get out of bed. He stood with his feet apart. Hanging on to the bunk frame with left hand as he pulled on his pants with his right and then ran, stopped, ran and staggered to the shower room door.

I couldn't sleep. When Dad ran, stop, ran and staggered back, he helped me out of bed, even helped me dress on the teeter-totter floor.

Getting around was tricky. The elderly man told us he wouldn't get out of bed until the rocking stopped or at least diminished. He asked us if we could bring him some fruit, an orange or a grapefruit, when we came back from breakfast.

"What's a grapefruit?" I asked.

"It looks like a big orange but is yellow," said the man.

"Oh," I said, "I don't think I've eaten one."

"Neither have I," said Dad, "We'll have to try one.

"Oh, they're refreshing, especially if one doesn't feel good," said the elderly gentleman.

Dad and I ran, stopped, ran and staggered toward the dining hall. There was a down stairway we had to negotiate. That was a challenge. As steady as I was on my feet, I had to hang on to the handrails. When the bow of the ship went downward, the stairway became as steep as a ladder. When the bow came up, it felt as if I was going up to go down. We made it to the dining hall. There weren't many people there. Some were just sitting, pale-faced, not eating. We looked around. No Mom, no Vija. We waited, ten, fifteen, twenty minutes, half an hour. No Mom, no Vija. I thought about eating, but as I debated, the contents of my stomach wanted to come into my throat. I held them back. We didn't know what to do. We waited for an hour. Dad drank a cup of black coffee. I ate a fig bar and wished I hadn't. Finally Dad suggested, "Let's go to our bunks."

"Sure, but by way of the latrine."

Before leaving, both of us ate a grapefruit. It was refreshing, especially under our circumstances. We asked for a paper bag, and took some grapefruits and oranges. We ran, stopped, ran and staggered to the latrine, but neither of us threw up. I noticed some had missed the mark and vomited on the wall and floor. That made me feel worse.

On the way to our bunks we passed several people vomiting in the hall. A young man was vomiting right by the doorway of our dormitory. The smell, the choking sounds, groans, moans and rudely expressed laments were nauseating. Swearing doesn't cure seasickness.

I was concerned about Mom and Vija. Their absence at breakfast meant they were both too seasick to come. Perhaps they were unable to run, stop, run and stagger anywhere. Many people were staying in bed, fearing they may fall and hurt themselves. Some couldn't make it to the latrine and threw up in their bunks.

We shared the oranges and grapefruit with the elderly gentleman. He knew what he was doing. The three of us didn't throw up, but the younger one on the fourth level did. I was glad he could run, stop, run and stagger to the latrine.

Dad was able to confirm that Mom, Vija and her mom were very seasick. My mother was receiving assistance from the ship's medics. There was nothing Dad and I could do to help them. I lay in my bunk, thinking about Mom and Vija. Dad, the older man and I survived on a diet of grapefruit and oranges. I did manage to sneak in some ice cream Dad brought me and two fig bars.

The storm raged for two and a half days, subsiding Tuesday morning, March 15th. About 8:30 a.m. Dad and I walked like normal human beings to the dining room for breakfast and were pleasantly surprised by Mom's presence. She looked very pale and fragile for the strong woman she was. She had been very sick, even coughing up some blood. If it hadn't been for the help the ship's doctor and medics gave her, she told us she might've died. She hadn't eaten anything since Saturday night. She was hungry, but even so none of the food on the breakfast buffet looked appetizing. I told her about the grapefruit and oranges. She ate one of each, drank some coffee with burnt white bread (toast) and said she felt much better. I asked about Vija and her mom. She told us they, too, had been very sick, even this morning they didn't feel like coming to the dining room. I encouraged Mom to take them some grapefruit and oranges. Mom sat with us while Dad and I ate a grapefruit then some scrambled eggs with bacon and black coffee. I, too, felt much, much better.

I had just stretched out on my bunk when the ship's sirens announced another emergency drill. The captain ordered everyone to don life jackets and assemble on the open deck.

I was angry with the inconsiderate captain. Dad and I put on our life jackets and headed to our designated area on the open deck above us. Once there I could observe the bow of the ship, the area assigned to Vija and our moms. In a few minutes all three were there, wearing their yellow life jackets. Vija and I made eye contact and I motioned her to stay on deck after the emergency drill. The drill was short and Vija stayed on deck.

I walked to her and noted how pale she was, rings around her eyes, hair straggly. She looked like she might faint any moment from weakness. She told me she was getting better and surprised me by asking if I would sit with her and her mom on the deck for a while.

"Sure Vija, more than glad to."

"Your nearness comforts me, strengthens me," she said but her mother scolded her as her dad and brother came, "Now, Vija, really!"

We sat silently on a wrought iron bench by the port side railing. The dark grey ocean was covered with white-capped waves. The waves smashed into the stem of the mighty ship's bow, sending spray onto the forward deck and lightly rocking the ship. A fairly strong wind was pushing low dark clouds towards the eastern horizon. The air was damp, salty and cool. I looked at my fragile Vija and shivered.

I asked Vija if she had eaten the grapefruit and oranges. She said she had and thanked me for the idea. I told her about the elderly gentleman who knew about seasickness. She had thrown up many times. With a little smile she told me her tummy was hurting. Her bunk was close to the bow, where the ship pitched the most. She could hear the waves smash into the bow and feel the ship shudder.

After her parents and brother left, Vija and I sat side by side on the ornate bench for about half an hour, listening to the wind chatter with the ship's superstructure. She looked at me with her tired eyes and told me she was getting cold and wanted to lie down inside where it was warmer. She invited me to have supper with her. That was a sign of recovery, I thought, as I watched her return to her dormitory.

I sat alone for a while and thought about my Vija, fragile and delicate. My nearness comforted her, strengthened her. Her nearness did the same for me and more. Her nearness encouraged me to face the future. Her nearness made every day complete. There were many boys on the ship; were there some my age? I didn't know nor did I care. I made no effort to meet any of them or make friends. To be with Vija fulfilled my day. To scurry to the bow and let the wind blow through our hair, causing our eyes to water, then retreat to the aft and watch the ship's wake dance and merge with the ocean waves was bliss. Will I ever get to dance with Vija, watch her twirl, curtsy and feel her soft hands in mine? Will I see her dance on the stage of her dreams? Oh my dear Vija, we'll be so far apart, separated by a continent.

"Your nearness comforts me, strengthens me," she had said. I felt that too when we just sat for many an hour on the ship's wrought iron benches sharing thoughts, feelings and hopes for our future. Sometimes we just sat in silence. When I was with Vija, I sensed happiness and openness for tomorrow. When she was sick I felt helpless beside her. Angry winds, foaming waters, please don't hurt my beautiful, slender angel, please let her get well.

Sensing the cold, I, too, retreated to my large and smelly bunk room. I had discovered a new kind of a relationship, a companionship that touches and uncovers feelings, a friendly relationship with an attractive girl.

Later Dad and I donned our winter coats and spent the afternoon on the deck watching the ship plow through the waves in front, leaving a white, churning wake behind where a carefree ocean fish would surface and leap. I felt lonesome and small, seeing the expanse of water all around me from horizon to horizon.

I had supper with Vija and her family. Everyone was feeling better. I enjoyed the conversation and thought them very nice people. I noted they too talked more about what we had left behind than where we were going. We also talked about the excellent quality and the enormous quantity of food on the ship. Vija's parents explained the way the ship's chefs were serving us was popular in America. Smorgasbord or buffet, eat-all-you-want-style, was an American way of dining; an easy way to serve large crowds. People can serve themselves, take what they want and how much they want, and go back and take some more if they're still hungry. Buffet style is better than the army style where you go through the assembly line, telling the servers what and how much you want, but the servers always slop more on your plate than you can eat, resulting in waste. I liked talking with Vija's parents. I learned how Americans liked to eat; something to look forward to in America. But that evening I was very careful about portions. That was difficult for me. Good food, some completely foreign to me, and I had to eat ever so conservatively. Vija, too, was watching, making sure I didn't eat too much. She ate like a bird.

In the morning of Wednesday the 16th of March, the ocean was calm. Dad and I explored the open deck once more, noting the ship had increased speed, taking advantage of the calm waters. We had fallen behind schedule during the storm and the captain was trying to get back on schedule. But the three knots faster speed brought also some bad news. Another storm was coming our way and the captain wanted to avoid it by sailing around it. But the storm changed its path and caught us head on.

By noon the ocean was high. The ship was turning into a giant teeter-totter again. I didn't mind it; I was used to it like a weathered sailor. I stuck to my grapefruit–orange diet, slipped in some ice cream and fig bars with condensed canned milk, and felt fine. A black sailor, one of the cooks, introduced me to a refreshing fruit juice, suggesting I refrain from the fig bars and canned milk, but oh well....? When I saw the roast beef, gravy and potatoes on the buffet the seasoned sailors were eating, it was punishment enough to refrain from them. I ate the fig bars and drank condensed canned milk straight out of the can; a delicious dessert after my main course of grapefruit and oranges!

The wind and waves continued to increase all afternoon, confining me to my bunk. Where could I go, who could I see? Vija's dormitory was off limits to me. I felt sorry for myself, lonely and bored for the first time in my life. The high, wooden fence in Riga confined me to a garden I loved. Now I was confined to a bunk, three layers up, with smelly seasick people all around, and I had counted two sturdy bulkheads separating me from Vija.

Thursday, March 17th, the storm continued to rage. I continued on my special diet and watched the sailors eat meat and potatoes in the dining room.

Friday, March 18th, the storm raged on. The most interesting activity of the day was to set the clock back another hour. This was the 5th time.

Saturday, March 19th, Mother Nature released her fury upon us. Gale force winds screamed through the ropes and masts on the deck above. The ship was rising and falling meters at a time. It was impossible to walk without continually hanging on to railings and walls. I prayed I wouldn't have to go to the latrine. I didn't think I could get there. People were moaning and vomiting as the ship slid into the valleys between the crests. I peered out my little porthole and saw waves, three perhaps four stories high, with angry spray on top, moving past. The ship smashed head on into angry mountains of water and I felt the ship's structure shudder as Vija had told me. What was happening in the bow to her and to Mom if the ship was pitching and lurching so savagely amidships? In the bow it was always worse. I wasn't feeling well. I feared for Vija and Mom. I couldn't stand fig bars and condensed milk any more. They nauseated me. The black cook was right, warning me not to eat fig bars.

As evening fell, the storm subsided and by midnight the ship was plying through gentle waves towards New York City, just two days away and two days late. We would have been in New York harbor March 19th but the storms delayed us.

Calmed by the gentle swaying of the mighty ship that brought us safely through a tempest of hurricane strength, I fell into a dreamless sleep.

Sunday morning, March 20th, was greeted by a calm sea. Even so, there weren't many people at breakfast when Dad and I met Mom in the dining room at 8:30 a.m. I didn't see Vija. After breakfast, the three of us walked the deck and admired the sea. The sky was cloudy, but here and there sunlight would break through the clouds, in beams, like slanting, transparent pillars supporting the heavenly dome, illuminating spots on the water to the brilliance of sparkling diamonds. Such beauty gave rise to feelings of regret that our journey was nearing its end. Regret also, that I had to spend so much of it in my bunk. We expected to see the shores of America the next day.

We were informed over the intercom that the ship's doctors would see all passengers before we landed. I wondered why? I thought we were done with physical exams. Dad thought this was because so many had been extremely seasick. Even as we were walking the deck, there were pale people sitting by the railing, bent over, holding their heads in their hands. Dad was right about the reason, but the way I was summoned to report to the doctor made me wonder if ocean waves can alter one's sex.

"Passenger one hundred thirty five, Kapeikis, Harija or Maria."

I think I heard Vija laugh in her dormitory, two

bulkheads away.

Sunday night we went to a Worship Service. It was a moving, emotional experience. The pastor and other speakers kept mentioning that for most of us, this Service would be our last in our native language. There were no two families going to the same city, even county. Vija was going to New York City, my family to Tacoma, Washington, Mrs. Rosental to Chicago. We were being scattered all over the United States. No one I had talked to had a relative or a countryman waiting at his or her destination. All of us would be met and welcomed by strangers.

The familiar liturgy, hymns, and Holy Scripture in Latvian were inspiring that night. We had been told we were the first D.P family going to Tacoma. Then for me, this was my last Worship in Latvian. The Estonians would worship after us. There were a scattering of other nationalities sailing with us though the majority of passengers were Latvian, Estonian and some Lithuanian D.P.'s from Germany.

I was deeply moved by the closing remarks of a teacher named Mr. Kalnins. "We cannot say that our journey is ending, but that it is at the midpoint. We must not say, with the mother climbing into a bus, 'My daughter is beautiful. She will marry a rich American and we will never return.' We cannot journey with a defeated faith. We will return. We will not be the generation who allowed our heritage to perish. Our ancestors did not allow that under more difficult, even hostile circumstances, nor will we. We will stay united; we will strive to lift Latvia to a place of honor and respect among the nations of the world, as did our ancestors during their days of slavery. We will follow in their footsteps. We will not be defeated. We will take on our journey, as bread for our souls, three precious treasures: Faith, Hope and Love. Faith and hope in God, and love for the people and land of our birth. For one more, and the last time, let us unite our voices in this, our floating Cathedral, in our National Anthem, God Bless Latvia." We stood and sang with our voices and with our hearts and souls.

Then there was silence, complete silence. I heard someone take a deep breath, a hand withdrawing a handkerchief from a pocket, a purse opening and closing, a sniffling nose, a tear being wiped from an eye. No one spoke. We left the dining-room-turned-Cathedral, in silence.

Monday, March 21st was pleasant. I climbed the stairwell to the open deck. Since we were in calm waters, I could be on the deck without a parent. I noticed the birds circling between the masts, forecasting landfall. I needed to be alone for a while, to sort things out and prepare myself for stepping onto American soil. All kinds of questions were racing through my mind. What was I really doing? Was I leaving Europe or was I going to America? Can I do both or must I choose and decide? Was it for me to choose and decide, or had others done that for me? I was content and happy in Latvia. I didn't start the war. I didn't invite the Russians or the Germans to occupy and rule Latvia. I was not a Communist or a Nazi. I understood and believed in democracy, freedom and equality. War, fought because of the ambitions of two ruthless dictators, forced me to leave Latvia, my country of birth, now in ruins. Stalin was in power and America considered him their ally. Why couldn't I stay in Germany? Why was I separated from my friends again? Soon I'll be separated also from Vija, my lovely, attractive travel companion? We chose to go to America. What will I do in America? I'll have a new life with unprecedented opportunities. Will I have what it takes to meet the new challenges? Two things I knew–I would never forget I was Latvian and I would do all in my power to convince America that Stalin's Communism is Evil; yes, spelled with a capital E. Once America and the world knew that, then Latvia will be free. I'll work hard, continue my education, accept responsibility and help my parents with the English language like Uncle Rudis helped with German. Without forgetting the past I shall turn to the future and learn to accept it.

I walked the deck, thinking, dreaming, preparing myself for tomorrow. I would step onto American soil ready to change the challenges of the unexpected into opportunities for the future.

The afternoon was very pleasant on the deck, much warmer than the days before. The breeze flowing over the ship was created by the ship itself as it steamed westward toward America. The sky was almost cloudless, though accented here and there by a white glowing castle-of-the-sky. Vija joined me. We talked and watched the birds, seagulls mostly, circle the ship and follow in its wake. Time went faster when Vija was with me. We kept our eyes on the western horizon. Our hearts beat a little faster, too, when we looked west over the ship's bow.

"Who will be the first to spot the shores of America?" we challenged each other.

People were coming up on the deck, and it was difficult to see over the heads of taller adults. Vija climbed onto the base of a bell tower, her skirts blowing in the breeze, and at once she announced, "I see land, I see tops of buildings, over there!" she pointed.

I climbed up beside her and saw it, too. Land to the northwest. The roofs of buildings emerged straight ahead out of the watery horizon. The skyscrapers of New York we had heard about, were rising out of the ocean before our eyes. People cheered! Some danced! Vija and I were speechless. My heart was pounding. I was seeing New York City rise as if out of the ocean waters.

The *General Muir*, with horns and whistles blowing and people cheering, steamed into New York harbor at about 4:00 p.m. and stopped six hundred meters off shore to anchor for the night. Because of the storms it took us eleven, instead of the anticipated nine, days to sail the Atlantic. All the passenger piers had ships in them. The General had to wait for its turn.

I stood, hanging on to the bell, transfixed. The tall, alabaster buildings fascinated me. So many of them, outdoing one another in reaching heavenward. I tried to count the stories. Impossible! I estimated, over there, 55, next, 62, 76 and the one with the pointed roof and spire must be at least 100 stories high. Every building was unharmed. I saw no ruins, no broken windows, no bomb damage anywhere. The shore was lined with trees. Some were in bloom. There was motion everywhere. People, and so many cars in colors I had never seen: red, yellow, blue, brown. Will I see a blue one without a roof? I heard horns. Close to shore I saw statues of bronze, alabaster, grey granite and stucco. Street cars were clanging. Lights on street corners changed colors. Red to green then red again. What? I noticed cars would stop when the lights turned red and then take off when they turned green. Traffic lights, not policemen, were directing autos in New York City.

I could see several bridges not far from our ship. A man pointed to what looked like an island, the home of all the magnificent buildings and said, "Manhattan Island." To the left of Manhattan Island, countless piers were reaching toward us with long grey freighters anchored alongside. Black cranes were unloading coal from the freighters into open railroad cars lined up on the piers. The city was alive with activity everywhere.

Vija and I stood on our perch until our hands began to hurt. We climbed down, and just in time. Our parents were beckoning us to go with them for supper–our last on the ship.

The dining hall was crowded tonight. It was impossible to find a spot where the seven of us could dine together. We had to dine separately. The atmosphere was electric, people talking loudly, laughing, proposing toasts, cheering. We took our plates and approached the buffet. Unbelievable! Roast turkey, ham, chicken, pork roasts, sausages, and an assortment of vegetables, breads, cakes and fruits. The chefs had prepared a banquet for our first night in New York, the United States of America.

After supper the seven of us went to gaze and marvel some more at New York City. We stood in the bow, Vija and I at the very tip. New York was stretched before us in full glory. The sun was setting, throwing long shadows from building onto building. Lights were coming on all over the city. Lights! Like stars in the sky, more and more windows dressed in a golden glow. Lights in the street glowed and sparkled. It was beautiful and I had come to this land to live, to grow, to have a new start in life, to do my best.

I looked at Vija. The lights from the city were changing the colors on her coat. Her hair was gently blowing in the wind. Her complexion was so fair. She was more beautiful than the city. She had come to live in New York; she belonged here. This will be her city. My heart went out to her, wishing her the very best–the happiness, the success, the fulfillment of her dreams we had talked about on the wrought iron benches of this ship. She sat there, legs crossed, elbow on her knee, left hand waving, pointing at me, sharing her dreams of the future. Vija, my Vija, the future is yours in this magnificent New York City, your city, your stage.

Vija and I stood in awestruck silence, mesmerized by the constant, endless procession of headlights. I noticed our parents had strolled toward amidships leaving Vija and me alone in the bow. Our hands would touch and our eyes would meet reflecting the lights from the shore.

"Harij, this is beautiful," she whispered.

"Yes, Vija, it is. And it's your new home."

"Think I'm up to it?"

"Yes, Vija, you are. Make your dreams come true."

"I'll try Harij, will you?"

"Yes, Vija, I will."

We had admired the city for some time and it was getting late.

Surrounded by the celestial view now reflected in the black water of the harbor, I thought of last night, the Worship Service, the singing. Through my mind were flowing the words and melody of "God Bless Latvia" when I heard in the distance an orchestra starting to play, a soprano singing. It was coming through the radio and the ship's intercom was amplifying the music.

In the distance spot lights were illuminating brightly something I hadn't noticed before in the harbor of New York: the Statue of Liberty. The music was the United States National anthem.

We stood transfixed once again, listening to the music. The music stopped and people applauded and cheered, then silence engulfed the ship and the harbor, interrupted only by an occasional warning from a distant lighthouse or a departing ship. Vija moved closer. Our parents were calling us. We faced each other and I held her soft hands in mine. Looking deeply into each other's tearful eyes we exchanged, for the last time, the words that had become so familiar to us, as waves from a parting ship splashed against the New York docks:

"Good night, Harij."

"Good night, Vija." I released her gentle hands.

Tuesday morning, the 22nd of March, 1949, at about 9:30 a.m., my parents and I cleared U.S. Customs and Immigration. We were in America.

We made it: from survival, to opportunity.

Epilogue

The unraveling of my elementary class and school in Haunstetten began as, one by one, my classmates also left for the United States, Canada or Australia. The school and camp were closed and the remaining Haunstettenites transferred to the nearby D.P. camp in Hochfeld.

From New York we crossed the United States by train, and settled in Tacoma, Washington, where my father worked in a foundry and I continued my education through to a university degree. I married the perfect woman, truly a Biblical "help meet" for me. We have children and grandchildren. I changed my profession in midlife, and retired with a sense of fulfillment and thankfulness to God for granting me the opportunity to experience two productive and satisfying careers, although not without heartaches and setbacks.

I served in the Ready Reserve of the United States Army twelve years as an officer, qualified in Air Defense and Field Artillery, Army Intelligence and Chaplaincy. Insignificant, yet it was my part of the Cold War, with the aim of bringing down the mighty Soviet Union and its version of Communism. Both Arnis and Imants also served in the U.S. Reserves.

I kept in touch with Arnis and Ojars until their untimely deaths. My parents, uncles and aunts have gone on to their eternal rewards. I was fortunate that they, too, came to America. As of the time of this writing, I'm in touch with Imants, who ran marathons four years into the twenty first century. I'm in contact with my teachers, Gunars and Jautrite Salins. I am also in touch with Vija's brother,

Vitauts who informed me that Vija passed away in 1988. She made New York City her home and fulfilled her dreams on the stages of the American Festival Ballet and the New York Metropolitan Ballet Companies. I was unable to locate other classmates – indeed we were scattered all over the world. Life moves on, new friendships form, sweet memories remain!

I will continue to record memories of my past. If you enjoyed Volume 1, watch for a sequel.

Harry G. Kapeikis
Penticton, British Columbia

Acknowledgments

Many thanks and miles of appreciation to my long time literary friends Louise Quandt of Naramata, British Columbia, and Donna Snethun of Spruce Grove, Alberta, for proofreading the manuscript; to Heidi Buckendahl of Oliver, British Columbia, for reviewing the book, helping with computer work and, together with PJ Perdue of Penticton, British Columbia, for creating the cover. I am also indebted to Jill Veitch of Kelowna, British Columbia, for final editing, revisions and formatting the book for publication. Thanks! Thanks! Thanks! A million thanks!

My grateful appreciation goes also to Yasmin John Thorpe, and Penny Smith, co-founders of the Penticton Writers and Publishers group, as well as fellow members, especially Klaus Sturze, for support, guidance and useful advice in the creative process.

Hugs and kisses to my wife, JoAnn, for her continuous support, countless hours of computer work, proofreading and encouragement. For that, and in celebration of our 50th Anniversary, this book is dedicated, in part, to her.

ISBN 142513400-9

9 781425 134006